BASHŌ'S HAIKU

Bashō's Haiku

Selected Poems by Matsuo Bashō

Matsuo Bashō

Translated by, annotated,
and with an Introduction by
David Landis Barnhill

STATE UNIVERSITY OF NEW YORK PRESS

Published by
State University of New York Press, Albany

© 2004 State University of New York

For information, address State University of New York Press,
194 Washington Avenue, Suite 305, Albany, NY 12210-2384

Production by Kelli Williams
Marketing by Michael Campochiaro

Library of Congress Cataloging in Publication Data

Matsuo Bashō, 1644–1694.
   [Poems. English. Selections]
   Bashō's haiku : selected poems by Matsuo Bashō / translated by
David Landis Barnhill.
      p. cm.
   Includes bibliographical references and index.
   ISBN-13: 978-0-7914-6165-5 (hardcover : alk. Paper)—
   978-0-7914-6166-2 (pbk :)
   ISBN 0-7914-6165-3 (alk. paper) — 0-7914-6166-1 (pbk. : alk. paper)
   1. Haiku—Translations into English. 2. Japanese poetry—Edo
period, 1600–1868—Translations into English. I. Barnhill, David
Landis. II. Title.
PL794.4.A227 2004
891.6'132—dc22
                                    2004005954

10 9 8 7 6 5 4

spruce fir trail

up through endless mist

into White Pass

sky

CONTENTS

PREFACE

"You know, Bashō is almost too appealing." I remember this remark, made quietly, offhand, during a graduate seminar on *haiku* poetry. I'm not sure the other student even noticed the comment, but it spoke volumes not only about the scholar, but about Bashō's impact on Japanese culture and now our own. It was about one hundred years ago that Bashō became known in the West through the translations of Basil Hill Chamberlain and, more importantly, the influence on the poet Ezra Pound. That influence expanded in midcentury, with R. H. Blyth's voluminous and high quality translations of *haiku* and the surge of American interest in Japanese culture following World War II. The last fifty years has seen increasing interest in Bashō among scholars, poets, nature writers, and environmental philosophers.

In this translation of Bashō's *haiku* and the accompanying volume, *Bashō's Journey: The Literary Prose of Matsuo Bashō*, I offer a collection of his poetry and prose that I hope will help extend that interest and his influence even further. It has been decades in the making, with a numerous people who have impacted it in a variety of ways. Professor Lee Yearley first introduced me to East Asian culture, the study of religion, and the intellectual life. Poets Kenneth Rexroth and Gary Snyder intensified my interest while enriching my perspective. Professors Edwin Good and Susan Matisoff were instrumental to my graduate work on Bashō, as was Makoto Ueda, whose scholarship on Bashō has been extraordinarily important. Friends Scott, Jerry, Phil, Zack, and Bill helped ensure the trip would be a long and strange one. My wife, enduring my solitary character and obsessive work, has been a true companion along the way. Guilford College provided a nourishing environment for someone dedicated to interdisciplinary approaches to learning. And I am grateful to Nancy Ellegate and the State University of New York Press for their support of this project.

Selected Chronology of the Life of Matsuo Bashō

1644   Matsuo Kinsaku (Bashō) is born in Ueno, Iga Province.

1656   Matsuo Yozaemon, Bashō's father, dies.

1662   Earliest extant poem.

1666   Death of Tōdō Yoshitada, Bashō's friend and fellow poet, son of his Lord.

1672   Dedicates a poetry contest he judged, *The Seashell Game (Kai ōi)*, at a Shinto Shrine. He moves to Edo.

1675   Participates in a linked verse *(haikai no renga)* gathering with Nishiyama Sōin (1605–82), the founder of the Danrin school. By now he has students, including Sugiyama Sampū (1647–1732) and Takarai Kikaku (1661–1707).

1676   Participates in two Danrin-style linked verse sequences, *Two Poets in Edo (Edo ryōgin shū)*.

1677   Begins to work at the waterworks department in Edo as he continues to be a rising star in the Danrin school.

1679   Becomes a lay monk.

1680   Two major collections by his school are published, *Twenty Solo Sequences by Tōsei's Disciples (Tōsei montei dokugin nijikkasen)* and *Haikai Contests*

(*Haikai awase*). He moves out of central Edo into a hut on the rustic outskirts in the Fukagawa district. His poetry begins to reflect the emotional intensity and spiritual depth of Chinese poetry.

1681   A disciple transplants a *bashō* (banana) tree at the hut. Before the year is over, the hut and the poet are known by that name. He practices Zen meditation under Butchō (1642–1716), and Zen and Chinese Daoism become influential in his poetry.

1683   The Bashō Hut is destroyed by fire in January. The first major anthology of his school, *Shriveled Chestnuts* (*Minashiguri*), is published. In August his mother dies.

1684   In September, begins a long journey to the West that will give rise to his first travel journal, *Journal of Bleached Bones in a Field* (*Nozarashi kikō*). During a visit in Nagoya, he leads five linked verse sequences (*kasen*) that will be published as *The Winter Sun* (*Fuyu no hi*).

1685   Visits his native village of Ueno to celebrate the New Year. After several other stops, he returns to Edo in the summer.

1686   Writes the unfinished *Critical Notes on the New Year Sequence* (*Hatsukaishi hyōchū*).

1687   Travels to Kashima Shrine to see the harvest moon, which results in *Kashima Journal* (*Kashima kikō*). He publishes *Collected Verses* (*Atsumeku*), a selection of thirty-four of his hokku. In late November, he sets off on a long journey to the west, which results in *Knapsack Notebook* (*Oi no kobumi*).

1688   Travels to Sarashina village to see the harvest moon, which results in *Sarashina Journal* (*Sarashina kikō*), and then returns to Edo in September.

1689   Leaves Edo in May for a very long journey to the north country and the west coast of Japan, which becomes the basis for *The Narrow Road to the Deep North* (*Oku no hosomichi*).

1690   Lives from May to August in the "Unreal Hut" by Lake Biwa, and then moves to his native village of Ueno. He begins to speak of his new poetic ideal of lightness (*karumi*).

1691   Spends late May at the "Villa of Fallen Persimmons" in the hills west of Kyoto, where he writes *Saga Diary* (*Saga nikki*). The linked-verse anthology *Monkey's Straw Raincoat* (*Sarumino*) is published. He returns to Edo in December.

1692   After many relatively quiet months, a new hut is built for him, and he becomes busy again as a haikai master.

1693   Tōin, a nephew he had looked after for many years, becomes ill, moves in with Bashō, and dies in April. Bashō begins to take care of Jutei, a woman with three children. In August he closes his gate to visitors.

1694   Begins a journey to the southwest in June in poor health. Two anthologies of his school are published, *The Detached Room* (*Betsuzashiki*) and *A Sack of Charcoal* (*Sumidawara*). On November 28, while in Osaka, he dies.

INTRODUCTION

THE HAIKU POETRY OF MATSUO BASHŌ

> stormy sea—
>   stretching out over Sado,
>   Heaven's River
> *araumi ya / sado ni yokotau / amanogawa*

Bashō was standing on the western shores of Japan looking out
upon the night sea. He was pausing on his long journey to the
"deep north" of Japan, and he could hear the crashing of the
waves. Miles beyond lay Sado Island. Sado was known as a
place of riches, where gold was being mined. But even more it
was known as a place where numerous people, including the
Emperor Juntoku, the Buddhist leader Nichiren, and the great
medieval Nō dramatist Zeami, had endured the enforced soli-
tude of exile. The poem begins with an exclamation of the vio-
lence and vastness of the water, the cutting word *ya* functioning
somewhat like an exclamation point. Then our consciousness is
brought to a focus on the melancholy island, small in the cold
sweep of ocean. The island lies in contrast to the ocean that sur-
rounds it, yet it harbors centuries of the emotional storm of
exile. Then our consciousness is pulled up and out across the
sky, as Heaven's River (the Milky Way) reaches from horizon to
horizon. As a metaphorical river, it flows in eternal tranquillity
above the storms of the sea and of human life, sparkling with a
scattered brightness more pure than gold. Bashō, the island, and
everything on earth seem to be alone yet together under the

stream of stars. Over the storm is silence; above the movement is a stillness that somehow suggests the flow of a river and of time; and piercing the darkness is the shimmering but faint light of stars.

The modern novelist Kawabata Yasunari was so moved by this verse that in the climax of his masterpiece, *Snow Country*, Bashō's River of Heaven becomes a principal actor. The protagonist Shimamura looks up into the night sky and feels himself floating into the Milky Way and wonders: "Was this the bright vastness the poet Bashō saw when he wrote of Heaven's River arched over a stormy sea?" A fire rages nearby, with sparks rising to the stars. "And the River of Heaven, like a great aurora, flowed through his body to stand at the edges of the earth. There was a quiet, chilly loneliness in it, and a sort of voluptuous astonishment." The novel concludes with this sentence: "As he caught his footing, his head fell back, and Heaven's River flowed down inside him with a roar" (Kawabata, 134, 137, 142).[1] The River of Heaven continues to flow today not only in the night sky, but also through sensitive readers of Bashō's poetry.

Bashō had come a long way by the time he wrote this poem, not only on his journey to the back country of Japan but in his life. Born in 1644, he grew up in a small town as a member of a low-ranking samurai family. While the still new Tokugawa Period (1600–1868) was characterized by feudal stability compared to the war-ravaged medieval period, the burgeoning affluence of the time opened up aesthetic transformation and social mobility. Literacy spread through many classes, and the merchant class in particular began to take up interest in the arts. The relatively new form of poetry of *haikai no renga*[2] (comic linked-verse) appealed both to the merchant class and to samurai. As a young man, Bashō began to participate in poetry gatherings with his friend Tōdō Yoshitada, the son of his family's Lord. In 1666, Yoshitada suddenly died, shaking Bashō into considering a departure from traditional feudal society. Because the arts were expanding, it was possible for some gifted writers to opt out of the strict class distinctions of farmer, samurai, artisan, and merchant and establish a livelihood as a master poet. Bashō did just that, heading first to the capital of Kyoto and then to the growing metropolis of Edo (now Tokyo). By 1680,

he had established himself as a successful poetry master, but dis-
satisfied with the superficial poetics of the time, he developed
his own aesthetics that reflected spiritual depth and aesthetic
subtlety, exemplified in the Sado Island poem. In the last ten
years of his life, he travelled often and wrote five travel journals.
In 1694, after starting out on yet another journey, he died in
Osaka. Shortly before his death he wrote:

ill on a journey:
    my dreams roam round
       over withered fields
tabi ni yande / yume wa kareno o / kakemeguru

The remarkable power of Bashō's poetry and prose contin-
ues today, expanding into cultures he could not have dreamed of.
His works, and the life he lived, have been influencing Western
literature since Ezra Pound popularized imagistic haiku a hun-
dred years ago. Over the past fifty years, his impact on poetry
has increased as distinguished poets such as Kenneth Rexroth,
Cid Corman, Sam Hamill, and Robert Hass have translated his
verse.[3] His influence is also increasing among nature writers,
such as John Elder and Gretel Ehrlich.[4] He continues as a master
poet to the growing number of haiku and haibun writers in Eng-
lish.[5] And recently the scholarly study of Bashō in the West has
reached a new level of insight.[6] My hope is that this translation
will help to extend his impact on Western culture.

HAIKAI, HOKKU, AND HAIKU

In studying Bashō's poetry, the modern reader is faced with a
seeming confusion of terms, in particular *haikai, hokku,* and
haiku. To clarify these terms, we need to step back in time to
classical Japanese poetry. The waka, a short poem with a
5-7-5-7-7 syllabic rhythm, was the principal verse form in clas-
sical literature beginning in the Heian Period (794–1186). Waka
poetics were characterized by highly refined sensibilities, vocab-
ulary, and themes severely restricted by aristocratic tastes, and
highly conventionalized associations in imagery.[7] *Renga,* a verse
form that became predominant in the medieval period (1186–

1600), continued the classical waka aesthetics while expanding the poetic structure. It is a linked-verse form usually composed by a group of poems, and consists of distinct but conjoined stanzas in alternating syllabic rhythms of 5–7–5, 7–7, 5–7–5, 7–7, and so on.[8]

The sixteenth and seventeenth centuries saw the rise of a "comic" form of linked verse, *haikai no renga*, which appealed to a broader audience. A number of different schools, with distinctive poetics and techniques, evolved, and Bashō's poetic school, *Shōmon*, was one form of *haikai no renga*. Bashō spoke more broadly of haikai art and the haikai spirit (*haii*), which included not only linked verse but also *haiga* (haikai painting) and *haibun* (haikai prose) and involved both earthy humor and spiritual depth. So it is most accurate to speak of Bashō as a master of "haikai" poetry.

In linked-verse, whether classical renga or its haikai form, the first stanza (hokku*)* sets the stage for the entire poem and is considered particularly important. One feature that distinguishes a hokku from other stanzas is that it must contain a season word (*kigo*), which designates in which season the poem was written in: hokku are by definition poems about the current season. A hokku also must be a complete statement, not dependent on the succeeding stanza.[9] Because of its importance to linked-verses and its completeness, haikai poets began to write them as semi-independent verses, which could be used not only as a starting stanza for a linked-verse, but also could be appreciated by themselves. So the individual poems that Bashō created are, properly speaking, "hokku."

"Haiku," on the other hand, is a modern word. It was popularized by the Masaoka Shiki (1867–1902), the first great modern haiku poet, as a way to distinguish his type of verse from its antecedents, haikai and hokku. In particular, Shiki emphasized that a haiku is a completely independent poem, not part of a linked-verse. During most of the twentieth century, Western scholars and translators used the term haiku for both modern haiku and premodern hokku. and haiku has thus come to be the generally accepted term in the West for both premodern and modern forms. In addition, Bashō's hokku now function in modern culture (both in Japan and the West) the same way Shiki's haiku does, as independent verses.

Such a situation poses a problem for translators. Should we be historically proper and speak of Bashō's hokku poems and haikai poetry, or should we accept the modern if anachronistic idiom and speak of his haiku poetry? Especially for translations intended for both a scholarly and a general audience, I simply don't think there is a fully satisfactory approach. As an indication of the complexity involved, the eminent scholar Haruo Shirane uses a combined approach in his *Early Modern Japanese Literature* (New York: Columbia University Press, 2002). He has sections on "Composing Haiku" (187) and "The Poetics of Haiku" (202) and yet speaks of Bashō's poems as hokku. In a similar way, I use the term hokku when talking about Bashō's verse and haikai when referring to his particular conception of art. However, I use the term haiku and the haiku tradition to refer to the poetic form more generally when I am referring to the long tradition that includes premodern hokku and modern haiku. And since haiku is the more familiar term, I have used it in the title of this book.

THE STRUCTURE OF HAIKU

It is common knowledge that the traditional form of a Japanese haiku is three lines with seven, five, and seven syllables. Unfortunately, this common knowledge is not quite accurate. As Hiroaki Sato has argued, Japanese hokku and haiku are not lineated in the way we are used to in the West. As it is written in Japanese script, it may be one line or two lines, and in printed editions it is virtually always presented as one line (horizontally, from top to bottom). As a result, Sato and a few others translate Japanese haiku and write American haiku in one line.

Concerning syllable count, the notion that haiku has a structure of seven, five, and seven syllables has led some Westerners, especially in the past, to translate Japanese haiku into English or write American haiku with that structure. It is particularly common in public schools to teach students to write haiku in this form. But the English syllable is different from the Japanese equivalent (*on*, sound). Japanese "syllables" are quite uniform, most of them consisting of a consonant and a vowel: *ka*, *ri*, *to*, and so forth. As a result, they are also very short.

English syllables have much greater variety in structure and length. Many English syllables would require two Japanese *on* to pronounce, and not a few would require three (for instance, "grape" would be pronounced something like "gu-re-pu" in Japanese). The result is that a Japanese haiku with five, seven, and five *on* is generally more concise than one with the same number of English syllables—and so a translation or an American haiku using 5–7–5 syllables will be longer. Also, in Japanese the five-seven-five has a more regular cadence because of the similarity in the length of the *on*. This is why I prefer to speak of the structure as a five-seven-five *rhythm*. In part for these reasons, few contemporary translators or Western haiku poets attempt to capture the five-seven-five pattern.

But the pattern is certainly there in the Japanese. For this reason, I don't agree with the one-line method of translating Japanese haiku. They are a three-part poem, and even though they are printed in one line, the Japanese reader is aware of that rhythm in a way that readers of one line of English cannot be. On the other hand, I agree that the conventional technique of using three separate lines in translation is also misleading: there is more flow in the original, even when there is a cutting word. As a result, I translate Bashō's hokku with overlapping and indented lines, to suggest both the three-part rhythm and the continuity of the original.

THE NATURE OF BASHŌ'S HOKKU

While haiku is one of the best known of foreign verse forms, the conventional understanding of it remains somewhat limited. In a conventional view, haiku is primarily an objective nature poem. It concerns the pure present—the haiku moment—and so allusions to the past and narrative content are not significant. The poem also presents the object in itself, rather than images with symbolic reference, with the poet writing within the solitude of his encounter with nature. As a result, the cultural context, whether it is the literary traditions or the circumstances of the poem, are unimportant. And so, too, titles or headnotes are not appropriate.

This view is probably the result of a number of different factors. Masaoka Shiki popularized the notion of haiku as *shasei* (a sketch of nature).[10] Zen, with its emphasis on the pure perception of things as they are, has also influenced this perspective. There may be more subtle Western influences as well, including the (now old) school of New Criticism, which maintained that a literary text stands as an independent entity and so cultural and biographical context is not significant. One could also speculate that the notion of objectivity popularized by the Scientific Revolution and the European Enlightenment may be at work here, in particular the notion that it is possible to understand the object as it exists beyond the limitations of subjectivity. And Western individualism, found both in the Protestant emphasis on the individual's encounter with the divine and the Romantic notion of the solitary artist transcending tradition, may be a factor.

As with most conventional views, there is considerable truth in this understanding of haiku. But it is also incomplete and misleading. Narrative content may be central to a haiku, as it was to many written by Bashō and the great poet Yosa Buson (1716–1784). As Haruo Shirane has demonstrated so well in his brilliant *Traces of Dreams*, cultural memory is a crucial part of Bashō's apprehension of the present, and allusions to the past are essential to our understanding of some of his hokku. Particularly important are what we might call "imbedded associations." Although sometimes Bashō employed a symbol, that is, something standing for something else (as a dove for peace), what is crucial to the entire Japanese literary tradition are conventions of reference and association that some images include. A bush warbler, for instance, is a bird of spring, particularly early spring, despite the fact that it is a common year-round resident throughout Japan. Part of the reason it has this seasonal association is that it is one of the first birds to sing in the new year. Its song is not only considered beautiful but is said to sound like the title of the Lotus Sutra (*Hokke-kyō*); it is as much an aural as a visual image. It is also associated with another image of early spring, plum blossoms. All of these meanings are embedded in the one word, *uguisu*.

Another important feature of haikai poetry is its social nature. *Haikai no renga* was usually made by a group of poets, and many of the hokku that seem to be poems of solitude served as the introduction to a communally created linked-verse.[11] In addition, many of Bashō's poems were "greeting" (*aisatsu*) poems, offered to a host (or even a place). That social context is integral to the meaning of the poem and is one of the reasons titles and headnotes are significant.[12] Like the literary associations, the social context of the haiku extends the richness of meaning of these brief poems.

NATURE IN HAIKU POETRY

The significance of nature in haiku poetry is well-known, but it is important to keep in mind the emphasis placed on seasons. As noted before, every hokku or haiku is supposed to be a poem of a season, indicated by one or more season words. The season word may, in fact, refer to a human activity, such as a religious ritual that is only performed in a particular season. But even here the human event implies a period of time in the natural world, with nature understood as a temporal process as much as collection of flora and fauna. Thus, every poem is located in both nature and time. (Most Japanese editions of haiku indicate the season and season word involved, as does this translation.)

There have been two apparently contrasting responses to the significance of nature in the haiku tradition. One holds that the poems are models of "nature poetry," particularly an imagistic portrait of the "thing-in-itself." The other view holds that the haiku tradition doesn't really concern true nature, but rather a culturalized nature that has been defined by tradition and thus is artificial.

First, it should be stated that Bashō was both an inheritor of his tradition's conventions about nature and a transformer of them. He applied "haikai twists" to some poetic conventions, expanding or even inverting some associations. Consider what is probably Bashō's most famous haiku:

old pond—
    a frog jumps in,
        water's sound
furuike ya / kawazu tobikomu / mizu no oto

This verse was striking in its time because the frog always had been an aural image that implied the resonant croaking in summer. Bashō was the first poet to present the frog not singing but leaping into the water—a very different sound, coming suddenly and yet seeming to linger in the ear the way the ripples spread out and slowly die away. Bashō was not completely tied to the restrictions of the tradition.

More importantly, we need to realize that the literary conventions are based on several assumptions that our own culture would do well to consider seriously. One is that plants, animals, and even scenes have a "true nature," just as humans do. A bush warbler, a pine, a moment of late autumn dusk when the light fades behind silhouetted trees: they are not mere objects but are characterized by certain qualities that make them distinctive. One can appreciate the true nature of a bush warbler most fully as it sings in early spring with the plum blossoms in bloom. A pine tree that grows in a manicured suburban lawn may grow straight, dense with needles, but the true nature of the pine is manifested by a one holding on at cliff-edge, bent, stunted, and with few needles because of a century of frigid wind. (This idea is the basis of Japanese pruning techniques and bonsai training.) And while we tend to think "beauty is in the eye of the beholder" and that emotions are subjective, the moment of the day's last light as autumn fades into winter (*aki no yūgure* or *aki no kure*) has a type of beauty and feeling that is in and of the scene itself. The Japanese held to an idea of "poetic essences" (*hon'i*), that captured the true nature of a thing and could be handed down in the literary tradition.[13]

A second assumption is that the natural world and the experience of nature are not wholly distinct. Each implies the other in a way that is similar to the school of phenomenology.[14] There is nature-that-we-are-conscious-of and consciousness-of-nature. The strict split between subject and object, subjectivity and objectivity, is not part of the East Asian tradition. It certainly is not a part of the Buddhist tradition, which emphasizes that the dichotomy between the ego-self and the world-out-there is the principal delusion that causes suffering and desires. In the Chinese poetic tradition, a principal goal was to achieve a unity of feeling and scene. A true poet has cultivated his sensibility to the point that his "subjective" feelings match the "objective" atsmosphere in the scene being experienced. Similarly, Bashō's aesthetic term *sabi* (loneliness) was a quality inherent in scene (such as autumn evening) as well as a feeling experienced by the refined poet. It was the culturally refined poet who could enter into and experience the true quality of scenes in nature.

A third assumption, related to the previous one, is that there are authoritative experiences of nature. Some experiences of nature are "truer"—more deeply insightful of the essential nature of things—than others. We can look to the experiences of great poets of the past as guides for what can and should be experienced when we see a bird, tree, or scene. In this way, great poets are similar to sages in Asian spiritual traditions who embody the experience of a deep insight. These authoritative aesthetic experiences can be codified in literary conventions.

A fourth assumption is that nature and culture are not separate. In the Chinese poetic tradition, writing and literature are human expressions similar in kind to the tracks of birds. Poetry is a natural expression of human feeling, akin to birdsong, an idea presented in the famous preface to the Japanese collection of court poetry, the *Kokinshū* (ca. 920). As the previous assumptions imply, it is the highly cultured person that can truly experience nature and express her feelings about it. "Culturized nature," if done with deep cultural insight into nature, is "true nature."[15]

So Bashō's "nature" is a combination of what we call the "natural world" and the Japanese tradition associated with it. In order to deepen the reader's understanding of the meaning of nature in his writings, I have tried to supply information both cultural and scientific, including genus and species when I could discover what they are.[16] For images used once or twice, the information is brief and found in the notes to poems. In the case of major nature images used frequently, I have supplied a glossary at the end of the book with more extensive information. My assumption is that the more we know of the nature images both culturally and scientifically, the fuller will be our understanding of the Japanese experience of nature, which will enrich our own experience of the complexity of the natural world and its relation to culture. Indeed, in designing the structure of this book, I have in mind not only students of Japanese literature and religion, but also naturalists and students of nature writing.

STAGES OF BASHŌ'S POETRY AND POETICS

Bashō's poetic style and aesthetic ideas went through many changes—except perhaps his view that a poet's style and aesthetics *should* undergo change.[17] We cannot here enter into a detailed discussion of those changes, but let me note a few major stages. In his early poetry, Bashō wrote under the influence of the Teimon school, established by Matsunaga Teitoku (1571–1653). This type of poetry drew on the imagery, diction, and elegant beauty of the court tradition while relying on verbal wit to amuse the reader. By 1672, his poetry was beginning to display the characteristics of the Danrin school, founded by Nishiyama Sōin (1605–1682). Under its influence, poets such as Bashō enjoyed greater freedom in subject matter, imagery, tone, and poetic composition. Courtly topics were subject to parody and classical allusions were given "haikai twists." Verbal wit continued to be used, but more to advance the comicly unorthodox perspective than to display classical erudition. In the late 1670s, Bashō began to use more frequently a technique of striking juxtaposition, in which two images were brought together but kept separate enough to suggest (rather than explain) a comparison.

By 1679, he had become a lay Zen monk, and the following year he moved out of the center of the bustling capital of Edo and took up residence in a hut by the Fukagawa River on the outskirts of the city. His hokku, sometimes accompanied by prose introductions, were showing an increasingly dark tone, some bordering on desolation. The following hokku, written in 1680, is sometimes said to be the first example of his mature style.

on a withered branch
    a crow has settled—
        autumn evening
kareeda ni / karasu no tomarikeri / aki no kure

He clearly was being influenced by the seriousness and depth of Chinese verse as well as the spiritual aesthetics of Zen.

In 1684, Bashō set forth on the first of his journeys that resulted in travel journals. By that time, his aesthetic of "loneliness" (*sabi*) was well-developed, and he had established his own school of poetry, *Shōmon*. Although Bashō had become a serious and mature poet, his haikai did retain humor. Part of the genius and appeal of Bashō was his ability to combine deeply spiritual poetics with an earthy humor. The period of 1689–1691, when he traveled to the Deep North of Japan and then spent time in the Kyoto area, Bashō's life was particularly rich in experiences of nature, stimulation by various disciples, and periods of productive solitude.

In the early 1690s, he began to emphasize lightheartedness and day-to-day subject matter, promoting a new aesthetic of "lightness" (*karumi*). This aesthetic reflected his renewed sense of the significance of the mundane dimension of life and art. It also helped him deal with an increasingly troubled spirit, something that became apparent in his writings after he returned to Edo in 1692. In 1694, frail but determined to continue the hard work of poetry, he set off again on a journey. He made it as far as Osaka, where he died in November. One can only imagine how his poetry might have evolved further if he had lived.

TRANSLATION STYLE AND PHILOSOPHY

As is obvious to those who know any Japanese, my style of translation tends toward the literal. This is not because I am striving for a correct scholarly translation, although accuracy in this sense is certainly a virtue. Rather, I believe the distinctive power of the original poem is usually captured most fully by staying close to what the original poem says and how it says it.

There are several major components of this approach. The first concerns the imagistic quality of many of the hokku. Bashō's hokku have been called a "poetry of nouns" because of its tendency to rely primarily on images rather than statement. We can look back at the Sado Island, crow on a withered branch, and old pond poems as examples. In each case we have the same pattern of noun, noun-verb, noun. Much of the dynamism of these poems is the stark imagism that turning them into a statement would only dilute. One could, for instance, translate the old pond as:

sitting by an old pond
    a frog jumps in
        giving off the sound of water.

Obviously this is an intentionally prosaic translation (although one could quote similar ones that have been published), but it illustrates how turning a series of images into a statement of an event robs the original of its power.

Another key component is the order in which the images are presented. Consider the following alternative translations of poems previously discussed:

Heaven's River
    stretches out over
        Sado Island

autumn evening:
    a crow has settled
        on a withered branch.

a frog jumps in
    and the water sounds:
        an old pond

The imagery of these versions is the same as in the original, but with the different image order these versions become quite different poems. The point is that many hokku are psychologically subtle, and the order of experiencing the images is critical to the poem's meaning. As we saw with the Sado Island poem, the movement from sea to island to sky is crucial to its effect. It is also crucial that the crow poem begins with the more general sense of autumn and settles, like a bird, on a withered branch, and that the old pond begins with the pond and ends with the resonating sound of water. If we are to capture in translation the complex experience of the Japanese poem, there must be a high priority on keeping the image order of the original.

Also worth consideration is the type of imagery—for instance, between noun and verb forms. Consider the following: "plovers cry," "the plovers' cry," and "the crying plovers." At one level all three images denote the same phenomenon, but the first one presents our mind with an image of an activity (crying), the second emphasizes the sound itself (the cry), and the third presents us with an object (the plovers). Subtle differences, to be sure, but poetry thrives on subtlety.

Another aspect of this approach to translating is the attempt to reproduce the laconic, abbreviated style of many hokku. It is tempting to add to the original verse explanations that might clarify it. Indeed, sometimes this is necessary, but I think it should be avoided whenever possible. Part of the meaning of some hokku is found in the very absence of words and lack of explanation. This is most notable in the case of cutting words (*kireji*), such as –*keri* (as in *tomarikeri*) and *ya* (as in *furuike ya*). These words separate the poem into two parts, and some of the power of the verse comes from the gap and tension between the parts.[18]

Sometimes, however, the laconic style results from words simply being left out—and left up to the reader to fill in. For instance,

usually hateful,
　　yet the crow too
　　　　in this dawn snow
higoro nikuki / karasu mo yuki no / ashita kana

bamboo shoots—
　　and my childhood
　　　　sketches of them
take no ko ya / osanaki toki no / e no susabi

Most translators have added explanatory fillers in order to make explicit what is implicit, or make specific what is ambiguous. The crow too is: beautiful, endearing, welcome . . . there are many words that could be used. But Bashō did not use them. Rather he left a "hermeneutical space," a gap in the meaning of the poem that invites the reader in to complete the poem in her own experience. To add the term "beautiful," for instance, only reduces the richness of the original. Similarly, most translators have explained the bamboo shoots, the old sketches, and the connection between them: the sketches resemble the bamboo shoots; the shoots remind him of his childhood; he used to love doing the sketches; the sketches were an artistic training, and so forth. All of these are possible interpretations of the original, but when one is specified, that lush multiplicity of interpretation is eliminated. Part of the richness of the hokku is in how the copresence of the two distinct but related elements of consciousness creates a complex psychological state: the sight of bamboo shoots growing before him and the memory of his sketches of those shoots when he himself was but a sprout of a man. There is nostalgia, a complex sense of the power of nature's growth, the relationship between that growth and both the maturing process and the growth of artistic ability, as well as a faint echo of his own advanced age. These poetic meanings are upheld by the absence of explanation, a gap between the two images, and an invitation to the reader to enter into the poem. We should not be in a hurry to eliminate ambiguity if it is part of the poetry of the original text.

Similarly, I usually avoid another type of explanation. Here the issue isn't an ambiguity in the original but the associations that are implied. The image of the *hototogisu*, a cuckoo, is often used by itself—in part because it conveniently consists of five syllables. By literary convention (stemming from but not limited to ornithological knowledge), the *hototogisu* is a bird of the summer; it is an aural rather than visual image, because it is more often heard than seen; its call is both beautiful and uncommon, so one anxiously awaits its song as summer comes on. Because it is an image of sound (and also because they may be uncomfortable with a one-word line), most translators will add a verb such as "to sing." This is accurate, but it is extra. A key part of the Japanese sensitivity to nature is its tendency to *hear* birds and tree breeze. Our experience of nature, which tends to be dominated by the ocular, will be enriched if we cultivate the Japanese sensibility of hearing, learn the birdsongs, and pay attention to the texture of wind through pines. It is a different kind of reading experience (and experience of nature) to say "the cuckoo sings" than to say "cuckoo" and *hear* the image.[19]

My general preference is obviously to let the reader come to the poem as it is in the original. This asks more of the reader, for it assumes the reader will bring to the text a knowledge of the traditional associations and won't be asking for footnotes embedded in the translation. Actually, I consider this a matter of respecting both the original text and the reader. I don't think the reader benefits by having the translator hold her hermeneutical hand by filling in the poem. As this approach asks more of the reader, it also asks more of the translator, not only because it is difficult to resist the tendency to explain the poem in the translation, but because the translator has to devise a format that can help the reader become learned enough to enter the poem on her own. (Notes to the poems, word-by-word translations, scientific names when known, and a glossary thus became essential for this translation.) And it asks more of the translator because the goal is not merely to communicate the basic sense of the original, but the structure and style that carries much of its meaning.

I want to be quick to note that none of these principles are absolute. Sometimes it is simply impossible to follow them, and other times a strict adherence to them would result in plain awkwardness. This is particularly true since one principle can work against the other. The translator may be left asking: should I maintain the image order, or change it in order to keep the type of imagery and avoid adding explanatory words? As any translator knows, translation is a craft of very relative success, and I am painfully aware of how often my translations fall short of my ideals.

TEXTS USED, TEXTUAL NOTES, AND ORGANIZATION

Depending on which complete edition you refer to, there are approximately 980 extant hokku by Bashō. I have translated 724, as well as numerous variants that give a sense of Bashō's creative process. I have not attempted a complete translation in order to avoid making the book unacceptably long and to avoid offering translations I thought did not work sufficiently well.

There are numerous excellent editions of Bashō's hokku, and I have referred to many in doing these translations. In general I have taken Kon Eizō's edition, *Bashō kushū*, as my standard, including the choice of title or headnote (of which there may be several versions). In some cases the combination of the headnote and the hokku constitute a haibun, which are included also in the companion volume of translations from his prose, *Bashō's Journey: The Literary Prose of Matsuo Bashō*. When his hokku are found in journals or haibun included in *Bashō's Journey*, I mention that in the notes.

Because knowledge of associations and circumstances are often crucial to the meaning of Bashō's hokku, I have included notes that give season, season word, year, and in many cases other information that seems important. A thorough commentary on over seven hundred of his hokku is not feasible, and frequently I had to battle my desire to add more information. I have also included in the notes a word-by-word dictionary-like translation that should help readers understand the poems better. They are also meant to encourage readers to create their own translations.

Traditionally Japanese verse is arranged by season rather than chronologically. I considered using a seasonal organization, but the reader would not be able to place the poems in the framework of Bashō's life. So I have used a combined format: the poems are listed chronologically, but I have emphasized the seasonal framework as well by organizing the translations by seasons within a given year. In the few cases where Bashō wrote a hokku out of season (see hokku 289, 375, 404, 415, 490, 714, 718, 723), I have kept the poem in its chronological context but highlighted the different seasonal context in the notes. Unfortunately, we do not know the exact date of composition of all of his verse and in some cases scholars offer different conjectures as to the time period. In general, I have followed Kon's dating, but sometimes when another scholar suggests a more specific year (e.g., 1684 instead of 1684–94), I have gone with the more specific, noting the uncertainty with a question mark after the date. To maintain the combined chronological and seasonal approach, I have grouped those known only by period (e.g., 1681–83) as a separate section, then grouped all those in that period according to the seasonal rhythm of spring, summer, fall, and winter. In the few cases of miscellaneous poems—those that lack a season word—I have ordered them chronologically within the season they were written (see hokku 66, 243, 354,

360, 405). However, in the case of several poems whose date of composition we do not know, I gave them a separate section (see hokku 114–16).

Premodern Japanese culture followed a lunar calendar: the new year began with the coming of spring, which was a different date each year although it was usually around late February. Winter, then, ranged over two of our calendar years, so to avoid confusion I give both years (e.g., winter, 1689–90). When known, I specify the date of composition of the poem (or of its earliest draft) in terms of both the lunar calendar and the Western Gregorian calender (e.g., 23rd of Third Month: May 12).

There are, of course, many translations of Bashō's hokku, and some of his poems have been translated innumerable times. In a few cases, especially when another translator has remained close to Bashō's original, my translation differs little from a predecessor—something that is true for earlier translators as well. I have avoided replication of earlier translations, but I also have avoided creating awkward translations simply in order to avoid similarity.

TRANSLATION
OF THE HOKKU

1662 TO 1669

1

Because spring began on the 29th

has spring come
    or has the year gone?
        second-to-last-day
haru ya koshi / toshi ya yukiken / kotsugomori

2

the moon's your guide:
    please come this way
        to a traveler's inn
tsuki zo shirube / konata e irase / tabi no yado

3

the old-lady cherry
    in bloom: a remembrance
        of her old age
ubazakura / saku ya rōgo no / omoiide

4

in the capital:
    ninety-nine thousand people
        blossom viewing
kyō wa / kuman-kusen kunju no / hanami kana

5
the blossoms are seen
   even by the eyes of the poor:
      demon thistle
hana wa shizu no / me ni mo miekeri / oni azami

6
blue flag irises
   looking just like their images
      in the water
kakitsubata / nitari ya nitari / mizu no kage

7
autumn wind
   through an open door—
      a piercing cry
akikaze no / yarido no kuchi ya / togarigoe

8
At the home of someone whose child had died

withered and bent over,
   the whole world upside down:
      bamboo in snow
shiore fusu ya / yo wa sakasama no / yuki no take

9
withering frost:
   melancholy blossoms
      through the flower field
shimogare ni / saku wa shinki no / hana no kana

10
the faces of blossoms,
   do they make you shy?
      hazy moon
hana no kao ni / hareute shite ya / oborozuki

11

among blossoms:
> grieving that I can't even open
>> my poem bag

hana ni akanu / nageki ya kochi no / utabukuro

12

blossoming waves:
> has snow returned to water,
>> flowering out of season?

nami no hana to / yuki mo ya mizu no / kaeribana

1670–79

13

like clouds drifting apart,
> a wild goose separates, for now,
>> from his friend

kumo to hedatsu / tomo ka ya kari no / ikiwakare

14

a hangover:
> but while the cherries bloom,
>> what of it?

futsukayoi / mono kawa hana no / aru aida

15

an acupuncurist
> pounding into my shoulder;
>> the cast off robe

haritate ya / kata ni tsuchi utsu / karakoromo

16

Musashi Plain—
> just an inch,
>> the deer's voice

musashino ya / issun hodo na / shika no koe

17
on the scales—
    Kyoto and Edo balanced
        in this spring of a thousand years
tenbin ya / kyō edo kakete / chiyo no haru

18
At Saya no Nakayama

still alive:
    under my traveler's hat,
        a bit of coolness
inochi nari / wazuka no kasa no / shita suzushimi

19
summer moon:
    leaving Goyu,
        in Akasaka
natsu no tsuki / goyu yori idete / akasaka ya

20
wind from Mt. Fuji—
    carrying it in my fan,
        a souvenir for those in Edo
fuji no kaze ya / ogi ni nosete / edo miyage

21
Cat in love

a cat's trysts:
    she crosses back and forth
        over a crumbling stove
neko no tsuma / hetsui no kuzure yori / kayoikeri

22
Summer rains

summer rains—
    offering his dragon lights,
        the city watchman
samidare ya / ryūtō aguru / bantarō

23
chopping a tree,
then looking upon the cut end—
tonight's moon
ki o kirite / motokuchi miru ya / kyō no tsuki

24
Winter showers

passing clouds—
like a dog running about and pissing,
scattered winter showers
yuku kumo ya / inu no kake-bari / murashigure

25
Frost

wearing a robe of frost,
the wind spread as its sleeping mat:
an abandoned baby
shimo o kite / kaze o shikine no / sutego kana

26
well—nothing's happened
and yesterday's come and gone!
blowfish soup
ara nani tomo na ya / kinō wa sugite / fukutojiru

27
the Dutch consul too
lies prostrate before Him:
spring of the Shōgun's reign
kabitan mo / tsukubawasekeri / kimi ga haru

28
a day of rain—
autumn in the world around
Boundary Town
ame no hi ya / seken no aki o / sakaichō

29
the Dutchmen too
   have come for the flowers:
      the horse saddle
oranda mo / hana ni kinikeri / umi ni kura

30
on a blue sea,
   waves fragrant with rice wine:
      tonight's moon
sōkai no / nami sake kusashi / kyō no tsuki

31
looking around,
   gazing intently, beholding:
      autumn in Suma
miwataseba / nagamureba mireba / suma no aki

32
morning snow:
   onion shoots rising
      mark the garden plot
kesa no yuki / nebuka o sono no / shiori kana

33
ah spring, spring,
   great is spring,
      etcetera
aa haru haru / ōinaru kana haru / to unmen

AUTUMN 1680

34
spider, what is it,
   in what voice—why—are you crying?
      autumn wind
kumo nani to / ne o nani to naku / aki no kaze

35
rose of sharon:
>in the hair of a naked child
>>a spray of flowers

hana mukuge / hadaka warawa no / kazashi kana

36
at night, stealthily,
>a worm in the moonlight
>>boring into a chestnut

yoru hisokani / mushi wa gekka no / kuri o ugatsu

37
in my humble view
>the netherworld must be like this—
>>autumn evening

gu anzuru ni / meido mo kaku ya / aki no kure

38
on a withered branch
>a crow has settled—
>>autumn evening

kareeda ni / karasu no tomarikeri / aki no kure

WINTER 1680–81

39
where's the winter shower?
>with umbrella in hand
>>the monk returns

izuku shigure / kasa o te ni sagete / kaeru sō

40
For nine springs and autumns, I lived austerely in the city. Now I have moved to the bank of the Fukagawa River. Someone once said, "Since of old, Chang-an has been a place for fame and fortune, so hard for a wayfarer empty-handed and pennliess." Is it because I'm impoverished myself that I can understand his feelings?

against the brushwood gate
    it sweeps the tea leaves:
        windstorm
shiba no to ni / cha o konoha kaku / arashi kana

41

Feelings on a cold night in Fukagawa

the oars' sound striking the waves,
    a bowel-freezing night —
        and tears
ro no koe nami o utte / harawata kōru / yo ya namida

42

The rich dine on meat; sturdy youths eat vegetable roots; but I
am poor:

snow morning:
    alone, I manage to chew
        dried salmon
yuki no ashita / hitori karazake o / kami etari

43

the rocks withered,
    the waters wilted—
        not even the feeling of winter
ishi karete / mizu shibomeru ya / fuyu mo nashi

SPRING 1681–83

44

wake up! wake up!
    let's be friends,
        sleeping butterfly
okiyo okiyo / waga tomo ni sen / nuru kochō

45

At a portrait of Zhuangzi

butterfly! butterfly!
    I would ask you about
        China's haikai
chō yo chō yo / morokoshi no haikai / kototowan

SUMMER 1681–83

46

The valor of the noonflower

even in snow
    the noonflower does not wither:
        the sun's light
yuki no naka wa / hirugao karenu / hikage kana

47

by the noonflower
    a rice-pounder cools himself:
        a sight so moving
hirugao ni / kome tsuki suzumu / aware nari

48

cuckoo:
    now there are no
        haikai masters
hototogisu / ima wa haikaishi / naki yo kana

AUTUMN 1681–83

49

white chrysanthemum, white chrysanthemum
    all that shame with your
        long hair, long hair
shiragiku yo shiragiku yo / haji nagakami yo / nagakami yo

WINTER 1681–83

50
Black Forest:
    so now what are you called?
        a morning of snow
kuromori o / nani to iu tomo / kesa no yuki

SPRING 1681

51
swarming in the waterweeds,
    the whitefish: if taken in hand
        they would vanish away
mo ni sudaku / shirauo ya toraba / kienubeki

52
Rika offered me a banana plant

having planted the *bashō*,
    now I despise them:
        the reed sprouts
bashō uete / mazu nikumu ogi no / futaba kana

SUMMER 1681

53
cuckoo,
    were you invited by the barley
        plumed with seed?
hototogisu / maneku ka mugi no / mura obana

54
in summer rains
    the crane's legs
        become short
samidare ni / tsuru no ashi / mijikaku nareri

55
foolishly, in the dark,
    he grabs a thorn:
        hunting fireflies
gu ni kuraku / ibara o tsukamu / hotaru kana

56
moonflowers white
    at night by the outhouse,
        torch in hand
yūgao no / shiroku yoru no kōka ni / shisoku torite

AUTUMN 1681

57
"live austere and clear!"
    Moongazer's recluse
        drinking song
wabite sume / tsukiwabisai ga / naracha uta

58
Feelings in my thatched hut

banana in a windstorm:
    a night of listening to rain
        dripping in the tub
bashō nowaki shite / tarai ni ame o / kiku yo kana

WINTER 1681–82

59
at a poor mountain temple,
    a kettle crying in the frost,
        the voice frigid
hinzan no / kama shimo ni naku / koe samushi

60
Buying water at this thatched hut

ice is bitter
    in the mouth of the rat
        quenching its thirst
kōri nigaku / enso ga nodo o / uruoseri

61
the year ending
    with echoes of pounding rice-cakes—
        a desolate sleep
kurekurete / mochi o kodama no / wabine kana

AUTUMN 1682

62
A response to Kikaku's firefly poem

one who breakfasts
    with morning glories:
        that's what I am
asagao ni / ware wa meshi kū/ otoko kana

63
crescent moon—
    a morning glory bud at night
        swelling
mikazuki ya / asagao no yūbe / tsubomuran

64
Thinking of old Du Fu

wind through his beard,
    lamenting late autumn:
        who is he?
higekaze o fuite / boshū tanzuru wa / ta ga kozo

65
in a world of rain
    life is like Sōgi's
        temporary shelter
yo ni furu mo / sarani sōgi no / yadori kana

WINTER 1682–83

66
my bedclothes are so heavy
    perhaps I'll see the snow
        from the sky of Wu
yogi wa omoshi / goten ni yuki o / miru aran

SPRING 1683

67
New Year's

First Day—
    deep in thought, lonely
        autumn's evening
ganjitsu ya / omoeba sabishi / aki no kure

68
is the bush warbler
    her spirit? asleep,
        a lovely willow
uguisu o / tama ni nemuru ka / taoyanagi

SUMMER 1683

69
sing cuckoo:
    you're the Sixth Month's
        plum blossoms
hototogisu / mutsuki wa ume no / hana sakeri

70

"That monk who's wearing a hat and riding a horse, where's he coming from, what's he after?" "That," replied the painter, "is a portrait of you on a journey." "Well, if so, bumbling wayfarer of the three worlds, watch out you don't topple from that horse."

the horse ambling,
> I see myself in a painting:
>> summer moor

uma bokuboku / ware o e ni miru / natsuno kana

WINTER 1683–84

71

A new Bashō Hut is built for me

listening to hail—
> my self, as before,
>> an old oak

arare kiku ya / kono mi wa moto no / furugashiwa

SPRING 1684–87

72

the bell fades away,
> the blossoms' fragrance ringing:
>> early evening

kane kiete / hana no ka wa tsuku / yūbe kana

73

eccentric—
> on grass devoid of fragrance,
>> a butterfly settles

monozuki ya / niowanu kusa ni / tomaru chō

SUMMER 1684–87

74

just as I scoop it,
  it rings in my teeth:
    spring water
musubu yori / haya ha ni hibiku / izumi kana

AUTUMN 1684–87

75

its sound clear,
  echoing to the Northern Stars:
    a fulling block
koe sumite / hokuto ni hibiku / kinuta kana

76

Receiving rice from someone

in the world,
  is it harvest time?
    my thatched hut
yo no naka wa / inekaru koro ka / kusa no io

77

This work does not quite fit the genre of travel journal. It's just
a record of the movements of the heart during scenes of moun-
tain bridges and country stores. Nakagawa Jokushi has applied
his painting colors to a scroll of the journal, making up for my
inability to depict the scenes in words. If others see his paint-
ings, I'll certainly feel ashamed.

spend nights on a journey,
  then you'll know my poems—
    autumn wind
tabine shite / waga ku o shire ya / aki no kaze

SPRING 1684–94

78
falling blossoms—
    birds too are startled:
      the dust of the koto
chiru hana ya / tori mo odoroku / koto no chiri

79
blooming wildly
    among the peach trees:
      first cherry blossoms
sakimidasu / momo no naka yori / hatsuzakura

80
a spring night:
    and with dawn on the cherries,
      it has ended
haru no yo wa / sakura ni akete / shimaikeri

81
squeaking in response
    to the young sparrows:
      mice in their nest
suzumeko to / koe nakikawasu / nezumi no su

82
At Lord Rosen's house

this too seems
    to be Saigyō's hut:
      a garden of blossoms
saigyō no / iori mo aran / hana no niwa

83
you too come out, bat:
    all these birds amid the blossoms
      of this floating world
kōmori mo / ideyo ukiyo no / hana ni tori

84
spring rain—
    blowing back and forth like straw coats,
        river willows
harusame ya / mino fukikaesu / kawa yanagi

85
the fragrance of plums:
    carrying me back
        to the cold
ume ga ka ni / oimodosaruru / samusa kana

86
butterflies and birds
    ceaselessly fluttering—
        clouds of blossoms
chō tori no / uwatsuki tatsu ya / hana no kumo

87
for one who says
    "I'm weary of my children"
        there are no blossoms
ko ni aku to/ mōsu hito ni wa / hana mo nashi

88
cherries in bloom
    throughout the world: to them too
        "hail Amida Buddha"
yo ni sakaru / hana ni mo nebutsu / mōshikeri

89
this mallet—
    long ago was it a camellia?
        a plum tree?
kono tsuchi no / mukashi tsubaki ka / ume no ki ka

SUMMER 1684–94

90
Bamboo, at Bokuin's house

not raining, yet
    on bamboo-planting day
        a raincoat and hat
furazu tomo / take uuru hi wa / mino to kasa

91
this hut:
    even the water rail hasn't found
        your door
kono yado wa / kuina mo shiranu / toboso kana

92
hydrangeas—
    at the time for summer clothes
        pale blue
ajisai ya / katabiradoki no / usuasagi

93
a squid-seller's call:
    indistinguishable from the
        cuckoo's
ikauri no / koe magirawashi / hototogisu

94
Awaiting the dawn at Taisui's house

periodic rain
    so no need to worry:
        rice sprouts
ame oriori / omou koto naki / sanae kana

AUTUMN 1684–94

95

Brushwood hut:
    the words sound
        so despicable and yet
in this world it is
    a thing of true delight
shiba no io / to kikeba iyashiki / nanaredomo /
yo ni konomoshiki / mono ni zo arikeru

This poem, included in the Sankashū, was written by the Priest
Saigyō when he visited a monk named Amidabō living in the
Higashiyama district of Kyoto. I delight in wondering what kind
of person that monk was. Here I offer a poem to a monk who
now spends his life in a grass hut.

this brushwood hut's
    moon; just as it was
        for Amidabō
shiba no to no / tsuki ya sonomama / amidabō

96

that's something to see—
    chrysanthemums after
        autumn's storm
midokoro no / are ya nowaki no / nochi no kiku

97

as the hackberry fruit falls
    the sound of starling wings—
        morning's windstorm
e no mi chiru / muku no haoto ya / asa arashi

98

Japanese lantern plant:
    fruit, leaves, and shells all
        the color of autumn leaves
hōzuki wa / mi mo ha mo kara mo / momiji kana

99
a chrysanthemum drops
    its dew, but when I pick it up:
        a brood bud
kiku no tsuyu / ochite hiroeba / nukago kana

100
my hut:
    a square of light
        from the window's moon
waga yado wa / shikaku na kage o / mado no tsuki

101
A motto: don't speak of other's shortcomings; don't brag about
your strengths

say something
    and the lips go cold:
        autumn wind
mono ieba / kuchibiru samushi / aki no kaze

102
what do they eat
    in their tiny house?
        autumn in willow's shade
nani kūte / koie wa aki no / yanagi kage

103
this temple:
    a garden full
        of banana plants
kono tera wa / niwa ippai no / bashō kana

104
mushroom—
    it's become so ragged
        it looks like a pine
matsudake ya / kabureta hodo wa / matsu no nari

105
a monkey showman
    with a little monkey jacket
        on a fulling block
saruhiki wa / saru no kosode o / kinuta kana

WINTER 1684–94

106
through the whole night
    did the bamboo freeze?
        morning frost
yo sugara ya / take kōrasuru / kesa no shimo

107
I've hit the bottom
    of my bag of discretion:
        year's end
funbetsu no / soko tatakikeri / toshi no kure

108
Words on a painting of bamboo

winter windstorm—
    hiding itself in bamboo,
        grown still
kogarashi ya / take ni kakurete / shizumarinu

109
with chrysanthemums gone,
    other than the radish
        there is nothing
kiku no nochi / daikon no hoka / sara ni nashi

110
At the memorial for Senka's father

my sleeves,
    dingy colored and cold:
        darkest gray
sode no iro / yogorete samushi / koi nezumi

111
a Motonobu painting:
    whence such a sad state?
        year's end
kohōgen / dedokoro aware / toshi no kure

MISCELLANEOUS 1684–94

112
these three
    of the moon and flowers:
        masters of the truth
tsuki hana no / kore ya makoto no / arujitachi

113
On a portrait of Hotei

so desirable—
    inside his satchel,
        moon and blossoms
monohoshi ya / fukuro no uchi no / tsuki to hana

114
Musashino fields—
    no hindrances now,
        your bamboo hat
musashino ya / sawaru mono naki / kimi ga kasa

SPRING 1684

115
spring begins—
    in a new year,
        ten quarts of old rice
haru tatsu ya / shinnen furuki / kome goshō

SUMMER 1684

116

are needles falling
   in the pine wind?
      the water's cool sound
matsukaze no / ochiba ka mizu no / oto suzushi

AUTUMN 1684

117

It was the first year of Jōkyō, autumn, Eighth Month. As I left
my ramshackle hut by the river, the sound of the wind was
strangely cold.

bleached bones
   on my mind, the wind pierces
      my body to the heart
nozarashi o / kokoro ni kaze no / shimu mi kana

118

autumn, ten years:
   now I point to Edo
      as the old home
aki totose / kaette edo o / sasu kokyō

119

On the day I crossed the Barrier, it was raining and all the
mountains were cloud-hidden.

misty rain,
   a day with Mt. Fuji unseen:
      so enchanting
kirishigure / fuji o minu hi zo / omoshiroki

120

with clouds and mist
   in a brief moment a hundred scenes
      brought to fulfillment
kumo kiri no / zanji hyakkei o / tsukushikeri

121

those who listen for the monkeys:
    what of this child
        abandoned in autumn's wind?
saru o kiku hito / sutego ni aki no / kaze ikani

122

Poem on horseback

roadside rose of
    sharon: devoured
        by my horse
michinobe no / mukuge wa uma ni / kuwarekeri

123

I arrived at Sayo-no-nakayama and was startled awake as if waking from a lingering dream in Du Mu's "Early Morning Departure"

dozing on my horse,
    with dream lingering and moon distant:
        smoke from a tea fire
uma ni nete / zanmu tsuki tōshi / cha no keburi

124

I visited Mutsubaya Fūbaku in Ise, resting my feet for about ten days. As night came on, I worshipped at the Outer Shrine. With shadows draped across the First Torii and sacred lanterns lit here and there, the "pine wind from the high peak" pierced my flesh and struck deep into my heart.

month's end, no moon:
    a thousand year cedar
        embraced by a windstorm
misoka tsuki nashi / chitose no sugi o / daku arashi

125

There's a stream in the lower end of Saigyō Valley. As I gazed at women washing potatoes:

potato-washing women:
 were Saigyō here,
  he'd compose a *waka*
imo arau onna / saigyō naraba / uta yoman

126

When I stopped at a teashop, a woman named Butterfly asked
for a poem refering to her name. She brought me some white
silk, and on it I wrote:

an orchid's scent—
 its incense perfuming
  a butterfly's wings
ran no ka ya / chō no tsubasa ni / takimono su

127

Visiting the thatched hut of a recluse living in tranquillity

ivy planted,
 and four or five stalks of bamboo
  in the windstorm
tsuta uete / take shigo hon no / arashi kana

128

I returned home at the beginning of Ninth Month. The Forget-
ting Grass by my mother's room had withered with frost, and
no trace of it remained. Everything from the past had changed.
The temples of my brothers and sisters were white, wrinkles
around their eyes. "We're still alive!"—it was all we could say.
My older brother opened a relic case and said, "Pay your
respects to Mother's white hair. Like Urashima with his jewelled
box, your eyebrows have aged." Then, for a time, we all wept.

should I take it in my hand
 it would melt in these hot tears:
  autumn frost
te ni toraba kien / namida zo atsuki / aki no shimo

129

We continued our pilgrimage into Yamato Province to a place
called Take-no-uchi in Katsuge District. This was Chiri's home-
town, so we rested our feet for a few days.

cotton-beating bow—
 as consoling as a lute
  deep in the bamboos
wata yumi ya / biwa ni nagusamu / take no oku

130
Visiting the Taima Temple on Mount Futagami, we saw a pine
in the courtyard that must have been a thousand years old, "big
enough to hide oxen." Though nonsentient, its connection to
the Buddha preserved it from the woodsman's axe. How fortu-
nate, how awesome!

monks, morning glories:
 how many died, and reborn;
  pine of the dharma
sō asagao / iku shinikaeru / nori no matsu

131
a house that knows no winter—
 the hulling of rice
  sounding like hail
fuyu shiranu / yado ya momisuru / oto arare

132
Spending the night at a certain temple lodging.

beat the fulling block,
 make me hear it—
  temple wife
kinuta uchite / ware ni kikaseyo ya / bō ga tsuma

133
The remains of Saigyō's thatched hut is off to the right of the
Inner Temple, reached by pushing a few hundred yards along a
faint woodcutter's path. It faces a steep valley—a stunning view.
The "clear trickling water" seems unchanged from of old, and
even now the drops trickle down.

dew trickles down:
 in it I would try to wash away
  the dust of the floating world
tsuyu tokutoku / kokoromi ni ukiyo / susugabaya

134

the imperial tomb has stood
for ages: what do you recall,
fern of longing?
gobyō toshi hete / shinobu wa nani o / shinobugusa

135

From Yamato I passed through Yamashiro, taking the Ōmi
Road into Mino. Beyond Imasu and Yamanaka lay the grave of
Lady Tokiwa. Moritake of Ise once wrote, "autumn's wind
resembling Lord Yoshitomo," and I had wondered what the
similarity was. Now I too wrote:

Yoshitomo's heart
it does resemble:
autumn wind
yoshitomo no / kokoro ni nitari / aki no kaze

136

At Fuwa Barrier

autumn wind—
just thickets and fields
at Fuwa Barrier
akikaze ya / yabu mo hatake mo / fuwa no seki

137

When I set off on my journey from Musashi Plain, I had
bleached bones by the roadside on my mind, but now:

not dead yet
at journey's end—
autumn evening
shini mo senu / tabine no hate yo / aki no kure

WINTER 1684–85

138

so harsh—
the sound of hail
on my cypress hat
ikameshiki / oto ya arare no / hinokigasa

139
At Hontō Temple in Kuwana:

winter peonies
　　and plovers, like
　　　　cuckoo in snow
fuyu botan / chidori yo yuki no / hototogisu

140
I went out to the beach in the predawn darkness

daybreak—
　　a whitefish, whiteness
　　　　one inch
akebono ya / shirauo shiroki / koto issun

141
Seeing a traveler

even a horse:
　　gazing up on it on a
　　　　morning of snow
uma o sae / nagamuru yuki no / ashita kana

142
Worshipping at Atsuta Shrine

even the fern of longing
　　is withered; buying rice-cakes
　　　　at an inn
shinobu sae / karete mochi kau / yadori kana

143
Running into early winter showers on the road

no rain hat
　　in the winter showers?
　　　　well, well!
kasa mo naki / ware o shigururu ka / ko wa nan to

144
a wild poem:

in winter's winds
    don't I look
        just like Chikusai
kyōku / kogarashi no / mi wa chikusai ni / nitaru kana

145
grass for my pillow:
    is a dog too being rained on?
        night's voices
kusa makura / inu mo shigururu ka / yoru no koe

146
Walking out to view the snow

market townsfolk!
    I'll sell you this hat,
        a snow umbrella
ichibito yo / kono kasa urō / yuki no kasa

147
snow upon snow:
    is tonight the twelfth month's
        full moon?
yuki to yuki / koyoi shiwasu no / meigetsu ka

148
Spending a day at the seashore

the sea darkening,
    a wild duck's call
        faintly white
umi kurete / kamo no koe / honoka ni shiroshi

149
Removing my straw sandals in one place, setting down my staff
in another, I kept spending nights on the road as the year drew
to a close.

the year gone,
    still wearing my bamboo hat
      and straw sandals
toshi kurenu / kasa kite waraji / hakinagara

SPRING 1685

150
Spending New Year's at a mountain hut back home

whose son-in-law?
    bearing fern fronds and rice-cakes
      this Year of the Ox
ta ga muko zo / shida ni mochi ou / ushi no toshi

151
a wayfaring crow:
    its old nest has become
      a plum tree
tabigarasu / furusu wa ume ni / narinikeri

152
On the road to Nara

yes it's spring—
    through nameless hills,
      a faint haze
haru nare ya / na mo naki yama no / usugasumi

153
Secluded in Second Month Hall

the water drawing—
    in the frozen night,
      the sound of monks' clogs
mizutori ya / kōri no sō no / kutsu no oto

154

At Single Branch Eaves in Takenouchi

a wren of a single branch:
        the fragrance of its plum blossoms
                throughout the world
yo ni nioi / baika isshi no / misosazai

155

I went to the capital, visiting Mitsui Shūfū's mountain villa at
Narutaki.

Plum Grove

the plums so white:
        yesterday did someone steal
                the cranes?
ume shiroshi / kinō ya tsuru o / nusumareshi

156

the dignified stature
        of the oak, indifferent
                to the blossoms
kashi no ki no / hana ni kamawanu / sugata kana

157

Meeting Priest Ninkō at Saiganji Temple in Fushimi

onto my robe
        sprinkle dewdrops from
                Fushimi's peach blossoms
waga kinu ni / fushimi no momo no / shizuku se yo

158

Crossing the mountains on the road to Ōtsu

on a mountain path,
        somehow so moving:
                wild violets
yamaji kite / naniyara yukashi / sumiregusa

159
A view of the lake

pine of Karasaki:
     more vague even
          than the blossoms
karasaki no / matsu wa hana yori / oboro nite

160
Sitting down for lunch at a traveler's shop

azaleas all arranged:
     in their shade, a woman
          tearing dried cod
tsutsuji ikete / sono kage ni hidara / saku onna

161
Poem on a journey

in a field of mustard,
     with flower-viewing faces:
          sparrows
nabatake ni / hanamigao naru / suzume kana

162
At Minakuchi I met a friend I had not seen for twenty years

our two lives:
     between them has lived
          this blossoming cherry
inochi futatsu no / naka ni ikitaru / sakura kana

163
A field of sunlight

butterflies only
     fluttering in this field
          of sunlight
chō no tobu / bakari nonaka no / hikage kana

164
blue flag irises
        stirring in my mind
            a hokku
kakitsubata / ware ni hokku no / omoi ari

SUMMER 1685

165
A monk from Hiru-ga-kojima in Izu Province, on pilgrimage
since last autumn, heard of me and came to Owari to join my
journey

well now, together
        let's eat ears of barley:
            a grass pillow
iza tomo ni / homugi kurawan / kusa makura

166
The Abbot of Engakuji, Daiten, had passed away early in First
Month. Shaken, I felt as if I was in a dream, and from the road
I sent word to Kikaku:

yearning for the plum,
        bowing before the deutzia:
            eyes of tears
ume koite / unohana ogamu / namida kana

167
Given to Tokoku

for the white poppy
        it tears off its wing:
            the butterfly's memento
shirageshi ni / hane mogu chō no / katami kana

168
Once again I stayed with Tōyō, and as I left for the Eastern
Provinces,

from deep in the
    peony's pistils, the bee's
        reluctant parting
botan shibe fukaku / wakeizuru hachi no / nagori kana

169
Stopping over in the mountains of Kai Province

my journey's horse
    solaced with barley:
        a night's lodging
yuku koma no / mugi ni nagusamu / yadori kana

170
At the end of Fourth Month, I returned to my hut, and as I rested from the weariness of the journey,

summer robes:
    still some lice
        I've yet to pick
natsugoromo / imada shirami o / toritsukusazu

AUTUMN 1685

171
All through the night the sky kept shifting between clear and cloudy, leaving us restless.

clouds now and then
    give us a rest:
        moonviewing
kumo oriori / hito o yasumeru / tsukimi kana

172
Three men living in Reiganjima visited my grass-thatched hut as night deepened. They all happened to have the same name, Shichirobei. Recalling Li Bo's poem about drinking alone, I playfully wrote:

with a full wine cup
 I drink to three names
  this evening
sakazuki ni / mitsu no na o nomu / koyoi kana

SPRING 1686

173
how many frosts
 has it endured—my banana plant
  is my New Year's pine
iku shimo ni / kokorobase-o no / matsu kazari

174
old fields—
 off to pick shepherd's purse blossoms
  with male companions
furu hata ya / nazuna tsumiyuku / otokodomo

175
looking closely:
 a shepherd's purse blossoming
  beneath the hedge
yoku mireba / nazuna hana saku / kakine kana

176
overcome with illness,
 I can't even eat a rice cake:
  peach blossoms
wazuraeba / mochi o mo kuwazu / momo no hana

177
Kannon Temple:
 looking off at its tiled roof
  in clouds of blossoms
kannon no / iraka miyaritsu / hana no kumo

178
My neighbor, priest Sōha, left his hut to go a journey

the old nest:
    so lonely it will be
        next door
furusu tada / aware narubeki / tonari kana

179
Grieving for Priest Tandō

falling to the ground,
    returning to the roots:
        a flower's farewell
chi ni taore / ne ni yori hana no / wakare kana

180
old pond—
    a frog jumps in,
        water's sound
furuike ya / kawazu tobikomu / mizu no oto

AUTUMN 1686

181
east and west,
    the pathos is the same:
        autumn wind
higashi nishi / awaresa hitotsu / aki no kaze

182
harvest moon—
    wandering round the pond
        all night long
meigetsu ya / ike o megurite / yomosugara

183
seeming like
    someone blind:
        moonviewing
zatō ka to / hito ni mirarete / tsukimi kana

184

just one possession,
     my world light
          as a gourd
mono hitotsu / waga yo wa karoki / hisago kana

185

Heading off to a certain place, I passed the night on a boat. At daybreak, I stuck my head out from under the thatched roof of the cabin, deeply moved by the late waning moon.

dawn comes—
     even on the night of the 27th,
          a crescent moon
akeyuku ya / nijūshichi ya mo / mika no tsuki

WINTER 1686–87

186

An old garden

flowers all withered,
     spilling their sadness:
          seeds for grass
hana mina karete / aware o kobosu / kusa no tane

187

Sent in reply to Priest Genki for his gift of sake

water so cold:
     it was hard for even a gull
          to fall sleep
mizu samuku / neiri kanetaru / kamome kana

188

A frigid night

the water jar cracks:
     in the frozen night
          I lie awake
kame waruru / yoru no kōri no / nezame kana

189
Hoping to view the first snow at my grass hut, whenever the sky clouded over I rushed home—many times I did this. Then, on the 8th of Twelfth Month, snow finally fell, a true joy:

first snow—
    great luck to be here
        in my own hut
hatsuyuki ya / saiwai an ni / makariaru

190
first snow—
    just enough to bend
        narciuss leaves
hatsuyuki ya / suisen no ha no / tawamu made

191
Snowy night at Fukagawa

drinking sake
    and now it's harder to sleep:
        night of snow
sake nomeba / itodo nerarene / yoru no yuki

192
A man named Sora has set up temporary lodging nearby, and morning and night we visit each other. When I cook something, he feeds the fire; when I make tea, he breaks up ice for water. By nature he loves quiet solitude, and our friendship is greater than gold. One evening he visited in a snowfall.

you start a fire,
    I'll show you something fun:
        a great ball of snow
kimi hi o take / yoki mono misen / yuki maruge

193
"moon and snow":
    so I've indulged myself
        to the end of the year
tsuki yuki to / nosabarikerashi / toshi no kure

SPRING 1687

194
Village plums

hey village kids,
    leave some plum branches:
        ox whips
sato no ko yo / ume orinokose / ushi no muchi

195
I went to see a certain person at his hermitage, but an old man caretaking the hut said, "the master is off on a temple pilgrimage." The plums by the hedge were in full bloom so I replied, "These will take his place—they look like him." To which he responded, "Well, they belong to the neighbors."

arriving when you were out,
    even the plums are far away
        beyond the hedge
rusu ni kite / ume sae yoso no / kakio kana

196
please don't forget:
    in the grove,
        a plum blossom
wasuru na yo / yabu no naka naru / ume no hana

197
All things are self-realized

at play in the blossoms,
    a horsefly: do not eat it
        friend sparrow
hana ni asobu / abu na kurai so / tomosuzume

198
A mountain cottage

nesting storks:
    viewed through branches
        of blossoms
kō no su mo / miraruru hana no / hagoshi kana

199
My grass-thatched hut

clouds of blossoms;
    the temple bell:
        Ueno? Asakusa?
hana no kumo / kane wa ueno ka / asakusa ka

200
all the long day
    singing, singing, yet not enough:
        a skylark
nagaki hi mo / saezuri taranu / hibari kana

201
mid the plain—
    attached to nothing,
        the singing skylark
haranaka ya / mono ni mo tsukazu / naku hibari

SUMMER 1687

202
cuckoo:
    singing singing as it flies,
        so very busy
hototogisu / nakunaku tobu zo / isogawashi

203
Self-portrait of a miserable man

my hair grown out,
    my face pale:
        summer rains
kami haete / yōgan aoshi / satsukiame

204
in the summer rains
    I'll go view the floating nest
        of a grebe
samidare ni / nio no ukisu o / mi ni yukan

205
My disciple Sanpū me sent a thin kimono as a summer gift

now look at me
 in this fine summer robe!
  a cicada kimono
ide ya ware / yoki nuno kitari / semigoromo

206
Enjoying the evening cool

I'll fall asleep drunk,
 the wild pinks blooming
  over the rocks
yōte nemu / nadeshiko sakeru / ishi no ue

207
I visited the overgrown old hut of a man who had gone into seclusion

you who raised melons:
 "would that you were here"
  in the evening coolness
uri tsukuru / kimi ga are na to / yūsuzumi

208
a little crab
 creeping up my leg:
  clear water
sazaregani / ashi hainoboru / shimizu kana

AUTUMN 1687

209
Sent to Rika:

lightning
 clenched in the hand:
  torchlight in the dark
inazuma o / te ni toru yami no / shisoku kana

210
Ransetsu painted a morning glory and then asked me to write a
verse on it

morning glory:
　　　even when painted poorly,
　　　　　it has pathos
asagao wa / heta no kaku sae / aware nari

211
field of bush clovers—
　　　be their shelter for a night:
　　　　　mountain dogs
hagi hara ya / hito yo wa yadose / yama no inu

212
The countryside

in the half harvested
　　　rice paddies, a crane—
　　　　　autumn in the village
karikakeshi / tazura no tsuru ya / sato no aki

213
peasant boy—
　　　husking rice, he pauses
　　　　　to gaze at the moon
shizu no ko ya / ine surikakete / tsuki o miru

214
taro leaves—
　　　awaiting the moon
　　　　　on the village's burnt field
imo no ha ya / tsuki matsu sato no / yakibatake

215
the moon swift,
　　　the branches still holding
　　　　　the rain
tsuki hayashi / kozue wa ame o / mochinagara

216

sleeping at a temple,
    reverent, with my true face:
        moon viewing
tera ni nete / makotogao naru / tsukimi kana

217

Before the Shrine

this pine sprouted
    in the age of the gods—
        so holy an autumn
kono matsu no / mibae seshi yo ya / kami no aki

218

Listening in tranquillity

bagworms:
    come hear their cry;
        a thatched hut
minomushi no / ne o kiki ni koyo / kusa no io

219

Rain at my thatched hut

rising again,
    the chrysanthemums faint
        after the rains
okiagaru / kiku honoka nari / mizu no ato

220

emaciated and yet
    somehow the chrysanthemum
        buds out
yase nagara / warinaki kiku no / tsubomi kana

WINTER 1687–88

221
"wayfarerer"
    will be my name;
        first winter showers
tabibito to / waga na yobaren / hatsushigure

222
Fuji

is one ridge
    clouded with winter showers?
        Fuji in snow
hito one wa / shigururu kumo ka / fuji no yuki

223
to the capital,
    half the sky left—
        clouds of snow
kyō made wa / mada nakazora ya / yuki no kumo

224
Staying over at Narumi

"gaze into
    the darkness of Star Cape":
        is this the plovers' cry?
hoshizaki no / yami o miyo to ya / naku chidori

225
so cold and yet
    a night sleeping together:
        so delightful
samukeredo / futari neru yo zo / tanomoshiki

226
At an inn on the journey

burning pine needles
    to dry my hand towel:
        the cold
go o taite / tenugui aburu / samusa kana

227
winter sun—
    frozen on horseback,
        my shadow
fuyu no hi ya / bashō ni kōru / kagebōshi

228
On the road to Irago, Etsujin was drunk riding on his horse

may it be snow and sand
    you fall into from your horse:
        drunk on sake
yuki ya suna / uma yori otochi yo / sake no yoi

229
a lone hawk:
    finding it brings such joy
        at Cape Irago
taka hitotsu / mitsukete ureshi / iragosaki

230
Cape Irago was close by, so I went to see it

Cape Irago:
    nothing can match
        the hawk's cry
iragozaki / niru mono mo nashi / taka no koe

231
I visited Tokoku, who was living in difficult circumstances at Cape Irago. From time to time I heard the cry of a hawk

more than dream
    the hawk of reality
        heartens me
yume yori mo / utsutsu no taka zo / tanomoshiki

232
According to the people here, this village is called "Hobi" because in olden times a retired emperor praised it, saying "preserve its beauty" (*ho bi*). I don't know where this might be written down, but such gracious sentiment is awe-inspiring.

plum and camellia:
       praise to their early bloom
             here in Hobi Village
ume tsubaki / hayazaki homen / hobi no sato

233
Atsuta Shrine after reconstruction

freshly polished,
       the sacred mirror too is clear:
             blossoms of snow
togi naosu / kagami mo kiyoshi / yuki no hana

234
At someone's gathering

smoothing it out,
       I'm off to snowviewing:
             my paper robe
tametsukete / yukimi ni makaru / kamiko kana

235
well then,
       let's go snow-viewing
             till we all fall down
iza saraba / yukimi ni korobu / tokoro made

236
Hakone Pass:
       someone seems to be crossing it
             this morning of snow
hakone kosu / hito mo arurashi / kesa no yuki

237
At the party of a certain person

searching out the plum fragrance
       I gaze up at the eaves
             of the warehouse
ka o saguru / ume ni kura miru / nokiba kana

238

the dew frozen,
    I soak it dry with my brush:
        the pure water spring
tsuyu itete / hitsu ni kumihosu / shimizu kana

239

resting on my journey,
    I watch the year-end housecleaning
        of the floating world
tabine shite / mishi ya ukiyo no / susu harai

240

I rented a horse at the village of Hinaga, mentioned in the poem
"From Kuwana I came with nothing to eat. . . .", so I could ride
up Walking-stick Hill. But my pack-saddle overturned and I was
thrown from the horse.

if only I had walked
    Walking-stick Hill:
        falling from my horse
kachi naraba / tsue-tsuki-zaka o / rakuba kana

241

my native home—
    weeping over my umbilical cord
        at year's end
furusato ya / heso no o ni naku / toshi no kure

1688–94

242

through gaps in snow,
    pale purple,
        sprouts of the *udo*
yuki ma yori / usu murasaki no / me udo kana

243

I'd like to sleep
    borrowing the scarecrow's clothes—
        midnight frost
karite nen / kakashi no sode ya / yowa no shimo

SPRING 1688

244

On New Year's Eve, reluctant to part with the passing year, I
drank deep into the night, and then slept through New Year's
morning:

on the *second* day
    I won't fail:
        flowering spring
futsuka ni mo / nukari wa seji na / hana no haru

245

Early spring

spring has risen
    only nine days now and
        these fields and mountains!
haru tachite / mada kokonoka no / noyama kana

246

even the heart of Akokuso
    I do not know:
        plum blossoms
akokuso no / kokoro mo shirazu / ume no hana

247

An area by Iga Castle yields what is known as coal. The odor is
repugnant.

give forth your fragrance!
    on a coal mining hill,
        plum blossoms
ka ni nioe / uni horu oka no / ume no hana

248
At a mountain cottage in Iga

even the sound
    of someone blowing his nose:
        plum blossoms
tebana kamu / oto sae ume no / sakari kana

249
withered grass—
    faint heat waves
        one or two inches high
kareshiba ya / yaya kagerō no / ichi ni-sun

250
sixteen foot Buddha:
    heat waves rising
        from the stone base
jōroku ni / kagerō takashi / ishi no ue

251
At Yamada in Ise Province

from what tree's
    blossoms I know not:
        such fragrance
nani no ki no / hana to wa shirazu / nioi kana

252
the shrine maidens:
    the loveliness of the lone plum here
        in blossom
okorago no / hito moto yukashi / ume no hana

253
Ichiu's wife

inside the shop curtains,
    in the quiet depths,
        plum blossoms of the north
nōren no / oku monofukashi / kita no ume

254
Meeting with Setsudō, son of Ajiro Minbu

out from an old plum tree
    grows a young sprout—
        plum blossoms
ume no ki ni / nao yadorigi ya / ume no hana

255
For the Priest Ryū Shosha

first I'll ask
    the names of things: these reeds
        with new leaves
mono no na o / mazu tou ashi no / wakaba kana

256
At a gathering in a grass-thatched hut

the taro is planted,
    the gate covered with vines'
        new leaves
imo uete / kado wa mugura no / wakaba kana

257
At Bōdai Temple

of this mountain's
    many sorrows, tell the tales
        old yam diggers
kono yama no / kanashisa tsuge yo / tokorohori

258
At Kusube

don't drop your dirt
    into my wine cup—
        flock of swallows
sakazuki ni / doro na otoshi so / muratsubame

259
At Rosō's house

my paper robe is wet,
    but I'll go break a branch:
        blossoms in the rain
kamiginu no / nurutomo oran / ame no hana

260
On the 15th, in the precincts of the Outer Shrine

inside the shrine's fences—
    so unexpected this portrait
        of Buddha entering nirvana
kami-gaki ya / omoi-mo-kakezu / nehan-zō

261
On the 17th day of Second Month, leaving Mt. Kamiji

be naked?
    not yet, with second month's
        windstorm
hadaka ni wa / mada kisaragi no / arashi kana

262
The first gathering of the monthly linked verse group at Yakushi
Temple

the first cherries blooming:
    right now, today,
        is such a fine day
hatsuzakura / orishimo kyō wa / yoki hi nari

263
The Honorable Tangan held a blossom-viewing party at his
villa. Things were just as in the old days.

so many many
    memories come to mind:
        cherry blossoms
samazama no / koto omoidasu / sakura kana

264
I spent time at "Gourd Bamboo Hut," resting from the difficulties of the journey

blossoms as my lodging
    from beginning to end—
        twenty days
hana o yado ni / hajime owari ya / hatsuka hodo

265
Two wayfarers with no abode in Heaven and Earth

the Yoshino cherries
    I will show you:
        cypress hat
yoshino nite / sakura mishō zo / hinokigasa

266
At Hatsuse

spring night—
    someone in retreat, so mysterious
        in a corner of the temple
haru no yo ya / komorido yukashi / dō no sumi

267
Hoso Pass, on the road from Tafu Peak to Ryūmon

higher than the lark:
    resting in the sky
        at the pass
hibari yori / sora ni yasurau / tōge kana

268
Dragon's Gate

the blossoms at Dragon's Gate:
    a splendid souvenir
        for my drinking friends
ryūmon no / hana ya jōgo no / tsuto ni sen

269
I'll tell my drinking friends
of these blossoms hanging
over the waterfall
sake nomi ni / kataran kakaru / taki no hana

270
During my pilgrimage through Yamato Province, I lodged at a
farmhouse for a night. My host showed me deep kindness and
warm hospitality.

in the shade of blossoms
it seems like a Nō play:
a journey's rest
hana no kage / utai ni nitaru / tabine kana

271
with a fan
drinking sake in the shadows—
falling cherry blossoms
ōgi nite / sake kumu kage ya / chiru sakura

272
were my voice good,
I'd chant from the Nō:
falling cherry blossoms
koe yokuba / utaō mono o / sakura chiru

273
Nijikō

petal after petal
mountain roses flutter down:
the sound of the rapids
horohoro to / yamabuki chiru ka / taki no oto

274
cherry blossom viewing:
admirable it is to walk
ten or twelve miles a day
sakuragari / kidoku ya hibi ni / go-ri roku-ri

275
with the sun darkening
    on the blossoms, it is lonely—
        a false cypress
hi wa hana ni / kurete sabishi ya / asunarō

276
    The moss pure spring

spring rain
    flowing down the tree:
        the pure water spring
harusame no / koshita ni tsutau / shimizu kana

277
    The moss pure spring

beginning to melt,
    I soak it dry with my brush:
        the pure water spring
ite tokete / hitsu ni kumihosu / shimizu kana

278
Yoshino

blossoms at their peak,
    with the mountains as always
        at daybreak
hanazakari / yama wa higoro no / asaborake

279
Mount Kazuraki

all the more I'd like to see it
    with dawn coming to the blossoms:
        the face of the god
nao mitashi / hana ni akeyuku / kami no kao

280
Mt. Kōya

for my father and mother
    I yearn so deeply—
        a pheasant's cry
chichi haha no / shikirini koishi / kiji no koe

281
Wakanoura

departing spring—
    I've finally caught up with it
        here at Wakanoura.
yuku haru ni / wakanoura nite / oitsukitari

SUMMER 1688

282
Clothes-changing day

removing a one layer
    I carry it over my shoulder:
        clothes-changing day
hitotsu nuide / ushiro ni oinu / koromogae

283
Buddha's birthday:
    on this day is born
        a little fawn
kanbutsu no / hi ni umareau / kanoko kana

284
Ganjin of Shōdaiji Temple endured seventy adversities in his attempts to come to Japan from China. He is said to have lost his sight due to the salt wind blown into his eyes. Worshipping at his sacred image:

with a young leaf
    I would wipe the tears
        from your eyes
wakaba shite / onme no shizuku / nuguwabaya

285
Departing from an old friend at Nara

deer horns
    developing their first branch:
        our separation
shika no tsuno / mazu hitofushi no / wakare kana

286
travel weary,
    just as I finally find lodging—
        wisteria blossoms
kutabirete / yado karu koro ya / fuji no hana

287
The lotus is called the Lord of Flowers. The peony is said to be
the wealthy noble among blossoms. But rice seedlings rise from
the mud, and are more pure than the lotus. In autumn, it yields
fragrant rice, richer than the peony. Thus one plant combines
the virtues of both, truly pure and rich.

villagers sing
    verses in the rice fields:
        the capital
satobito wa / ine ni uta yomu / miyako kana

288
At a certain person's house in Osaka

iris blossoms:
    conversations about them are
        one joy of the journey
kakitsubata / kataru mo tabi no / hitotsu kana

289
Suma

the moon is here
    yet there seems an absence:
        summer in Suma
tsuki wa aredo / rusu no yō nari / suma no natsu

290
seeing the moon
        yet something is lacking—
                summer in Suma
tsuki mite mo / mono tarawazu ya / suma no natsu

291
The sky of mid-Fourth Month was still misty and the moon of
the brief night was exceptionally lovely. The mountains were
dark with young leaves, and at dawn, the time the cuckoo sings,
light began to fall upon the sea. The high plain was reddened
with waves of wheat, and white poppies were visible among the
eaves of the fishers' huts.

the faces of the fishers
        were seen first—
                poppy flowers
ama no kao / mazu miraruru ya / keshi no hana

292
is it crying from an arrow
        from the fishers of Suma?
                cuckoo
suma no ama no / yasaki ni naku ka / hototogisu

293
Temple of Suma—
        hearing the unblown flute
                in the deep shade of trees
sumadera ya / fukanu fue kiku / koshitayami

294
cuckoo:
        off where it disappears—
                a single island
hototogisu / kieyuku kata ya / shima hitotsu

295
Spending the night at Akashi

octopus traps—
    fleeting dreams under
        summer's moon
takotsubo ya / hakanaki yume o / natsu no tsuki

296
in the summer rains
    one thing unhidden—
        the bridge of Seta
samidare ni / kakurenu mono ya / seta no hashi

297
While I was thinking of my upcoming journey on the Kiso
Road, I was staying at Ōtsu and I went to see the fireflies at
Seta.

these fireflies,
    like the moon
        in all the rice paddies
kono hotaru / tagoto no tsuki ni / kurabemin

298
Fireflies

held in my eye:
    with Yoshino's blooms
        Seta's fireflies
me ni nokoru / yoshino o seta no / hotaru kana

299
falling from
    a grass blade, and flying away:
        a firefly
kusa no ha o / otsuru yori tobu / hotaru kana

300
At Ōtsu

summer in the world:
    floating on the lake
        over waves
yo no natsu / kosui ni ukamu / nami no ue

301
Coolness

moonflowers—
    and in autumn,
        various gourds
yūgao ya / aki wa iroiro no / fukube kana

302
Gathering on the 5th day of Sixth Month, the first year of Genroku

noonflower,
    with a short night's sleep:
        daytime
hirugao no / mijikayo neburu / hiruma kana

303
Hearing that Chine had died, I sent a message to Kyorai from Mino

and now also
    the clothes of the deceased—
        summer airing
naki hito no / kosode mo ima ya / doyōboshi

304
I would lodge here
    until the days the goosefoot
        has grown a staff
yadorisen / akaza no tsue ni / naru hi made

305

Responding to an invitation from a certain Rakugo, I enjoy the cool under the pines of Mount Inaba, soothing the hardships of my journey

mountain cove—
　　I would nourish my body
　　　　with this field of melons
yamakage ya / mi o yashinawan / uribatake

306

I would compare them
　　to a delicate child: flowers
　　　　of a summer field
moroki hito ni / tatoen hana mo / natsuno kana

307

Mount Inaba

a temple bell too
　　seems to be ringing:
　　　　cicada's cry
tsukigane mo / hibiku yō nari / semi no koe

308

A certain Kisaburō lives in quiet retreat at the base of Mt. Inaba and has invited me over to enjoy the cool of evening.

castle ruins—
　　pure water from the old well
　　　　is what I'll seek first
shiro ato ya / furui no shimizu / mazu towan

309

Going to see fishermen using cormorants on the Nagara River in Mino

so fascinating,
　　but then, so sad:
　　　　cormorant fishing boat
omoshirōte / yagate kanashiki / ubune kana

310
in this place
    all that meets the eye
        is cool
kono atari / me ni miyuru mono wa / mina suzushi

311
summer has come
    yet just one leaf on
        the one-leaf-fern
natsu kite mo / tada hitotsu ha no / hitoha kana

AUTUMN 1688

312
3rd day of the month

like nothing
    it's been compared to:
        the crescent moon
nanigoto no / mitate ni mo nizu / mika no tsuki

313
In the rice fields at the Treasury of the Dharma Temple

after the reaping—
    from the side of a field of early rice
        a snipe's call
kari ato ya / wase katakata no / shigi no koe

314
Congratulations on a new house

such a fine house—
    out back, sparrows delight
        in the millet field
yoki ie ya / suzume yorokobu / sedo no awa

315
A View of Narumi

early autumn—
        the ocean and the rice fields
                all one green
hatsuaki ya / umi mo aota no / hitomidori

316
First day of autumn

weary of the journey,
        how many days like today?
                autumn's wind
tabi ni akite / kyō iku ka yara / aki no kaze

317
lotus pond—
        left as they are, unplucked,
                for the Festival of Spirits
hasu ike ya / orade sono mama / tamamatsuri

318
The fifth year of Jōkyō, Seventh Month, 20th day. I was entertained at Chōkō's "Bamboo Leaf Eaves" hut.

With millet and grass
        not a thing wanting:
                grass-thatched hut
awa hie ni / toboshiku mo arazu / kusa no io

319
Butterfly on a chrysanthemum blossom

deep into autumn—
        a butterfly sipping
                chrysanthemum dew
aki o hete / chō mo nameru ya / kiku no tsuyu

320
not hidden
    at this house: vegetable soup
        with red pepper
kakusanu zo / yado wa najiru ni / tōgarashi

321
Yasui departing on a journey

seeing you off,
    your back in the distance—
        lonely autumn wind
miokuri no / ushiro ya sabishi / aki no kaze

322
seeing friends off,
    being seen off, and now:
        autumn in Kiso
okuraretsu / okuritsu hate wa / kiso no aki

323
so many plants,
    each with its own
        brilliant blossom
kusa iroiro / ono ono hana no / tegara kana

324
Friends saw me off at the outskirts of town and we shared a few drinks

morning glories
    oblivious to all the drinking
        are in full bloom
asagao wa / sakamori shiranu / sakari kana

325
trembling, teetering,
    now even more dew-like—
        lady flowers
hyoro hyoro to / nao tsuyukeshi ya / ominaeshi

326
its inside I'd like
      to line with lacquer:
            moon at the inn
ano naka ni / makie kakitashi / yado no tsuki

327
the hanging bridge—
      grasping for dear life,
            ivy vines
kakehashi ya / inochi o karamu / tsuta katsura

328
high hanging bridge—
      what first comes to mind
            is the Meeting with the Horses
kakehashi ya / mazu omoiizu / uma mukae

329
Mt. Obasute

her face—
      an old woman weeping alone:
            moon as companion
omokage ya / oba hitori naku / tsuki no tomo

330
moon of the sixteenth
      and still I linger here
            near Sarashina
izayoi mo / mada sarashina no / kōri kana

331
biting deep within,
      the pungent radish:
            autumn wind
mi ni shimite / daikon karashi / aki no kaze

332
chestnuts of Kiso:
    for those of the floating world,
        my souvenir
kiso no tochi / ukiyo no hito no / miyage kana

333
Zenkōji Temple

the moon's light—
    four gates, four sects
        yet only one
tsuki kage ya / shimon shishū mo / tada hitotsu

334
blowing away
    the rocks: Asama's
        autumn windstorm
fukitobasu / ishi wa asama no / nowaki kana

335
The old master of this lotus pond loves chrysanthemums. Yesterday, there was a celebration at Mount Lu, and today we drink the rest of the wine, each of us sporting with making verse. We wonder now, who among us will enjoy good health next year on this day?

the sixteenth night moon?
    or is it this morning's lingering
        chrysanthemums?
izayoi no / izure ka kesa ni / nokoru kiku

336
emaciated in Kiso
    and still not recovered:
        late harvest moon
kiso no yase mo / mada naoranu ni / nochi no tsuki

337
the ivy leaves
    are tinged with the past:
        autumn foliage
tsuta no ha wa / mukashi mekitaru / momiji kana

338
departing autumn—
    wrapping my body
        in the narrow bedding
yuku aki ya / mi ni hikimatou / minobuton

339
chrysanthemums and
    cockscombs: every flower cut
        for Nichiren's death day
kiku keitō / kiri tsukushikeri / omeikō

WINTER 1688–89

340
winter seclusion:
    again I'll lean back against
        my old post
fuyugomori / mata yorisowan / kono hashira

341
five or six of us
    lined up before the tea cakes:
        the sunken hearth
itsutsu mutsu / cha no ko ni narabu / irori kana

342
I had heard the good name of the Buddhist layman Dōen of
Daitsūan Hut. With warm feelings toward him, I promised that
we would meet, but before that day could come, he passed away
like the frost of an early winter evening. Hearing that today is
the first anniversary of his death,

I long to imagine
    how you looked—your staff
        of withered wood
sono katachi / mibaya kareki no / tsue no take

343

Grieving over Rika's wife

lying down,
    the futon pulled up:
        cold, desolate night
kazuki fusu / futon ya samuki / yo ya sugoki

344

At the memorial of a certain person

do they extinguish even
    the banked charcoal?
        the sound of hissing tears
uzumibi mo / kiyu ya namida no / niyuru oto

345

Jūzō of the province of Owari is known as Etsujin, a name that
comes from the place where he was born. Now he hides himself
in the city, but only to supply himself with some food and fuel.
If he works two days, he plays the next two; if he works three
days, he plays the next three. He loves his wine, and he sings
from the *Tales of the Heike* when he's drunk. A true friend
indeed.

that snow we saw:
    this year also
        has it fallen?
futari mishi / yuki wa kotoshi mo / furikeru ka

346

On a snowy night I playfully sought a *dai* hood, using the two
words "buying rice" as my topic

off to buy rice
    with a snow covered bag—
        my winter hood
kome kai ni / yuki no fukuro ya / nagezukin

347
are you a companion
        to these creepers secluded away?
            winter vegetable seller
sashikomoru / mugura no tomo ka / fuyuna uri

SPRING 1689

348
New Year's Day:
        it's the sun in each field
            that brings such longing
ganjitsu wa / tagoto no hi koso / koishikere

349
so enticing—
        in the spring of this year too
            the sky of wayfaring
omoshiro ya / kotoshi no haru mo / tabi no sora

350
morning and evening,
        as if someone waits for me at Matsushima:
            my unfulfilled love
asa yosa o / taga matsu shima zo / katagokoro

351
Second year of Genroku, Second Month, at Tōzan's lodging

heat waves
        shimmering from the shoulders
            of my paper robe
kagerō no / waga kata ni tatsu / kamiko kana

352
red-blossom plums—
        unseen love engendered
            by the courtly blind
kōbai ya / minu koi tsukuru / tamasudare

353
Worshiping at Futamigaura

doubt it not:
 the blossoms of the tide also show
  spring upon this bay
utagau na / ushio no hana mo / ura no haru

354
even the creepers:
 their new leaves lovely
  at the dilapidated house
mugura sae / wakaba wa yasashi / yabure ie

355
a skylark's singing,
 and keeping to its rhythm,
  a pheasant's cry
hibari naku / naka no hyōshi ya / kiji no koe

356
On a painting of someone drinking sake

no moon, no blossoms,
 just drinking sake
  all alone
tsuki hana mo / nakute sake nomu / hitori kana

357
Giving my grass hermitage to a family with daughters

a grass hut too
 has a season of moving:
  a doll's house
kusa no to mo / sumikawaru yo zo / hina no ie

358
young sweetfish
 seeing off the whitefish:
  departure
ayu no ko no / shirauo okuru / wakare kana

359
departing spring—
     birds cry, in the fishes'
          eyes are tears
yuku haru ya / tori naki uo no / me wa namida

360
Muro no Yashima

with threads of
     heat waves it is interwoven:
          the smoke
itoyū ni / musubitsukitaru / kemuri kana

361
the sun about to sink,
     and the threading heat waves
          departing
irikakaru / hi mo itoyū no / nagori kana

362
a village where no
     bells ring: what, then,
          of spring evenings?
kane tsukanu / sato wa nani o ka / haru no kure

363
Spending a lonely spring evening in a country cottage

the sunset bell too
     cannot be heard:
          spring evening
iriai no / kane mo kikoezu / haru no kure

SUMMER 1689

364
so holy:
     green leaves, young leaves,
          in sun's light
ara tōto / aoba wakaba no / hi no hikari

365
for a while
    secluded at a waterfall—
    start of the summer retreat
shibaraku wa / taki ni komoru ya / ge no hajime

366
In search of Suitō of Yoze in Nasu Province

a man carrying fodder:
    I'll make him our guide
    across this summer field
magusa ou / hito o shiori no / natsuno kana

367
Concerning the beautiful views at Master Shūa's residence

mountains too
    move into the garden—
    a summer parlor
yama mo niwa ni / ugokiiruru ya / natsuzashiki

368
    A grass-thatched hut
        less than five feet square:
    regrettable indeed
        to build even this—
    if only there were no rains
tateyoko no / goshaku ni taranu / kusa no to o /
musubu mo kuyashi / ame nakariseba

I knew of this poem by Priest Butchō, but seeing the hut is far
more stirring than only having heard of it. Deeply moved, my
heart feels purified.

even woodpeckers
    don't damage this hut:
        summer grove
kitsutsuki mo / io wa yaburazu / natsu kodachi

369
rice fields and barley—
    and among them also
        summer's cuckoo
ta ya mugi ya / naka ni mo natsu no / hototogisu

370
in the summer mountains
    praying before the clogs:
        setting off
natsuyama ni / ashida o ogamu / kadode kana

371
On a painting of a crane and banana tree

a crane cries—
    that shriek will surely tear
        the banana leaves
tsuru naku ya / sono koe ni bashō / yarenubeshi

372
The deputy of the mansion sent me off with a horse. The groom leading the way asked, "Could you please write me a poem card?" "Such a refined request," I thought.

across the plain,
    turn my horse over there!
        cuckoo
no o yoko ni / uma hikimuke yo / hototogisu

373
As two monks on a pilgrimage to see the Deep North, we visited Shinohara in Nasu, and then thought of hurrying to see the "Killing Rock" of Sesshōseki. But rain kept pouring down, so we decided to stop over here first.

falling from high above—
    at a Takaku lodging,
        cuckoo
ochikuru ya / takaku no shuku no / hototogisu

374
The Killing Stone

the stench of the stone—
    the summer grass red,
        the scorching dew
ishi no ka ya / natsugusa akaku / tsuyu atsushi

375
The "willow where the crystal stream flows" stands on a foot-
path by a rice field in Ashino village. Several times the district
official, someone named Kohō, had said "I'd love to show you
the willow," and I always had wondered where it might be. And
now finally I stand in that willow's shade.

a whole rice paddy
    planted—I depart
        from the willow
ta ichimai / uete tachisaru / yanagi kana

376
from the west? from the east?
    above all in the rice sprouts
        the sound of the wind
nishi ka higashi ka / mazu sanae ni mo / kaze no oto

377
Crossing the Shirakawa Barrier

the beginning of all art—
    in the deep north
        a rice-planting song
fūryū no / hajime ya oku no / taueuta

378
The Chinese written character "chestnut" consists of "tree" and
"west," so the chestnut tree is supposed to be related to the
Buddha Amida's Western Pureland. They say that throughout
his life the Bodhisttva Gyōgi used the wood of this tree for his
staff and the pillars of his hut.

people of the world
    don't discern this blossom—
        chestnut by the eaves
yo no hito no / mitsukenu hana ya / noki no kuri

379
About five miles east of the post-town of Sukagawa is the Ishikawa Waterfall, which I've longed to see. At this time the water level had increased dramatically from the rains, and I was told it was impossible to cross.

summer rains:
    enough water to drown
        the waterfall
samidare wa / taki furiuzumu / mikasa kana

380
planting seedlings
    with the hands—ancient patterns
        from the fern of longing
sanae toru / temoto ya mukashi / shinobuzuri

381
satchel and sword, too,
    displayed for Fifth Month:
        carp streamers
oi mo tachi mo / satsuki ni kazare / kaminobori

382
the Takekuma Pine:
    show it to him,
        late-blooming cherries
takekuma no / matsu misemōse / osozakura

Kyohaku gave me this hokku as a farewell gift, so I wrote,

since the cherries bloomed,
    I've longed to see this pine: two trunks
        after three month's passage
sakura yori / matsu wa futaki o / mitsukigoshi

383
Rainhat Island—
　　where is it this rainy month
　　　　along muddy roads?
kasashima wa / izuko satsuki no / nukarimichi

384
I'll bind blue flags
　　around my feet:
　　　　sandal cords
ayamegusa / ashi ni musuban / waraji no o

385
islands and islands—
　　shattered into a thousand pieces,
　　　　summer's sea
shimajima ya / chiji ni kudakete / natsu no umi

386
At Takadachi in Ōshū Province

summer grass:
　　all that remains
　　　　of warriors' dreams
natsugusa ya / tsuwamonodomo ga / yume no ato

387
all the summer rains:
　　have they left it untouched?
　　　　Hall of Light
samidare no / furinokoshite ya / hikaridō

388
From Narugo Hot Springs we intended to head into Dewa
Province across Shitomae Barrier. Few travelers use this road, so
the border guards were deeply suspicious, and it was a long time
before they allowed us to pass. When we made the crest of a
high ridge, the sun was already down. We spotted a border
guard's house and sought a night's lodging there. But then heavy
rain and wind lashed us for three days, so we holed up in the
mountains in a thoroughly cheerless place.

fleas, lice,
   a horse peeing
      by my pillow
nomi shirami / uma no shitosuru / makura moto

389
making coolness
   my lodging:
      lying at ease
suzushisa o / waga yado ni shite / nemaru nari

390
crawl out here!
   under the silkworm nursery,
      the croak of a toad
haiide yo / kaiya ga shita no / hiki no koe

391
Seeing safflowers in bloom at Mogami

eye-brow brushes
   come to mind:
      safflower blossoms
mayuhaki o / omokage ni shite / beni no hana

392
stillness—
   sinking into the rocks,
      cicadas' cry
shizukasa ya / iwa ni shimiiru / semi no koe

393
gathering all
   the summer rains, the swift
      Mogami River
samidare o / atsumete hayashi / mogamigawa

394
At the home of Fūryū

at this water's source
   I would seek for an ice house:
      willow tree
mizu no oku / himuro tazunuru / yanagi kana

395
At Seishin's house

the wind's fragrance
   also suggests the south:
      Mogami River
kaze no ka mo / minami ni chikashi / mogamigawa

396
so grateful—
   perfumed with snow,
      the South Valley
arigata ya / yuki o kaorasu / minamidani

397
coolness—
   the crescent moon faint
      over Black Feather Mountain
suzushisa ya / hono mikazuki no / haguroyama

398
cloud peaks,
   how many have crumbled away:
      Moon Mountain
kumo no mine / ikutsu kuzurete / tsuki no yama

399
at Yudono,
   forbidden to speak,
      my sleeves wet with tears
katararenu / yudono ni nurasu / tamoto kana

400
his jewel-like spirit—
 it returns to Mt. Haguro,
  moon of the law
sono tama ya / haguro ni kaesu / nori no tsuki

401
moon? blossoms?
 to such questions,
  just four sleepers snoring
tsuki ka hana ka / toedo shisui no / ibiki kana

402
10th day of Sixth Month, second year of Genroku, after a seven-day devotional retreat at Mt. Haguro:

surprising freshness—
 after departing the mountains of Dewa,
  the first eggplant
mezurashi ya / yama o ideha no / hatsunasubi

403
thrusting the hot sun
 into the sea:
  Mogami River
atsuki hi o / umi ni iretari / mogamigawa

404
Kisagata—
 in the rain, Xi Shi asleep,
  silk tree blossoms
kisagata ya / ame ni seishi ga / nebu no hana

405
The evening rain ended, a certain person of the area guided me by boat into Kisagata Bay.

clearing at evening—
 cooling off under the cherry flowers
  with blossoms on the waves
yūbare ya / sakura ni suzumu / nami no hana

406
the Shallows—
    a crane with legs wet,
      the sea cool
shiogoshi ya / tsuru hagi nurete / umi suzushi

407
Mount Atsumi—
    all the way to Fuku Bay,
      the evening cool
atsumiyama ya / fukuura kakete / yūsuzumi

AUTUMN 1689

408
the Seventh Month—
    even the sixth night
      is different
fumizuki ya / muika mo tsune no / yo ni wa nizu

409
Looking out toward Sado Island from a post town called Izu-
mozaki in Echigo

stormy sea—
    stretching out over Sado,
      Heaven's River
araumi ya / sado ni yokotau / amanogawa

410
At the home of Dr. Hosokawa Shunan

in your medicinal garden
    which flowers should be
      my night's pillow?
yakuran ni / izure no hana o / kusamakura

411
skewering sea breams
    with cool willow twigs—
        a fisherman's wife
kodai sasu / yanagi suzushi ya / ama ga tsuma

412
in the same house
    prostitutes, too, slept:
        bush clover and moon
hitotsuya ni / yūjo mo netari / hagi to tsuki

413
the scent of early rice—
    cutting through the fields, on the right,
        the Rough Shore Sea
wase no ka ya / wakeiru migi wa / arisoumi

414
so red, red,
    the sun relentless and yet
        autumn's wind
akaaka to / hi wa tsurenaku mo / aki no kaze

415
I was invited to a certain grass hut

autumn is cool:
    let each hand set to peeling
        melons and eggplants
aki suzushi / tegoto ni muke ya / uri nasubi

416
A man named Isshō had become well-known for his devotion to
the way of haikai, but last winter he died. His elder brother held
a linked verse gathering as a memorial.

grave too move!
    my wailing voice:
        autumn wind
tsuka mo ugoke / waga naku koe wa / aki no kaze

417
At a place called Little Pine

a lovely name—
      Little Pine, where the wind wafts
            over bush clover and miscanthus
shiorashiki / na ya komatsu fuku / hagi susuki

418
At the house of Kansei

drenched passersby—
      they too are captivating:
            bush clover in rain
nurete yuku ya / hito mo okashiki / ame no hagi

419
so pitiful—
      under the helmet,
            a cricket
muzan ya na / kabuto no shita no / kirigirisu

420
Yamanaka—
      no need to pluck chrysanthemums:
            the fragrance of these springs
yamanaka ya / kiku wa taoranu / yu no nioi

421
peach tree,
      don't let your leaves fall:
            autumn wind
momo no ki no / sono ha chirasu na / aki no kaze

422
Fishing fires, one of the ten famous scenes of Yamanaka

by the fishing fires,
      a bullhead—under the waves
            choking in tears
isaribi ni / kajika ya nami no / shita musebi

423
leaving the hot-springs:
  tonight my skin
   will be cool
yu no nagori / koyoi wa hada no / samukaran

424
leaving the hot springs,
  looking back how many times —
   beneath the mist
yu no nagori / iku tabi miru ya / kiri no moto

425
from this day forth—
  the inscription washed away
   by dew on my hat
kyō yori ya / kakitsuke kesan / kasa no tsuyu

426
Visiting the Kannon temple at Nata

whiter than
  the stones of Stone Mountain:
   autumn's wind
ishiyama no / ishi yori shiroshi / aki no kaze

427
I would sweep the garden
  before departing: in the temple,
   falling willow leaves
niwa haite / idebaya tera ni / chiru yanagi

428
scribbled on,
  now the fan is torn up:
   memories at departure
mono kaite / ōgi hikisaku / nagori kana

429

I crossed the bridge at Asamutsu. The popular pronunciation is
Asamuzu, but in the "Bridge" section of Sei Shonagon's *Pillow
Book*, it is writen "Asamutsu."

Asamutsu—
    on a moon-viewing journey
      a dawn departure
asamutsu ya / tsukimi no tabi no / akebanare

430

Tamae

behold the moon!
    while the reeds at Jewel Bay
      are still uncut
tsukimi seyo / tamae no ashi o / karanu saki

431

Hina-ga-dake

tomorrow's moon:
    does it augur rain?
      Hina-ga-dake
asu no tsuki / ame uranawan / hina-ga-dake

432

At Hyōchi Castle

is this the mountain
    where Yoshinaka awoke?
      a moon of sorrow
yoshinaka no / nezame no yama ka / tsuki kanashi

433

The sea of Kei

the eight scenes
    of various provinces and now
      the moon at Kei
kuniguni no / hakkei sara ni / kei no tsuki

434
1689, gazing at the moon in Tsuruga Bay, I visited Kei Shrine
and heard of the tradition of the Yugyō Abbots.

the moon so pure
    on the sand carried here
        by the Pilgrim Priests
tsuki kiyoshi / yugyō no moteru / suna no ue

435
Fifteenth night, and as the innkeeper had predicted, rain falls

harvest moon—
    the north country weather
        so uncertain
meigetsu ya / hokkoku biyori / sadamenaki

436
On the same night, the innkeeper told us a story. "There's a
temple bell deep in the sea. Once the provincial governor sent
divers to search for it. And they found it, but it was upside
down, so there was no way they could pull it up."

where's the moon?
    the temple bell sunk
        to the bottom of the sea
tsuki izuku / kane wa shizumeru / umi no soko

437
At the beach

not just the moon:
    because of rain, even sumō
        has been called off
tsuki nomi ka / ame ni sumō mo / nakarikeri

438
At the harbor

the ancient name
    "Deer Antler" so lovely:
        the autumn moon
furuki na no / tsunuga ya koishi / aki no tsuki

439
loneliness—
    superior even than Suma,
      autumn on this beach
sabishisa ya / suma ni kachitaru / hama no aki

440
between the waves—
    mingling with tiny shells,
      bits of bush clover blossoms
nami no ma ya / kogai ni majiru / hagi no chiri

441
Drawn to Color Beach

drop your little petals,
    bush clover, on the little shells:
      our little cup
kohagi chire / masuho no kogai / kosakazuki

442
still not a butterfly
    as autumn deepens:
      a rape-worm
kochō ni mo / narade aki furu / namushi kana

443
When I open my door, to the west there is the mountain called
Ibuki. There are no blossoms; there is no snow. Only the self-
sufficient grandeur of the mountain.

just as it is—
    not even needing the moon:
      Mt. Ibuki
sonomama yo / tsuki mo tanomaji / ibukiyama

444
Written impromptu at Mr. Josui's villa

peacefully secluded here,
     I would love to pick fruit
          and the grains of grass
komoriite / ko no mi kusa no mi / hirowabaya

445
bloom quickly,
     the ninth is near:
          chrysanthemum blossoms
hayaku sake / kunichi mo chikashi / kiku no hana

446
A certain Sogyū, who lives in Seki, visited me at my lodging in
Ōgaki. The blossoms Sōgi refered to in "White Wisteria Slope"
were fragrant, just as when he wrote of them.

wisteria beans:
     I'll make them my poetry
          with the blossoms gone
fuji no mi wa / haikai ni sen / hana no ato

447
At Bokuin's villa

hermitage—
     moon, chrysanthemums,
          and an acre of rice
kakurega ya / tsuki to kiku to ni / ta san-tan

448
For a painting

Saigyō's sandals:
     hang them as well
          with the pine's dew
saigyō no / waraji mo kakare / matsu no tsuyu

449

like a clam from its shell,
    setting off for Futami:
        departing autumn
hamaguri no / futami ni wakare / yuku aki zo

450

I stayed over at the house of Yūgen in the Ise Province. His wife
was in complete accord with the wishes of her husband, faithful
in every way, and she soothed a traveler's weary heart. When
Akechi fell into poverty, his wife cut her hair so she could pre-
pare a renga gathering. Recalling now her selfless nature,

moon, be lonely—
    I want to tell of
        Akechi's wife
tsuki sabi yo / akechi ga tsuma no / hanashi sen

451

The Inner Shrine had already been moved, but I worshipped at
the Outer Shrine during its Ritual of Renewal.

for holiness,
    everyone's been shoving each other:
        the Shrine Renewal
tōtosa ni / mina oshiainu / gosengū

452

At a place called Nakamura in Ise Province

autumn winds:
    now the graveyard of Ise
        is even more desolate
aki no kaze / ise no hakahara / nao sugoshi

453

Futami

Saigyo's inkstone?
    I pick it up — dew
        on the concave rock
suzuri ka to / hirou ya kuboki / ishi no tsuyu

454
Shuei-in

entering the gate:
    by the sago palm,
        an orchid's fragrance
mon ni ireba / sotetsu ni ran no / nioi kana

455

transforming itself
    every single day:
        a cotton rose
edaburi no / higoto ni kawaru / fuyō kana

WINTER 1689–90

456
first winter shower:
    even the monkey seems to want
        a little straw coat
hatsushigure / saru mo komino o / hoshigenari

457
for the people in this house
    send down winter showers
        no matter the cold
hitobito o / shigure yo yado wa / samukutomo

458
mushroom gathering—
    in danger of getting drenched in
        a cold evening shower
takegari ya / abunaki koto ni / yūshigure

459
winter garden—
    the moon too a thread:
        an insect's song
fuyuniwa ya / tsuki mo ito naru / mushi no gin

460

on a folding screen
    a mountain is painted:
        winter seclusion
byōbu ni wa / yama o egaite / fuyugomori

461

Playing with children in the hills

in the first snow
    let's make beards
        from rabbit fur
hatsuyuki ni / usagi no kawa / hige tsukure

462

First day of eleventh month, second year of Genroku, for a linked verse at Ryōbon's house

hey kids!
    let's run around
        in the hail!
iza kodomo / hashiri arikan / tamaarare

463

Visiting the Southern Capital, I yearned for the eventual building of the Buddha Hall

first snow—
    for the Great Buddha, when
        will the columns be raised?
hatsuyuki ya / itsu daibutsu no / hashiradate

464

Song on a journey

off to the mountain castle
    of Ide, hiring a palanquin:
        early winter showers
yamashiro e / ide no kago karu / shigure kana

465
were they walking
　　around Chōshō's grave too?
　　　　bowl beating
chōshō no / haka mo meguru ka / hachitataki

466
With many people visiting my grass hut in Zeze,

if it hails
　　I'll cook and serve
　　　　wicker-caught whitebait
arare seba / ajiro no hio o / nite dasan

467
why does it head
　　to the market at year's-end?
　　　　a flying crow
nani ni kono / shiwasu no ichi ni / yuku karasu

SPRING 1690

468
Greeting the New Year near the capital

the man wearing
　　a straw mat, who is he?
　　　　blossoms of spring
komo o kite / tarebito imasu / hana no haru

469
With a person heading to Zeze

let's go see
　　the Festival of the Otter:
　　　　deep in the hills of Seta
kawauso no / matsuri mite koyo / seda no oku

470
a bush warbler
    drops its hat:
        camellia blossom
uguisu no / kasa otoshitaru / tsubaki kana

471
In my home village, having sown seeds of the three vegetables in
my brother's garden

spring rain—
    just beginning to sprout,
        eggplant seedlings
harusame ya / futaba ni moyuru / nasubidane

472
this tiny seed
    I do not belittle:
        red pepper
kono tane to / omoikonasaji / tōgarashi

473
Catching my interest in the mountains of Iga during the year of
the horse,

seed potatoes—
    with cherries blooming,
        the vegetable seller on his rounds
taneimo ya / hana no sakari ni / uriariku

474
At Mr. Kōboku's

pine-filled berms
    and blossoms – a manor built
        deep in the forest
dote no matsu / hana ya kobukaki / tonozukuri

475
Blossom viewing

beneath a tree,
    both soup and fish salad:
        cherry blossoms!
ki no moto ni / shiru mo namasu mo / sakura kana

476
so fitting—
    bean-flour rice balls
        while blossom hunting
niawashi ya / mame no komeshi ni / sakuragari

477
heat waves—
    the saiko's threadlike leaves
        in a thin haze
kagerō ya / saiko no ito no / usugumori

478
butterfly wings:
    how many times fluttering
        over the wall's roof
chō no ha no / ikutabi koyuru / hei no yane

479
It is said that long ago Hanagaki Village in Iga was made impe-
rial land to protect the double blossom cherry trees of Nara.

the whole village:
    are they all descendants
        of the blossom guards?
hitosato wa / mina hanamori no / shison ka ya

480
"it eats snakes"—
    hearing this, how ghastly
        the call of the pheasant
hebi kuu to / kikeba osoroshi / kiji no koe

481

An Account of Pure Washed Hall

from the four directions,
    blossoms are blowing in:
        waves of the grebe
shihō yori / hana fukiirete / nio no nami

482

Gazing upon the lake, lamenting the passage of spring

spring departs:
    with those of Ōmi
        I join the lament
yuku haru o / ōmi no hito to / oshimikeru

483

the solitary nun
    aloof in her straw hut:
        white azalea
hitori ama / waraya sugenashi / shirotsutsuji

SUMMER 1690

484

Staying over at Seta, I worshiped at Ishiyama temple at dawn and saw the Genji room there.

daybreak:
    in the lingering lavender
        a cuckoo calls
akebono wa / mada murasaki ni / hototogisu

485

Moving into the Unreal Dwelling behind Ishiyama Temple

for now I'll rely
    on the pasania tree:
        summer grove
mazu tanomu / shii no ki mo ari / natsu kodachi

486
you're the butterfly
　　I'm Zhuangzi's
　　　　dreaming heart
kimi ya chō / ware ya sōji ga / yumegokoro

487
summer grass—
　　before you come,
　　　　I'll hunt out the snakes
natsugusa ya / ware sakidachite / hebi karan

488
neither to evening
　　nor morning does it belong:
　　　　melon blossom
yūbe ni mo / asa ni mo tsukazu / uri no hana

489
the sun's path—
　　hollyhocks turn with it
　　　　in summer rains
hi no michi ya / aoi katamuku / satsukiame

490
fragrant orange—
　　when? in what field?
　　　　cuckoo
tachibana ya / itsu no no naka no / hototogisu

491
Firefly viewing at Seta

firefly viewing—
　　the boatman is drunk,
　　　　the boat unsteady
hotarumi ya / sendō yōte / obotsukana

492
in the capital,
>   yet longing for the capital—
>   cuckoo

kyō nite mo / kyō natsukashi ya / hototogisu

493
"The evening cool at riverside, Fourth Avenue," they call it. From early Sixth Month with its evening moon to the moon at dawn just past mid-month, people line up along the river in platforms drinking sake and feasting as they party all night long. Women wrapped in showy sashes, men sporting fashionably long coats, with monks and old folks intermingling, even apprentices to coopers and blacksmiths, everyone carefree and leisurely, singing up a storm. Yes, indeed, life in the capital!

river breeze—
>   wearing pale persimmon robes,
>   the evening cool

kawakaze ya / usugaki kitaru / yūsuzumi

494
A recluse named Tōko from the Naniwa area came to meet this untalented teacher.

don't take after me:
>   cut in two,
>   a musk melon

ware ni niru na / futatsu ni wareshi / makuwauri

495
my hut:
>   that the mosquitoes are small
>   is all I can offer

waga yado wa / ka no chiisaki o / chisō kana

496
The fleeting transience of life

soon to die,
  yet no sign of it:
   a cicada's cry
yagate shinu / keshiki wa miezu / semi no koe

AUTUMN 1690

497
On Tanabata

do not peek
  even through silk tree leaves:
   the stars' light
nebu no ki no / hagoshi mo itoe / hoshi no kage

498
At a thatched hut by Kiso Yoshinaka's grave, my heart was
drawn to the cemetery

Festival of Spirits:
  today too at the crematorium
   smoke rises
tamamatsuri / kyō mo yakiba no / kemuri kana

499
dragonfly—
  unable to hold on
   to the grass blade
tonbō ya / toritsuki kaneshi / kusa no ue

500
wild boars too
  are blown along:
   autumn windstorm
inoshishi mo / tomo ni fukaruru / nowaki kana

501

Unchiku, a monk in Kyoto, painted a picture—perhaps a self-portrait—of a monk with his face turned away. He asked me to write a legend on it, so I wrote: You are over sixty, and I nearly fifty. Together in a dream, we present the forms of dreams. Here I add the words of one asleep:

turn this way,
    I too am lonely:
        autumn evening
kochira muke / ware mo sabishiki / aki no kure

502

plucking out white hairs—
    under the pillow,
        a cricket
shiraga nuku / makura no shita ya / kirigirisu

503

harvest moon—
    children lined up along
        the temple veranda
meigetsu ya / chigotachi narabu / dō no en

504

harvest moon—
    turning toward the sea,
        the Seven Komachis
meigetsu ya / umi ni mukaeba / nana komachi

505

Moonviewing at an old temple

moonviewing—
    in the room not a single
        beautiful face
tsukimi suru / za ni utsukushiki / kao mo nashi

506
At our first linked verse party at Masahide's house

the moon about to rise—
    everyone with hands on knees
        in the room
tsuki shiro ya / hiza ni te o oku / yoi no yado

507
by a paulownia tree,
    a quail is crying
        inside the garden wall
kiri no ki ni / uzura naku naru / hei no uchi

508
A virtuous monk once said, "Superficial Zen is the root of grave
flaws," and I appreciate his words.

lightning,
    yet unenlightened:
        so admirable
inazuma ni / satoranu hito no / tattosa yo

509
At Katada

a sick goose
    falling in the night's cold:
        sleep on a journey
byōgan no / yosamu ni ochite / tabine kana

510
a fisher's hut:
    mingling with small shrimp,
        crickets
ama no ya wa / koebi ni majiru / itodo kana

511

At Shōzui Temple in Katada

sipping morning tea,
    the monk is peaceful:
        chrysanthemum blossoms
asacha nomu / sō shizukanari / kiku no hana

512

I spent a number of days in Awazu, where there was a man who
loved the tea ceremony. He gathered chrysantheum flowers
from a nearby beach and invited me to tea.

a butterfly too comes
    to sip the vinegar:
        chrysanthemum salad
chō mo kite / su o suu kiku no / namasu kana

WINTER 1690–91

513

On the road to my hometown

early winter showers—
    enough to blacken the fields'
        freshcut stubble
shigururu ya / ta no arakabu no / kuromu hodo

514

a cricket
    crying forgetfully:
        the brazier
kirigirisu / wasurene ni naku / kotatsu kana

515

Recalling days of old

frost has come,
    but a wild pink blossom
        on the wooden brazier
shimo no nochi / nadeshiko sakeru / hioke kana

516
winter winds—
    cheeks swollen in pain,
        someone's face
kogarashi ya / hohobare itamu / hito no kao

517
On a journey

first snow—
    the color of the knapsack
        of a wandering priest
hatsuyuki ya / hijiri kozō no / oi no iro

518
Traveling the Shinano Road

snow falling—
    miscanthus for the shrine hut
        still uncut
yuki chiru ya / hoya no susuki no / karinokoshi

519
plovers rising:
    as early evening deepens,
        winds storm down Mt. Hiei
chidori tachi / fukeyuku shoya no / hiei oroshi

520
A journey

year-end house cleaning:
    through the cedar trees,
        a windstorm
susuhaki wa / sugi no ki no ma no / arashi kana

521
A poetry gathering to see the year off

for half a day,
    companions to the gods—
        seeing the year off
hanjitsu wa / kami o tomo ni ya / toshiwasure

522

Sojourning in the capital, every night I heard the melancholy sound of a pilgrim beating his bowl while seeking alms.

dried salmon and also
    a Kūya pilgrim's emaciation:
        the depths of winter
karazake mo / kūya no yase mo / kan no uchi

523

hold for a moment
    the sound of slicing soybeans:
        bowl beating
natto kiru / oto shibashi mate / hachitataki

524

flying down
    on the stones of Stone Mountain:
        hail storm
ishiyama no / ishi ni tabashiru / arare kana

525

usually hateful,
    yet the crow too
        in this dawn snow
higoro nikuki / karasu mo yuki no / ashita kana

526

At Ōtsu

on low hills too:
    a mountain windstorm swirling
        the tree leaves
sanshaku no / yama mo arashi no / ko no ha kana

527

on Hira and Mikami
    snow mantles across the peaks:
        a bridge of snowy egrets
hira mikami / yuki sashiwatase / sagi no hashi

528
Responding to a request from Jōkō Ajiyari:

Ah, admirable, admirable! The bamboo hat is admirable. The straw coat is admirable. What kind of person bestows this to us, what person makes such a painting, this vision from a thousand years, appearing right here? Now with this form, the spirit too appears. The coat so admirable, the hat so admirable.

so admirable—
    even on a day without snow,
        straw coat and bamboo hat
tōtosa ya / yuki furanu hi mo / mino to kasa

529
hidden
    in the late winter waters:
        a diving grebe
kakurekeri / shiwasu no umi no / kaitsuburi

530
At Otokuni's new house

buying a house,
    and lending it to me:
        seeing the year off
hito ni ie o / kawasete ware wa / toshiwasure

SPRING 1691

531
Kiso's character:
    sprouting strongly through the snow,
        the spring grass
kiso no jō / yuki ya haenuku / haru no kusa

532
At Otokuni's house

plum blossoms and fresh greens
    at the Mariko stopover
        and that yam porridge
ume wakana / mariko no shuku no / tororojiru

533

Early spring in the mountains of Iga

mountain village
     and the New Year's dancers are late:
          plum blossoms
yamazato wa / manzai ososhi / ume no hana

534

moonrise gathering—
     carrying a plum branch,
          a novice mountain ascetic
tsukimachi ya / ume katageyuku / koyamabushi

535

so lazy—
     finally roused from bed:
          spring rain
bushōsa ya / kakiokosareshi / haru no ame

536

emaciated
     by love and barley?
          the lady cat
mugimeshi ni / yatsururu koi ka / neko no tsuma

537

year upon year—
     fertilizing the cherry trees:
          blossom dust
toshidoshi ya / sakura o koyasu / hana no chiri

538

drinking it all up,
     let's make it into a flower vase:
          the four liter wine barrel
nomiakete / hanaike ni sen / nishōdaru

539
for a moment
    it hangs above the blossoms:
        the night's moon
shibaraku wa / hana no ue naru / tsukiyo kana

540
old and infirm—
    my teeth bite sand
        in the dried seaweed
otoroi ya / ha ni kuiateshi / nori no suna

541
a mountain rose—
    I should stick it in my hat
        just like a branch
yamabuki ya / kasa ni sasubeki / eda no nari

542
On a picture

mountain roses—
    when tea ovens at Uji
        are so fragrant
yamabuki ya / uji no hoiro no / niou toki

543
a night of darkness—
    having lost its nest,
        a plover crying out
yami no yo ya / su o madowashite / naku chidori

SUMMER 1691

544
grievous junctures—
    the human fate of becoming
        a bamboo shoot
uki fushi ya / take no ko to naru / hito no hate

545
Arashiyama's
    bamboo grove so dense—
        the wind threading through
arashiyama / yabu no shigeri ya / kaze no suji

546
citron blossoms—
    let's recall the olden days:
        the food preparing room.
yu no hana ya / mukashi shinoban / ryōri no ma

547
cuckoo:
    filtering through the vast bamboo grove
        the moon's light
hototogisu / ōtakeyabu o / moru tsukiyo

548
sunk in sorrow,
    make me feel loneliness:
        mountain cuckoo
uki ware o / sabishigarase yo / kankodori

549
clapping hands,
    and dawnlight in the echo:
        summer moon
te o uteba / kodama ni akuru / natsu no tsuki

550
bamboo shoots—
    and my childhood
        sketches of them
take no ko ya / osanaki toki no / e no susabi

551
ears of barley—
    tinted in the tears
        of crying skylarks
mugi no ho ya / namida ni somete / naku hibari

552
day by day
    the barley reddens toward ripeness:
        singing skylarks
hitohi hitohi / mugi akaramite / naku hibari

553
devoid of talent,
    I wish only to sleep:
        raucous warblers
nō nashi no / nemutashi ware o / gyōgyōshi

554
Regretting tomorrow's departure from the Villa of Fallen Persimmons, I walked around gazing at all the rooms from back to front.

summer rains—
    poem cards peeled off,
        their traces on the wall
samidare ya / shikishi hegitaru / kabe no ato

555
wrapping rice dumplings:
    with one hand she puts back
        her fallen hair
chimaki yū / katate ni hasamu / hitaigami

556
Sixth Month:
    the burning heat of someone
        suffering from flu
minazuki wa / fukubyō yami no / atsusa kana

AUTUMN 1691

557
Early Autumn

early autumn—
    the rolled up mosquito net
        now a bedcover
hatsuaki ya / tatami nagara no / kaya no yogi

558
a begonia,
    the color of watermelon blossoms,
        in full bloom
shukaidō / suika no iro ni / sakinikeri

559
autumn's wind blowing
    and yet how green
        the chestnut burs
akikaze no / fukedomo aoshi / kuri no iga

560
seedhead of the reed—
    seized by demons
        of the Rashōmon gate
ogi no ho ya / kashira o tsukamu / rashōmon

561
in the cowshed,
    the dusky sound of mosquitoes:
        lingering summer heat
ushibeya ni / ka no koe kuraki / zansho kana

562
Thinking of constructing a hut, Kukū asked for a poem on a
painting of Kenkō.

the color of autumn:
    not even a pot
        of rice-bran mash
aki no iro / nukamiso tsubo mo / nakarikeri

563
loneliness—
  dangling from a nail,
    a cricket
sabishisa ya / kugi ni kaketaru / kirigirisu

564
The night of the fifteenth

friends who've given rice:
  tonight they're my guest
    at moonviewing
yone kururu / tomo o koyoi no / tsuki no kyaku

565
Harvest moon

Mii Temple,
  I'd love to knock on its gate:
    tonight's moon
miidera no / mon tatakabaya / kyō no tsuki

566
At Katada, on the night of the 16th

open the lock
  let the moon shine in—
    Floating Temple
jō akete / tsuki sashireyo / ukimidō

567
how easily it rose
  and now it hesitates,
    the moon in clouds
yasuyasu to / idete izayou / tsuki no kumo

568
sixteenth night moon—
  just enough time to boil shrimp
    in the night's darkness
izayoi ya / ebi niru hodo no / yoi no yami

569
harvest moon:
  though it's a second time . . .
   this moon at Seta
meigetsu wa / futatsu sugite mo / seta no tsuki

570
rice-field sparrows
  in the tea fields—
   their refuge
ina suzume / chanokibatake ya / nigedokoro

571
the hawk's eyes
  have darkened now:
   calling quail
taka no me mo / ima ya kurenu to / naku uzura

572
At the home of Sanshi in Tatsugaoka

gaze at the buckwheat, too,
  and make them envious:
   bushclover in the fields
soba mo mite / kenarigaraseyo / nora no hagi

573
grass-thatched hut—
  as day darkens I'm given
   chrysanthemum wine
kusa no to ya / higurete kureshi / kiku no sake

574
along the bridge beam
  endures the fern of recollection:
   farewell moon
hashigeta no / shinobu wa tsuki no / nagori kana

575
nine times awakened
    yet it's still the moon
        before dawn
kokono tabi / okite mo tsuki no / nanatsu kana

576
mushroom—
    a leaf from an unknown tree
        sticking to it
matsudake ya / shiranu ko no ha no / hebaritsuku

577
beneath the noodles
    building up the fire:
        the night's cold
nyūmen no / shita takitatsuru / yosamu kana

578
autumn wind—
    a paulownia tree being blown,
        now frost on the ivy
akikaze ya / kiri ni ugokite / tsuta no shimo

579
rice threshing,
    an old woman's good fortune:
        chrysanthemum blossom
ine koki no / uba mo medetashi / kiku no hana

WINTER 1691–92

580
Fourth year of Genroku, Tenth Month, staying over at Mr.
Riyū's place at Menshō Temple. It has been a hundred years
since this temple was moved here from the village of Hirata. As
it says in the record of contributions for the temple, "Bamboo
and trees grow densely, and the earth and rocks are aged with
moss." A truly venerable grove, deeply moving in its aura of
great age.

the ambience
    of a hundred years: this garden's
        fallen leaves
momotose no / keshiki o niwa no / ochiba kana

581

so very precious:
    are they tinting my tears?
        falling crimson leaves
tōtogaru / namida ya somete / chiru momiji

582

Words in praise of this garden

finely-crafted,
    now the garden is enlivened:
        early winter shower
tsukurinasu / niwa o isamuru / shigure kana

583

deep-rooted leeks
    washed pure white:
        so cold
nebuka shiroku / araiagetaru / samusa kana

584

Enjoying myself at Sensen's house

time to time
    gazing on Mt. Ibuki:
        winter seclusion
oriori ni / ibuki o mite wa / fuyugomori

585

An impromptu verse at Mr. Kōsetsu's villa

has the withering wind
    added some color?
        a bloom out of season
kogarashi ni / nioi ya tsukeshi / kaeribana

586
narcissus—
  and the white paper screen,
    reflecting each other
suisen ya / shiroki shōji no / tomoutsuri

587
its color
  whiter than the peach:
    narcissus bloom
sono nioi / momo yori shiroshi / suisenka

588
At Suganuma's house

weary of the capital,
  ah this cold whipping wind—
    winter dwelling
kyō ni akite / kono kogarashi ya / fuyuzumai

589
At Kōgetsu's house

awaiting the snow,
  the faces of the wine lovers—
    lightning flash
yuki o matsu / jōgo no kao ya / inabikari

590
winter winds blow
  the rocks sharpened
    among the cedars
kogarashi ni / iwa fukitogaru / sugima kana

591
I worshiped at the Hōrai temple in the province of Mikawa.
Back on the road, my old illness cropped up, and I spent a night
at an inn at the foot of the mountain.

praying for a warm bed,
    it has now appeared:
        sleep along the journey
yogi hitotsu / inori idashite / tabine kana

592

As early winter showers fell desolately, I sought a night's lodging. I dried my wet clothes by the hearth fire and scooped water to my mouth. The master of the inn treated me with kindness, comforting for a while the troubles of the journey. As the day ended, I laid down under the lamp, took out my ink and brush set, and started to write. Noticing this, he earnestly asked for a poem to remember our one moment of meeting.

putting up at an inn
    I am asked my name:
        early winter showers
yado karite / na o nanorasuru / shigure kana

593

With no settled place in this world, for the last six or seven years I've spent my nights on the road, suffering many illnesses. Unable to forget dear friends and disciples of many years, I finally made my way back to the Musashi Plain. Day after day they have come visit my poor hut, and I offer this verse in reply:

somehow
    still alive—snow on
        withered miscanthus
tomokakumo / narade ya yuki no / kareobana

594

the gods gone
    everything desolate among
        the dead leaves
rusu no ma ni / aretaru kami no / ochiba kana

595

arrowroot leaves
    with their face exposed:
        morning frost
kuzu no ha no / omote misekeri / kesa no shimo

596
geese clamoring
    on rice fields at Toba—
        frigid rain
kari sawagu / toba no tazura ya / kan no ame

597
fishes, birds,
    their heart we do not know:
        seeing the year off
uo tori no / kokoro wa shirazu / toshiwasure

SPRING 1692

598
a spring unseen:
    on the back of a mirror,
        plum blossoms
hito mo minu / haru ya kagami no / ura no ume

599
so enviable:
    far north of the floating world,
        mountain cherry blossoms
urayamashi / ukiyo no kita no / yamazakura

600
bush warbler—
    pooping on the rice cake
        at the edge of the veranda
uguisu ya / mochi ni funsuru / en no saki

601
Parting gift for one heading east

know my heart:
    with a blossom,
        a begging bowl
kono kokoro / suiseyo hana ni / goki ichigu

602
cats in love:
>   when it's over, from the bedroom
>   a hazy moon

neko no koi / yamu toki neya no / oborozuki

603
Sauntering

counting them as I pass:
>   house after house,
>   the plums and willows

kazoekinu / yashiki yashiki no / ume yanagi

604
"Rich in moon and bloosoms": at my hut there are a peach and
cherry tree; for my disciples there are Kikaku and Ransetsu.

in my two hands,
>   peach and cherry blossoms—
>   and mugwort rice-cake

ryō no te ni / momo to sakura ya / kusa no mochi

SUMMER 1692

605
The first anniversary of Fuboku's death: a linked verse gathering

the sound of a
>   cuckoo singing—
>   an old inkstone box

hototogisu / naku ne ya furuki / suzuribako

606
cuckoo cries—
>   five-foot spears
>   of blue flags

hototogisu / naku ya goshaku no / ayamegusa

607
Sixth Month—
    though there is sea bream,
        this pickled whale meat
minazuki ya / tai wa aredomo / shiokujira

608
on the Chinese gable,
    the setting sun . . . growing faint:
        evening cool
kara hafu no / irihi ya usuki / yūsuzumi

AUTUMN 1692

609
On the subject of wildflowers of the fields

they make me forget
    the heat of summer's pinks:
        wildflowers of the fields
nadeshiko no / atsusa wasururu / nokiku kana

610
under the crescent moon
    the earth is shrouded with mist:
        buckwheat blossoms
mikazuki ni / chi wa oboro nari / soba no hana

611
Words on transplanting banana trees

banana leaves
    will hang by the pillars:
        moon over the hut
bashō-ba o / hashira ni kaken / io no tsuki

612
harvest moon—
    swelling up to my gate,
        the cresting tide
meigetsu ya / mon ni sashikuru / shiogashira

613

Evening party at Fukagawa

green was just right
    and yet now it's a
        a red pepper
aokute mo / arubeki mono o / tōgarashi

614

Near the end of the Fukagawa river, the moon shining into a boat at a place called "Five Pines"

upriver and
    now downriver—
        moon's companion
kawakami to / kono kawashimo ya / tsuki no tomo

615

Enjoying the Onagizawa with Tōkei

traveling with autumn
    I would go all the way to
        Komatsu River
aki ni soute / yukabaya sue wa / komatsugawa

616

autumn departs
    yet something holds promise—
        green tangerines
yuku aki no / nao tanomoshi ya / aomikan

WINTER 1692–93

617

For a linked verse gathering at Kyoriku's cottage, 3rd day of Tenth Month, fifth year of Genroku

just today,
    let's all be old:
        first winter shower
kyō bakari / hito mo toshiyore / hatsushigure

618
opening the hearth—
    the aging plasterer
        with sideburns of frost
robiraki ya / sakan oiyuku / bin no shimo

619
salted sea breams,
    their gums too are cold:
        the fish store
shiodai no / haguki mo samushi / uo no tana

620
sweeping the garden,
    the snow forgotten:
        a broom
niwa hakite / yuki o wasururu / hahaki kana

621
banked charcoal—
    against the wall,
        the guest's shadow
uzumibi ya / kabe ni wa kyaku no / kagebōshi

622
into my moon and flower
    folly, I'll drive a needle:
        start of deep winter
tsuki hana no / gu ni hari taten / kan no iri

623
my heart
    so oddly at ease:
        Twelfth Month
nakanaka ni / kokoro okashiki / shiwasu kana

SPRING 1693

624
New Year's Day

year after year—
    the monkey wearing
        a monkey's mask
toshidoshi ya / saru ni kisetaru / saru no men

625
slowly spring
    is taking shape:
        moon and plum
haru mo yaya / keshiki totonou / tsuki to ume

626
On a portrai of Master Shrimp

a whitefish—
    opening its black eyes
        in the net of the Law
shirauo ya / kuroki me o aku / nori no ami

627
On an propitious day in Second Month, Zekitsu had his head shaven and entered medical school, and I offered him my congratulations.

on this First Horse Day,
    a fox must have shaved
        your head
hatsu uma ni / kitsune no sorishi / atama kana

628
Words of farewell to monk Sengin
a crane's black
    robe of feathers—
        clouds of blossoms
tsuru no ke no / kuroki koromo ya / hana no kumo

SUMMER 1693

629
cuckoo:
>   its call stretching out
>   across the water
hototogisu / koe yokotau ya / mizu no ue

630
going beyond even
>   the art of wind and moon:
>   peony blossoms
fūgetsu no / zai mo hanare yo / fukamigusa

631
As Kyoriku sets off on the Kiso Road

emulate the heart
>   of a wayfarer:
>   pasania blossoms
tabibito no / kokoro ni mo niyo / shii no hana

632
learn from the journey
>   of a sorrowing wayfarer:
>   flies of Kiso
uki hito no / tabi ni mo narae / kiso no hae

633
moonflower—
>   sticking my drunken face
>   out the window
yūgao ya / yōte kao dasu / mado no ana

634
children!
>   noonflowers have bloomed,
>   and I'll peel a melon
kodomora yo / hirugao sakinu / uri mukan

AUTUMN 1693

635
Komachi's poem

with flooding waters
        the stars too sleep on their journey—
                upon a rock
takamizu ni / hoshi mo tabine ya / iwa no ue

636
without dropping
        its bright white dew,
                a bush clover sways
shiratsuyu mo / kobosanu hagi no / uneri kana

637
first mushroom—
        just a few days into the season,
                autumn dew
hatsutake ya / mada hikazu henu / aki no tsuyu

638
Autumn, the sixth year of Genroku: wearied of people, I locked
my gate.

morning glories—
        locked during daytime,
                my fence gate
asagao ya / hiru wa jō orosu / mon no kaki

639
When I had shut my gate in Fukagawa

morning glories—
        even they, too, are not
                my friend
asagao ya / kore mo mata waga / tomo narazu

640
fish stench:
on top of waterweed
dace entrails
namagusashi / konagi ga ue no / hae no wata

641
sixteenth night moon—
ever so slightly
the darkening begins
izayoi wa / wazuka ni yami no / hajime kana

642
Lamenting the death of Matsukura Ranran

in autumn's wind,
sadly broken,
a mulberry staff
akikaze ni / orete kanashiki / kuwa no tsue

643
3rd day of Ninth Month, visiting his grave

have you seen it?—
on the seventh night, over your grave,
the third-day moon
mishi ya sono / nanuka wa haka no / mika no tsuki

644
Mourning Tōjun

the moon has set;
all that remains is
the four corners of his desk
iru tsuki no / ato wa tsukue no / yosumi kana

645
chrysanthemums blooming—
in a stonemason's yard
amid the stones
kiku no hana / saku ya ishiya no / ishi no ai

WINTER 1693–94

646

on the gold screen
   a pine of great age—
      winter seclusion
kinbyō no / matsu no furusa yo / fuyugomori

647

Sixth year of Genroku, 9th day of the first month of winter, visiting Sodō's chrysanthemum garden. The Chrysanthemum Festival is held today, the 9th day of the Tenth Month, because in Ninth Month the chrysanthemums had not yet budded. As a Chinese poem says, "The Chrysanthemum Festival is any time they are in bloom," and it's not unprecedented for the Festival to be postponed. So though it's winter, we're encouraged to write poems on the autumn chrysanthemum.

chrysanthemum fragrance—
   in the garden, the sole
      of a worn-out sandal
kiku no ka ya / niwa ni kiretaru / kutsu no soko

648

winter chrysanthemums—
   rice bran spilling over them
      from a nearby hand mill
kangiku ya / konuka no kakaru / usu no hata

649

winter chrysanthemum—
   heating sweet wine
      in front of the window
kangiku ya / amazake tsukuru / mado no saki

650

wrapped warm
   in its feather robe,
      the duck's feet
kegoromo ni / tsutsumite nukushi / kamo no ashi

651
On the topic of harvesting radishes

up in the saddle
    sits a little boy—
        radish harvest
kuratsubo ni / kobōzu noru ya / daikonhiki

652
When the huge bridge over Fukagawa River was half completed

first snow—
    coating the bridge
        under construction
hatsuyuki ya / kakekakaritaru / hashi no ue

653
Eating vegetable roots, I talked all day with samurai

a samurai gathering:
    pungent as a radish is
        their talk
mononofu no / daikon nigaki / hanashi kana

654
20th of Tenth Month, an impromptu verse at Fukagawa

the pathos of
    the birdseller's geese:
        Festival of Ebisu
furiuri no / gan aware nari / ebisukō

655
Ebisu Festival:
    vinegar salesman decked out
        in formal wear
ebisukō / suuri ni hakama / kisenikeri

656
The *Shin-Ryōgoku* Bridge being completed,

everyone heads off,
     grateful for the bridge:
          frosted roadway
mina idete / hashi o itadaku / shimoji kana

657
still alive
     all frozen into one:
          sea slugs
ikinagara / hitotsu ni kōru / namako kana

658
year-end housecleaning:
     hanging his own shelf,
          a carpenter
susuhaki wa / ono ga tana tsuru / daiku kana

659
and also a night
     a thief came calling:
          year's end
nusubito ni / ōta yo mo ari / toshi no kure

SPRING 1694

660
decorations of the immortals:
     I'd love to hear from Ise
          the first news of the year
hōrai ni / kikabaya ise no / hatsudayori

661
in the plum's fragrance,
     suddenly the sun—
          mountain path
ume ga ka ni / notto hi no deru / yamaji kana

662
as if touching
   a boil, willow branches
      bending
haremono ni / sawaru yanagi no / shinae kana

663
bush warbler—
   behind the willow,
      in front of the grove
uguisu ya / yanagi no ushiro / yabu no mae

664
in the plum's fragrance
   the single term "the past"
      holds such pathos
ume ga ka ni / mukashi no ichiji / aware nari

665
Buddha's Nirvana Day —
   wrinkled hands together,
      the sound of the rosaries
nehane ya / shiwade awasuru / juzu no oto

666
forty or fifty feet
   in the sky, raindrops
      in the willow
hakkuken / sora de ame furu / yanagi kana

667
spring rain—
   dripping down the wasp's nest
      from the leaking roof
harusame ya / hachi no su tsutau / yane no mori

668
a green willow
 drooping into mud:
  low tide
aoyagi no / doro ni shidaruru / shiohi kana

669
spring rain—
 mugwort spreading out
  among the roadside grass
harusame ya / yomogi o nobasu / kusa no michi

SUMMER 1694

670
Sent to Tōrin in his new house (words for my own painting)

this dew isn't cold—
 the nectar of a
  peony blossom
samukaranu / tsuyu ya botan no / hana no mitsu

671
hidden in the bushes,
 do the tea-pickers too hear it?
  cuckoo
kogakurete / chatsumi mo kiku ya / hototogisu

672
deutzia—
 over it, dark, a willow
  bending back
unohana ya / kuraki yanagi no / oyobigoshi

673
hydrangea—
 and a thicket as a little garden
  for the cottage
ajisai ya / yabu o koniwa no / betsuzashiki

674
Seventh year of Genroku, Fifth Month, I set off from Edo, and
for those who saw me off, these words:

ears of barley
    clutched for support:
        bidding farewell
mugi no ho o / chikara ni tsukamu / wakare kana

675
especially when
    it comes into view—
        Fuji in Fifth Month
me ni kakaru / toki ya kotosara / satsuki fuji

676
bush warbler—
    in a grove of bamboo shoots
        singing its old age
uguisu ya / take no koyabu ni / oi o naku

677
summer rains—
    a silkworm ill
        in the mulberry field
samidare ya / kaiko wazurau / kuwa no hata

678
Entering Suruga Province

Suruga road—
    orange blossoms too
        have the scent of tea
surugaji ya / hanatachibana mo / cha no nioi

679
summer rains:
    blow that sky down,
        Ōi River
samidare no / sora fukiotose / ōigawa

680

At Nagoya in Owari

on a journey through the world,
        tilling a small field,
                back and forth
yo o tabi ni / shiro kaku oda no / yukimodori

681

When Yasui was building a hermitage

for coolness
        this Hida craftsman
                has the blueprint
suzushisa o / hida no takumi ga / sashizu kana

682

Stopping over at the house of the hermit Yamada

"the water rail calls there"
        people say, and so
                staying over at Saya
kuina naku to / hito no ieba ya / sayadomari

683

coolness—
        naturally, the branches
                of a wild pine
suzushisa ya / suguni nomatsu no / eda no nari

684

having carried brushwood,
        the horse returns—
                wine casks for rice-planting
shiba tsukeshi / uma no modori ya / tauedaru

685

At Yamei's house

coolness
        portrayed in painting:
                bamboos of Saga
suzushisa o / e ni utsushikeri / saga no take

686
clear cascade stream—
    has its water been drawn up
        for these jelly noodles?
kiyotaki no / mizu kumasete ya / tokoroten

687
Sixth Month—
    the clouds laid out on its peak,
        Windstorm Mountain.
rokugatsu ya / mine ni kumo oku / arashiyama

688
clear cascade stream —
    falling into the waves,
        green pine needles
kiyotaki ya / nami ni chirikomu / aomatsuba

689
in morning dew,
    dirty and cool,
        a mud-smeared melon
asatsuyu ni / yogorete suzushi / uri no tsuchi

690
At Kyokusui's house

summer night—
    at dawn, scattered leftovers
        of chilled food
natsu no yo ya / kuzurete akeshi / hiyashimono

691
While at Kyokusui's house, we chose the poetic topic "farm life."

fanning the rice,
    his wife prepares a special treat—
        the cool of evening
meshi augu / kaka ga chisō ya / yūsuzumi

692

plates and bowls too
    faint in twilight:
        evening cool
sarabachi mo / honoka ni yami no / yoisuzumi

693

Seventh year of Genroku, 21ˢᵗ day of Sixth Month, at
Bokusetsu's hut in Ōtsu

as autumn approaches
    our hearts are drawn together—
        a four-and-a-half mat room
aki chikaki / kokoro no yoru ya / yojōhan

AUTUMN 1694

694

At Honma Shume's house, hanging on the back wall of a Nō
stage, is a portrait of skeletons playing flute and drum. Is human
life any different than the sporting of skeletons? Zhuangzi used
a skull for his pillow and didn't distinguish dream from real-
ity—truly, this evokes the character of our lives.

lightning—
    through the face,
        miscanthus plumes
inazuma ya / kao no tokoro ga / susuki no ho

695

so cool:
    feet against a wall
        in a midday nap
hiyahiya to / kabe o fumaete / hirune kana

696

a narrow path,
    wire grass blossoms
        filled with dew
michi hososhi / sumotorigusa no / hana no tsuyu

697
At Yadō's house

tanabata—
       autumn is truly here
          as night begins
tanabata ya / aki o sadamuru / yo no hajime

698
While I was in Ōtsu in the summer of seventh year of Genroku, my elder brother wrote to invite me to return home for the Bon Festival.

the whole family
       white-haired, leaning on canes:
          a graveyard visit
ie wa mina / tsue ni shiraga no / haka mairi

699
Upon hearing that the nun Jutei had died

do not think
       you did not count:
          Festival of Spirits
kazu naranu / mi to na omoiso / tamamatsuri

700
lightning—
       into the darkness
          a night-heron's cry
inazuma ya / yami no kata yuku / goi no koe

701
the color of the wind—
       planted wild,
          the garden in autumn
kazairo ya / shidoro ni ueshi / niwa no aki

702
a village grown old:
       no house without
          a persimmon tree
sato furite / kaki no ki motanu / ie mo nashi

703
winter melons—
   all of them now
      with changed faces
tōgan ya / tagai ni kawaru / kao no nari

704
under the harvest moon,
   mist at the foot of the mountains
      haze over the rice paddies
meigetsu ni / fumoto no kiri ya / ta no kumori

705
seeming to be
   blossoms of the harvest moon:
      cotton field
meigetsu no / hana ka to miete / watabatake

706
cockscombs—
   with geese arriving,
      now deeper crimson
keitō ya / kari no kuru toki / nao akashi

707
may the hokku that come
   be unlike our faces:
      first cherry blossoms
kao ni ninu / hokku mo ideyo / hatsuzakura

708
new rice-straw
   is appearing . . . with
      early winter showers
shinwara no / desomete hayaki / shigure kana

709
I was visited by Tojū of Ise at my mountain hermitage

I'll serve buckwheat
    while they're blossoming:
        mountain path
soba wa mada / hana de motenasu / yamaji kana

710
departing autumn—
    with their hands outspread,
        chestnut burs
yuku aki ya / te o hirogetaru / kuri no iga

711
crying "beeeee" . . . ,
    the lingering sound so sad:
        night deer
bii to naku / shirigoe kanashi / yoru no shika

712
chrysanthemums'
    fragrance — in Nara, many
        ancient Buddhas
kiku no ka ya / nara ni wa furuki / hotoketachi

713
At Dark Pass

in the scent ofchrysanthemums,
    climbing through the dark
        at festival time
kiku no ka ni / kuragari noboru / sekku kana

714
penetrating even
    the lair of a wild boar—
        cricket's cry
inoshishi no / toko ni mo iru ya / kirigirsu

715
On the 13th, while visiting the Sumiyoshi market

buying a measuring box
    I then changed my mind:
        moonviewing
masu kōte / funbetsu kawaru / tsukimi kana

716
At Kiryū's house

autumn already passing:
    in the cold drizzle
        a waning moon
aki mo haya / baratsuku ame ni / tsuki no nari

717
On the 21st of Ninth Month, at Shioe Shayō's house

autumn's night
    has been struck and shattered:
        a genial conversation
aki no yo o / uchikuzushitaru / hanashi kana

718
My thoughts

this road—
    with no one on it,
        autumn dusk
kono michi ya / yuku hito nashi ni / aki no kure

719
wind in the pines—
    swirling round the eaves
        as autumn ends
matsukaze ya / noki o megutte / aki kurenu

720
Thoughts on a journey

this autumn:
    why do I feel so old?
        into the clouds, a bird
kono aki wa / nande toshiyoru / kumo ni tori

721
white chrysanthemum:
    gazing closely,
        not a speck of dust
shiragiku no / me ni tatete miru / chiri mo nashi

722
At Keishi's house, with the topic "Accompanying a boy under
the moon"

the moon is clear—
    accompanying my boy lover
        frightened by a fox
tsuki sumu ya / kitsune kowagaru / chigo no tomo

723
deepening autumn:
    the man next door,
        what does he do?
aki fukaki / tonari wa nani o / suru hito zo

WINTER 1694

724
Written during illness

ill on a journey:
    my dreams roam round
        over withered fields
tabi ni yande / yume wa kareno o / kakemeguru

NOTES

NOTES TO THE INTRODUCTION

1. Kawabata, Yasunari, *Snow Country,* trans. Edward G. Seidensticker (New York: Berkley, 1960). I have altered slightly Seidensticker's translation, in which the image of Heaven's River is rendered "the Milky Way."

2. For terms such as *haikai* and *hokku,* see comments later in this introduction and the glossary.

3. Kenneth Rexroth, *A Hundred Poems from the Japanese* (New York: New Directions, 1964); Cid Corman and Kamaike Susumu, *Back Roads to Far Towns: Bashō's Oku-no-hosomichi* (New York: Mushinsha, 1968); Sam Hamill, *Bashō's Ghost* (Seattle: Broken Moon, 1989); Robert Hass, *The Essential Haiku: Versions of Bashō, Buson, and Shiki* (Hopewell, NJ: Ecco Press, 1994).

4. See John Elder, *Following the Brush: An American Encounter with Classical Japanese Culture* (Boston: Beacon Press, 1993), and *Imagining the Earth: Poetry and the Vision of Nature* (Urbana: University of Illinois Press, 1985); Gretel Ehrlich, *Islands, The Universe, Home* (New York: Penguin, 1991).

5. Cor van den Heuvel, ed., *The Haiku Anthology: English Language Haiku by Contemporary American and Candian Poets* (New York: W. W. Norton, 1999); Bruce Ross, ed., *Journey to the Interior: American Versions of Haibun* (Rutland, Vt.: Tuttle, 1998).

6. Makoto Ueda's *Matsuo Bashō* (New York: Twayne, 1970) remains a useful introduction to his life and writings, and his *Bashō and His Interpreters: Selected Hokku with Commentary* (Stanford: Stanford University Press, 1991), a translation of 255 of Bashō's hokku along selected Japanese commentaries, is invaluable. Haruo Shirane, *Traces of Dreams: Landscape, Cultural Memory, and the Poetry of Bashō* (Stanford: Stanford University Press, 1998), provides a learned discussion of some of the cultural traditions at work in Bashō's writings. Peipei Qiu's detailed analyses of the Daoist influence on Bashō is illuminating.

7. For a helpful introduction to waka, see Earl Miner, *An Introduction to Japanese Court Poetry* (Stanford: Stanford University Press, 1968).

8. See Earl Miner, *Japanese Linked Poetry: An Account with Translations of Renga and Haikai Sequences* (Princeton: Princeton University Press, 1979), and Hiroaki Sato, *One Hundred Frogs: From Renga to Haiku to English* (New York: Weatherhill, 1983).

9. Very occasionally there are "miscellaneous" hokku, with no season word. In renga, while other stanzas may or may not have a season word, in the opening hokku it is required. And also very occasionally a poet might write a poem about a season other than the current one.

10. For a discussion of Shiki's impact on our understanding of haiku, see Shirane, *Traces of Dreams*.

11. For a discussion of the religious significance of the communal dimension of renga, see Gary Ebersole, "The Buddhist Ritual Use of Linked Poetry in Medieval Japan," *Eastern Buddhist* 16 (1983): 50–71.

12. Most translators of Bashō's poetry have left out the title or headnote. Ueda, *Bashō and His Interpreters,* and Shirane, *Traces of Dreams,* are notable exceptions. See Shirane, *Traces of Dreams,* 160–184, for a valuable discussion of greeting poems.

13. For a helpful discussion of poetic essences, see Shirane, *Traces of Dreams*.

14. For an application of this literary approach to Chinese poetry, see James J. Y. Liu, *Chinese Theories of Literature* (Chicago: University of Chicago Press, 1975).

15. For a fuller discussion of this idea, see the introduction to the companion volume of this book, *Bashō's Journey: The Literary Prose of Matsuo Bashō.*

16. In some cases, it was difficult or impossible for me to find out the genus and species, and in others experts give different names. One can dream of a "field guide" to Japanese literature, which would include a thorough scientific and cultural description of plants and animals, with not only photographs but also recordings of the sounds of nature (e.g., bird songs, pine wind) that are so important to the literature.

17. For Bashō's principle of the unchanging and the ever-changing, see Shirane, *Traces of Dreams*, 263–269. For a discussion of Bashō's stylistic development, see Ueda, *Matsuo Bashō.*

18. For a discussion of the effect of cutting words, see Shirane, *Traces of Dreams*, 82–115.

19. Probably the only bird we commonly do this with is the owl.

NOTES TO THE HOKKU

The season of the hokku is followed by the season word(s). One asterisk indicates the image is discussed in the section "Major Nature Images in Bashō's Hokku." Also see the glossary for images related to the moon (tsuki*) and blossoms (hana*), which are used so frequently, I have not included an asterisk. Two asterisks indicate that the term is discussed in the glossary.

1662 to 1669

1 spring ? came / year ? gone / second-to-last-day
   • Winter: Second-To-Last Day. 1662–63 (29th of Twelfth Month; February 7). Bashō's first dated hokku. Among the oddities of the lunar calendar, spring occasionally starts one or two days before the lunar New Year. The verse alludes to several poems. One is by Ariwara

Motokawa (888–953): "During the old year / spring has come. / The remaining days: / should we call them / last year / or this year?" (*toshi no uchi ni / haru wa ki ni keri / hitotose o / kozo to ya iwamu / kotoshi to ya iwamu*). Another is in *The Tales of Ise* (10th c.): "Did you come / or did I go? / I can't remember / was it dream or reality? / was I asleep or awake?" (*kimi ya koshi / ware ya yukiken / omōezu / yume ka utsutsu ka / nete ka samete ka*).

2   moon ! guide / this-way to please-enter / journey 's lodging
   • Autumn: moon. 1663. The hokku alludes to a line from the Nō play *Tengu on Mount Kurama* where the blossoms are the guide.

3   old-lady-cherry / bloom ! old-age 's / memories
   • Spring: old-lady cherry blossom (*sakura**). 1664. This type of cherry blooms before the leaves appear. The poem can be read as "blooming in old age is memorable," or "blooming in old age recalls her prime." The poem refers to a Nō play in which an old samurai states that dying in battle will be memorable.

4   Kyoto as-for / ninety-nine-thousand crowd 's / blossom-viewing !
   • Spring: blossoms viewing. 1666. The capital of Kyoto was said to have ninety-eight thousand households.

5   blossom as-for poor 's / eye to also appear / demon thistle
   • Spring: blossoms; demon thistle. 1666. Demons were thought to be invisible. The demon thistle has thorns and a scarlet blossom.

6   iris / resemble ! resemble / water 's image
   • Summer: iris (*kakitsubata**). 1666. A parody of a line in the Nō play *Blue Flag Iris* (*Kakitsubata*): "they look just alike, the *kakitsubata* and *ayame*."

7   autumn-wind 's / door's opening ! / piercing-voice
   • Autumn: autumn wind (*akikaze**). 1666. Bashō uses word-play to suggest the sharpness of the wind and the voice: *yari* means both "sliding" (door) and "spear"; *kuchi* means both "opening" and "mouth."

8   withered bent ! / world as-for upside-down 's / snow 's bamboo
   • Winter: snow. 1666–67. *Yo* means "joint" (of bamboo) as well as "world."

9   withering-frost in / bloom as-for depression 's / blossom
     field !
     • Winter: withered by frost. 1666–67.
10   blossom 's face / at timid do ! / hazy-moon
     • Spring: hazy moon; blossoms. 1667.
11   blossoms at not-open / grieve ! my 's / poem-bag
     • Spring: blossoms. 1667. *Akanu* means both "not open"
     and "not be tired of." "Poem-bag" was for carrying
     manuscripts of verse. An earlier version has the more
     conventional *ware* for *kochi*.
12   waves 's blossom as / snow also ? water 's / returning-
     flower
     • Winter: out-of-season blossoms, snow. 1668–69. *Nami
     no hana* refers to white wave caps. *Kaeribana*, literally
     "returning flower," is a flower that blooms after its
     normal season.

1670–79

13   cloud as separate / friend ! ! goose 's / living-separation
     • Spring: departing geese (*kari no wakare**). 1672. Bashō
     wrote this for his friend Jō Magodayū before Bashō
     departed for Edo. *Kari* means both "goose" and "tem-
     porary." The first line has been read also as "separated
     by clouds" or "beyond the clouds."
14   hangover / thing ? blossom <nom.> / is interval
     • Spring: blossoms. 1673–79.
15   acupuncturist ! / shoulder into needle hit / cast-off-robe
     • Autumn: pounding clothes (implied). 1675. The hokku
     parodies the classical poetic topic of a country woman
     pounding a fulling block, in this case a "Chinese robe,"
     another meaning of *karakoromo*.
16   Musashi Plain ! / one-inch extent 's / deer 's voice
     • Autumn: voice of the deer (*shika**). 1675. Musashi
     Plain, extending north and west of Tokyo, is the largest
     in Japan.
17   scales ! / Kyoto Edo equal-weigh / thousand-generation 's
     spring
     • Spring: spring. 1676. Kyoto was the old imperial capi-
     tal, and Edo (Tokyo) the new capital of the Tokugawa
     shogunate.

18 life is / scanty 's hat 's / under coolness
- Summer: cool (*suzumi**). 1676. Written during a journey to his hometown. Bashō finds cool shade only under his traveler's hat, rather than while resting under trees. The hokku alludes to a waka by Saigyō (1118–90): "Did I ever think / I would pass this way again, / so many years now gone by? / It's been such a long life / Saya-between-the-Hills" (*toshi takete / mata koyubeshi to / omoiki ya / inochi narikeri / saya-no-naka yama*).

19 summer 's moon / Goyu from leaving / Akasaka !
- Summer: summer moon. 1676. Goyu and Akasaka were two post towns very close to each other on the famous highway from Edo to Kyoto. The summer night, and thus the moon's passage, is considered very brief.

20 Fuji 's wind ! / fan in carry / Edo souvenir
- Summer: fan. 1676. Bashō is on his way from Edo to his hometown. The fan implies summer heat, and a cool wind from Mt. Fuji, near Edo, would be welcome indeed.

21 cat 's wife / cook-stove 's crumble from / come-and-go
- Spring: cats in love. 1677. Refers to a story in the *Tales of Ise* about Ariwara no Narihira (825–80) who visits his lover by going over a crumbled wall. A typical Danrin** parody of classical literature.

22 summer-rains ! / dragon-candle offer / city-guard
- Summer: summer rains (*samidare**). 1677. Mirages of light that sometimes appeared out on the ocean were thought to come from dragons offering candles to the gods of the sea. City watchmen lit lanterns in the night.

23 tree <acc.> cut / cut-end see ! / today 's moon
- Autumn: tonight's moon. 1677.

24 go cloud ! / dog 's run-urine / scattered-winter-showers
- Winter: scattered winter showers (*shigure**). 1677–78. An earlier version has for the second line "a dog running and barking" (*inu no nigeboe*).

25 frost <acc.> wear / wind <acc.> spread-sleep 's / abandoned-child !
- Winter: frost. 1677–78. This hokku alludes to a waka by Fujiwara no Yoshitsune (1169–1206): "Crickets

cry— / in the frosty night / on a frigid mat / I will spread out a sleeve / and sleep alone" (*kirigirisu / naku ya shimoyo no / samushiro ni / koromo kata shiki / hotori ka mo nen*). An earlier version has for the second line "spreading out a sleeve" (*komoro kata shiku*).

26 oh anything ! is-not ! / yesterday as-for passing / blowfish
   • Winter: blowfish. 1677–78. Blowfish soup is delicious but can be deadly.

27 consul too / is-prostrate / lord 's spring
   • Spring: spring. 1678. Every year the Dutch consul in Nagasaki paid a formal visit to the shōgun in Edo.

28 rain 's day ! / world's autumn <acc.> / Sakaichō
   • Autumn: autumn. 1678. Sakaichō, literally "boundary city," was a lively entertainment area of Edo, set off from the dreary city outside its boundaries.

29 Hollander also / blossom for come / horse on saddle
   • Spring: blossoms. 1679. See notes to hokku 28. The hokku alludes to an earlier waka by Minamoto Yorimasa (1104–1180): "When the flowers bloom, / please let me know," / I said to the forest ranger, / and now he comes. / Saddle my horse! (*hana sakaba / tsugemu to iishi / yamazato no / tsukai wa kitari / uma ni kura oke*).

30 blue-sea 's / wave rice-wine smell / today 's moon
   • Autumn: tonight's moon. 1679. *Tsuki* can mean "wine cup" as well as "moon."

31 look-around / gaze see / Suma 's autumn
   • Autumn: autumn. 1679.

32 morning 's snow / onion <acc.> garden 's / mark !
   • Winter: morning snow; onion. 1679–80. In classical waka, *shiori* refers to breaking branches to mark a trail.

33 ah spring spring / is-large ! / <quote> etc.
   • Spring: spring. 1680.

Autumn 1680

34 spider what <quote> / sound <acc.> what <quote> cry / autumn 's wind
   • Autumn: autumn wind (*akikaze**). 1680. The poem plays off of a passage in the *Pillow Book* (1002?) of Sei

Shōnagon (966?–1025?) in which the bagworm was
said to make a faint plaintive cry of *chichiyo chichiyo*
("father! father!").

35   flower rose-of-sharon / naked child 's / spray-of-flower !
   • Autumn: rose of sharon (*mukuge**). 1680. The hokku
     alludes to a waka by Yamabe Akahito (fl. 724–737):
     "The splendid courtiers / in their leisure: / all day long /
     they play at dressing their hair / with cherry blossoms"
     (*momoshiki no / ōmiyabito wa / itoma are ya / sakura
     kazashite / kyō mo kurashitsu*).

36   night secretly / insect as-for moonlight 's / chestnut <acc.>
     dig
   • Autumn: moonlight; chestnut (*kuri**). 1680. It is the
     night of the 13th of Ninth Month, the "later harvest
     moon," which is also called the "Chestnut Moon." The
     poem gives a haikai twist to a line from a Chinese poem
     by Fu Wen, "Night rain secretly burrows into the moss
     on the rocks," while creating an unusual connection
     between a chestnut and the moon.

37   fool ponder to / hell also this ! / autumn 's evening
   • Autumn: autumn evening (*aki no kure**). 1680. The first
     line was used by scholars commenting on classical texts.

38   withered branch on / crow <subj.> has-landed / autumn 's
     evening
   • Autumn: autumn evening (*aki no kure**). 1681 (Third
     Month; April-May). One of Bashō's most famous
     poems, which is said to have initiated his mature style.
     Two paintings illustrating this poem have one crow, but
     an earlier painting of an earlier version of the hokku has
     seven crows (*karasu**) in a large tree and twenty in the
     air. (The earlier version uses a different verbal ending:
     tomaritaru.) *Aki no kure* can be interpreted as evening
     in autumn and as evening *of* autumn: late autumn.

Winter 1680–81

39   where winter-shower / umbrella <acc.> hand in carrying /
     return monk
   • Winter: winter showers (*shigure**). 1680–81. The hokku
     alludes to a prose poem by the Chinese poet Chang Tu:

"The vast reach of misty rain begins to clear, and a heron appears, standing on the winter shore. Far off where the fog ends, a monk returns to a temple in the dusk."

40 brushwood 's door in / tea <acc.> tree-leaves rake / windstorm !
   • Winter: raking tree leaves. 1680–81. Written soon after he moved into the *Bashō-an* hut on the outskirts of Edo. In the haibun "The Brushwood Gate."

41 oar 's voice waves <acc.> hitting / bowels freeze / night ! tears
   • Winter: frozen. 1680–81. Written during a period when Bashō's poetry was turning away from his earlier, more superficial style toward the depth and melancholy of Chinese verse. It is in "broken meter," with the first line having ten syllables instead of five, with the cutting word *ya* placed in an unusual way that breaks up the last line. In the haibun "Old Beggar" and "Words on a Cold Night."

42 snow 's morning / alone dried-salmon <acc.> / eat able
   • Winter: snow; dried salmon. 1680–81. The headnote refers to a statement by the Chinese Sung philosopher Wang Xinmin: "One who can get by chewing vegetable roots can achieve a hundred things."

43 rock wither / water wilt ! / winter also is-not
   • Winter: winter. 1680–81. This hokku shows Bashō's transition from Danrin** to a "Chinese style": there is a haikai twist of expectation of what withers and wilts, but deep melancholy rather than wit is the motive.

Spring 1681–83

44 arise arise / my friend into make / sleep butterfly
   • Spring: butterfly *(chō*)*. 1681–83? An earlier version has the headnote "Drinking Alone" and a last line of "drunken butterly" *(you kochō)*.

45 butterfly ! butterfly ! / China's haikai / will-ask
   • Spring: butterfly *(chō*)*. 1681–1683. Another version reads: "of China's haikai / I would ask of you: / fluttering butterfly" *(morokoshi no / haikai towan / tobu kochō)*.

Summer 1681–83

46   snow 's within as-for / noon-face not-wither / sunlight !

- Summer: noonflower *(hirugao*)*. 1681–83. Draws on a pasage from the *A Zen Forest: Sayings of the Masters*, a popular Zen phrase book, in which enlightenment is compared to the resilience of the banana *(bashō*)* plant in snow and the plum blossom in full sun.

47   noon-face at / rice pound cool / pathos is

- Summer: noonflower *(hirugao*)*; cool *(suzumi*)*. 1681–83? An earlier version has "rest" *(yasumu)* instead of cool.

48   cuckoo / now as-for haikai-master / is-not world !

- Summer: cuckoo *(hototogisu*)*. 1681–83. Poetry pales before the beauty of the cuckoo's song, and poets fall silent. Danrin** style humorous exagerration.

Autumn 1681–83

49   white chrysanthemum ! white chrysanthemum ! / shame long-hair ! / long-hair !

- Autumn: white chrysanthemum *(kiku*)*. 1681–83. A playful use of an expression from the Chinese Daoist text *Zhuangzi*, attributed to Zhuangzi (Chuang Tzu, ca. 300 B.C.E.): "If your life is long, your shames are many." The long and narrow petals of the chrysanthemum recall white hair, as does the flower's long blossoming season. The rhythm of this hokku is a highly unusual, said to be 10–7–5.

Winter 1681–83

50   black-forest / what <quote> say although / morning 's snow

- Winter: morning of snow. 1681–83.

Spring 1681

51   water-weed in swarm / whitefish ! if-take / will-surely-disappear

- Spring: whitefish *(shirauo*)*. 1681. The poem gives a haikai twist to the conventional image of dew vanishing from one's hand.

52 bashō plant / first hate reed 's / two-leaves !
  • Spring: bud of a reed (*ogi**). 1681. His disciple Rika (dates unknown) offered a banana plant as a gift for his hut, but the ogi reeds common in that swampy area competed with it. The banana plant flourished, however, and not long after, his hut and the poet himself were called by the name of this plant.

Summer 1681

53 cuckoo / invite ? barley 's / flock miscanthus
  • Summer: cuckoo *(hototogisu**)*, barley (*mugi**). 1681. The hokku gives a haikai twist to a conventional image of being beckoned by miscanthus (*susuki**) plumes in the wind.
54 fifth-month-rain in / crane 's leg / short become
  • Summer: summer rains (*samidare**). 1681. The hokku plays off a passage from the *Zhuangzi*: "A wild duck's legs are short, but it would grieve if they were lengthened. A crane's (*tsuru**) legs are long, but it would bemoan having them shortened." Syllable rhythm is 5–5–7.
55 folly in dark / bramble <acc.> grab / firefly !
  • Summer: firefly *(hotaru**)*. 1681. An example of a Danrin**-style allegorical hokku, in this case referring to the darkness of greed and being blindly absorbed in one's goals.
56 evening-face <nom.> / white night 's outhouse on / candle hold
  • Summer: moonflower (*yūgao**). 1681. The hokku gives a haikai twist to a passage from *Tale of Genji* (*Genji monogatari*, ca. 1000) in which Prince Genji reads a poem from Lady Yūgao by torchlight.

Autumn 1681

57 aesthetic-poverty live / moon-gazer 's / Nara-gruel song
  • Autumn: moon. 1681. *Wabi*** refers to an aesthetic poverty, in which austerity and loneliness cultivate artistic and spiritual sensitivity. *Sumu* means both "to dwell"

and "to be clear." Moongazer is a fictional name for a recluse. The particular drinking song here refers to a porridge of beans, chestnuts, and so forth, cooked with tea, the kind of simple meal associated with a *wabi* recluse. In the haibun "Live Austere."

58   banana windstorm doing / tub in rain <acc.> / hear night !
   • Autumn: windstorm (*nowaki**). 1681. Interpretations differ about whether the tub is outside (to wash hands? to catch rainwater?) or inside (suggesting a leak). The broad leaves of the banana (*bashō**) plant flap in the wind and tear easily, and they are a traditional image of impermanence. In the haibun "Sleeping Alone in a Grass Hut."

Winter 1681–82

59   poor-temple 's / kettle frost in cry / voice is-cold
   • Winter: frost; cold. 1681–82 (Twelfth Month). In haibun "Old Beggar."

60   ice bitter / rat 's throat <acc.> / moisten
   • Winter: frozen. 1682, late Twelfth Month. Bashō had to buy water because the water by his hut was unsuitable for drinking. The hokku is based on a passage from the *Zhuangzi*: "A sewar rat drinks from a river, just enough to quench his thirst." In the haibun "Old Beggar."

61   ending-ending / rice-cake <acc.> echo 's / austere-sleep !
   • Winter: rice-cake making. 1681–82 (late Twelfth Month). Rice-cakes were made for the upcoming New Year's celebration. In the haibun "Old Beggar."

Autumn 1682

62   morning-glory with / I as-for meal eat / man !
   • Autumn: morning glory (*asagao**). 1682. Takarai Kikaku (1661–1707), one of Bashō's disciples, wrote the hokku: "as for me: / inside a grass gate, / a firefly eats nettles" (*kusa no to ni / ware wa tade kū / hotaru kana*). This was based on a proverb, "some insects eat nettles,"

roughly "every one to his own taste, and some prefer what seems bitter."

63   three-day-moon ! / morning-glory 's evening / swell-seem
- Autumn: crescent moon. 1682. A morning glory bud is narrow and before the sun rises, when the crescent moon is up, it begins to swell.

64   beard-wind <acc.> blowing / late-autumn grieve as-for / he <nom.> who
- Autumn: late autumn. 1682. The poem draws on a line from Chinese poet Du Fu: "Leaning on a staff of chenopod, lamenting the world: who is he?" The rhythm of the poem is 8–8–4 syllables, closer to Chinese-style verse.

65   world in pass-time also / especially Sōgi / shelter !
- Miscellaneous (no season word). 1682 (mid-Sixth Month; August). *Furu* means both "pass time" and "rain." The poem concludes the haibun "Under a Rain-hat," which associates him with Chinese and Japanese wayfaring poets who also wore such a hat. Bashō's hokku draws on a verse by the renga master Sōgi (1421–1502): "In a world of rain / life is like a temporary shelter / from a wintry shower" (*yo ni furu mo / sarani shigure no / yadori kana*). Sōgi's poem in turn alludes to an earlier poem by Lady Sanuki (1141?–1217?): "Life in this world / is suffering / yet over this cedar house / the first winter showers / pass so easily" (*yo ni furu mo / kurushiki mono o / maki no ya ni / yasuku mo suguru / hatsu-shigure*). Note that there is a difference of only one word between Bashō's verse and Sōgi's.

Winter 1682–83

66   bed-clothes as-for heavy / Wu in snow <acc.> / see perhaps
- Winter: bedclothes; snow. 1682–83. The hokku plays on lines from the Chinese poet Ko Shi: "My hat is heavy with the snows from the sky of Wu; / my shoes are fragrant with the blossoms from the land of Chu."

Spring 1683

67   first-day ! / when-think lonely / autumn 's evening
  • Spring: first day. 1683.
68   bush-warbler <acc.> spirit as sleep ? / lovely-willow
  • Spring: willow (*yanagi**), bush warbler (*uguisu**). 1683.
    The poem alludes to the famous story in the *Zhuangzi*
    where Zhuangzi dreams he is a butterfly, but when he
    awakes, he wonders if he is in fact a butterfly dreaming
    that he is Zhuangzi. In addition, it was popular belief
    that the spirit of a person could leave the body when it
    was asleep.

Summer 1683

69   cuckoo / sixth-month as-for plum 's / blossom bloomed
  • Summer: cuckoo (*hototogisu**). 1683. As plum (*ume**)
    blossoms are signs of the beginning of spring, the
    cuckoo's song is considered the harbinger of summer,
    and poets often wait impatiently for its first call.
70   horse clip-clop / me <acc.> painting in see / summer-
    moor !
  • Summer: summer moor. 1683. *Bokuboku* is an ono-
    matopoeia for the sound of horse's hoofs. Commenta-
    tors differ whether the scene is one of tranquillity or of
    frustration at the horse's slow pace. There are four ear-
    lier versions, three with different meanings from the
    final one: "a summer horse ambling, / I see myself in a
    painting: / dense growth" (*kaba bokuboku / ware o e ni
    miru / shigeri kana*); "a summer horse ambling, / I feel
    as if I see myself / in a painting" (*kaba bokuboku / ware
    o e ni miru / kokoro kana*); "a summer horse trudges, /
    I feel as if I see myself / in a painting" (*kaba no chikō /
    ware o e ni miru / kokoro kana*). The second of these
    has a headnote "Composed with difficulty on the road
    to a place called Gunnai in Kai Province." In the haibun
    "Praise for Painting of 'Summer Moor,'" which is a
    response to a painting of a monk-like figure on horse-
    back, who the painter identifies as Bashō.

Winter 1683–84

71 hail listen ! / this self as-for before 's / old-oak
   • Winter: hail. 1683–84. The oak holds its withered leaves through the winter.

Spring 1684–87

72 bell disappear / flower 's scent as-for strike / evening !
   • Spring: fragrance of blossoms. 1684–87.

73 curiosity ! / not-smell grass on / settle butterfly
   • Spring: butterfly *(chō*)*. 1684–87. One of several poems in which Bashō highlights—and implicity praises—something in nature that lacks or ignores conventional beauty.

Summer 1684–87

74 scoop from / quickly teeth in echo / spring !
   • Summer: spring (source of water). 1684–87.

Autumn 1684–87

75 voice is-clear / northern-stars to echo / fulling-block
   • Autumn: fulling block *(kinuta*)*. 1684–87. The Northern Stars are what we call the "Big Dipper." Based on the Chinese verse by Liu Yuanshu: "Across the Northern Stars, wild geese fly; / beneath the moon of the southern tower, winter clothes are fulled."

76 world 's inside as-for / harvest time ? / grass 's hut
   • Autumn: harvest. 1684–87.

77 pass-a-night-on-a-journey / my poems <acc.> know ! / autumn 's wind
   • Autumn: autumn wind *(akikaze*)*. 1684–87. In the haibun "Introduction to a Scroll of *Journal of Bleached Bones in a Field*," in which Bashō disparages his first travel journal.

Spring 1684–94

78 fall blossoms ! / bird also surprised / koto 's dust
   • Spring: falling blossoms. 1684–94. Music's power was said to be able to make dust move, and the second line echoes a passage in *The Tale of Genji*. Written on a

painting of a koto, a classical stringed instrument.

79   bloom-disordered / peach 's among from / first cherry-
blossoms
   • Spring: first cherry blossom (*sakura**); peach (*momo**).
     1684–94.

80   spring 's night as-for / cherry-blossoms onto opening / it
has closed
   • Spring: spring night; cherry blossom (*sakura**). 1684–94.

81   sparrow-child with / voice call-exchange / mice 's nest
   • Spring: young sparrows (*suzume**). 1684–94.

82   Saigyō / 's hut also may-be / blossom 's garden
   • Spring: blossoms. 1684–94. A greeting poem for Naitō
     Rosen (1655–1733), a haikai poet and patron.

83   bat also / come-out floating-world 's / blossom among bird
   • Spring: blossoms. 1684–94.

84   spring-rain ! / straw-raincoat blow-back / river willow
   • Spring: spring rain *(harusame**)*; river willow (*yanagi**).
     1684–94.

85   plum 's scent with / carry-back / cold !
   • Spring: plum (*ume**). 1684–94. Here the fragrance of
     plums recalls winter's cold.

86   butterfly bird 's / restless rise ! / blossom 's cloud
   • Spring: butterfly *(chō**)*; clouds of blossoms. 1684–94.

87   child to weary <quote> / say person to as-for / blossom
also is-not
   • Spring: blossoms. 1684–94.

88   world in bloom / blossom to also nembutsu / speak
   • Spring: blossoms. 1684–94. Amida is the popular
     Buddha of infinite compassion, and the *nembutsu* is the
     term for the chant "*namu Amida Butsu*" (hail Amida
     Buddha), a common form of worship.

89   this mallet <nom.> / past camellia ? / plum 's tree ?
   • Spring: camellia (*tsubaki**); plum (*ume**). 1684–94. The
     mallet first was used for fulling clothes by rural women,
     but now has become a flower vase treasured by the
     nobility. In the haibun "Praise for the Mallet," in which
     Bashō remarks that the uncertain and shifting fate of this

piece of wood is shared by the poor and wealthy alike, a
fact that should undercut both resentment and smugness.

Summer 1684–94

90 not-rain yet / bamboo plant day as-for / raincoat and rainhat
  • Summer: bamboo planting day. 1684–94. 13th day of
    Fifth Month was traditionally the day to plant bamboo.
    An earlier version has the cutting word *ya* instead of *wa*.
91 this hut as-for / water-rail even not-know / door !
  • Summer: water rail (*kuina**). 1684–94. In the haibun,
    "An Account of Kosen's Residence," where Bashō
    praises the rustic simplicity and remoteness of his host's
    house. A greeting poem for his host.
92 hydrangea / summer-kimono time 's / light-blue
  • Summer: hydrangea (*ajisai**); summer clothes. 1684–94.
93 squid seller 's / voice indistinguishable / cuckoo
  • Summer: cuckoo (*hototogisu**), squid. 1684–94.
94 rain occasionally / think thing is-not / rice-sprouts !
  • Summer: rice sprouts. 1684–94. "Awaiting the dawn"
    refers to a custom of inviting a friend over to stay up all
    night and view the dawn on certain propitious days on
    the First, Ninth, or in this case Fifth Month.

Autumn 1684–94

95 brushwood 's door's / moon ! as-it-is / Amidabō
  • Autumn: moon. 1684–94. An earlier version has "grass
    hut" (*kusa no to*) instead of "brushwood hut." This is
    the haibun "Amidabō."
96 worthy 's / that ! windstorm 's / after 's chrysanthemum
  • Autumn: windstorm (*nowaki**); chrysanthemum
    (*kiku**). 1684–94. Another version, with *mo* ("also")
    instead of *no* in the first line, appears on a painting by
    Bashō of chrysanthemums and bamboo.
97 hackberry 's fruit fall / gray-starling 's wing-sound ! /
    morning windstorm
  • Autumn: fruit of the hackberry; gray starling. 1684–94.
    The hackberry, or *enoki* (*Celtis sinensis var. japonica*),
    has round red-brown fruit in late autumn. Gray

Starlings, or *mukudori* (*Sturnus cineraceus*), favor the fruits. They are found in large flocks, and their sudden winging up startles the morning calm like a windstorm.

98   Japanese-lantern-plant as-for / fruit also leaf also shell also / autumn-foliage !

- Autumn: Japanese lantern plant; autumn foliage. 1684–94. The plant, also known as bladder cherry, is the perennial *Physalis alkekengi*. The "shell" refers to the red calyx that covers the fruit.

99   chrysanthemum 's dew / fall when-pick-up / brood-bud !

- Autumn: chrysanthemum (*kiku**); dew (*tsuyu**). 1684–94. A brood bud forms on an axil and when it is ripe, it falls and can propagate a new plant. Another example of Bashō looking closely at the details of nature.

100 my hut as-for / square 's light <acc.> / window 's moon

- Autumn: moon. 1684–94.

101 something speak-when / lips are-cold / autumn 's wind

- Autumn: autumn wind (*akikaze**). 1688–94. The motto is based on a Chinese proverb.

102 what eating / small-house as-for autumn 's / willow shade

- Autumn: autumn. 1684–94.

103 this temple as-for / garden full 's / banana !

- Autumn: banana (*bashō**). 1684–94.

104 mushroom ! / worn extent as-for / pine 's appearance

- Autumn: mushroom. 1684–94. The Japanese word for this mushroom literally means "pine mushroom."

105 monkey-showman as-for / monkey 's small-jacket <acc.> / fulling-block !

- Autumn: fulling block (*kinuta**). 1684–94.

Winter 1684–94

106 night throughout ? / bamboo freeze / morning 's frost

- Winter: frost; freezing. 1684–94.

107 discretion 's / bottom strike / year 's end

- Winter: year's end. 1684–94. A discretion bag was supposed to be a bag with excuses and other means of dealing with year-end debts.

108 winter-wind ! / bamboo in hide / become-quiet
- Winter: winter wind (*kogarashi**). 1684–94.

109 chrysanthemum 's after / turnip 's other / again is-not
- Winter: radish. 1684–94. The sophisticated chrysanthe-mum (*kiku**) is replaced by the lowly radish.

110 sleeve 's color / is-dirty cold / dark gray
- Winter: cold. 1684–94. Senka was a disciple in Edo.

111 Kanō-Motonobu / source pathos / year 's end
- Winter: year's end. 1684–94. *Kohōgen* was Kanō Motonobu, a principal painter in the famous Kanō school of painting. Bashō discovered a great painting at an end of the year sale, perhaps a family whose wealth had disappeared and in desperation was selling off great art in order to deal with debts.

Miscellaneous 1684–94

112 moon flower 's / this ! truth 's / master
- Miscellaneous (no definitive season word). 1684–88 (1685?). In the haibun "Praise for a Painting of Three Sages," which was written on a portrait of the renga poet Sōgi and the haikai poets Yamazaki Sōkan (16th century) and Arakida Moritake (1473–1549). The por-trait was painted by Bashō's disciple Morikawa Kyoriku (1656–1715).

113 desireable ! / bag 's within 's / moon and blossom
- Miscellaneous: no season word. 1684–94. Hotei is the round-bellied god of good fortune. The term "moon and blossoms" implies both the natural world as a whole and poetry about nature.

114 Musashino-fields ! / touch thing is-not / you 's hat
- Miscellaneous. 1684–94.

Spring 1684

115 spring begin ! / new-year old / rice five-shō
- Spring: spring begins; New Year. 1684 (probably New Year's day: February 16). Bashō's disciples helped sup-port him by giving rice. Two earlier versions have dif-ferent first lines: "so fitting" (*niawashi ya*) and "I'm rich" (*ware tomeri*).

Summer 1684

116 pine-wind 's / falling-leaves ? water 's / sound is-cool
   • Summer: cool (*suzumi**). 1684?

Autumn 1684

117 bones-exposed-in-a-field <acc.> / heart into wind 's / pene-
   trate body !
   • Autumn: piercing my body. 1684. This is the opening
     hokku in Bashō's first travel journal, *Journal of
     Bleached Bones in a Field*, as he imagines himself dying
     by the roadside.
118 autumn ten years / on-the-contrary Edo <acc.> / point
   old-home
   • Autumn: autumn. 1684. On his departure from Edo in
     Journal of Bleached Bones in a Field. His hometown
     was Ueno, but he had been living in Edo for over twelve
     years.
119 mist-rain / Fuji <acc.> not-see day ! / interesting
   • Autumn: mist (*kiri**). 1684. In *Journal of Bleached
     Bones in a Field*, where Bashō was crossing a mountain
     pass at Hakone Barrier, famous for its view of Mt. Fuji.
120 cloud mist 's / short-time hundred-scenes <acc.> / exhaust
   • Autumn: mist (*kiri**). 1684. In the haibun "On Mount
     Fuji." The haibun associates Mt. Fuji with two mythical
     peaks in Daoist lore. The final verb of the hokku, literally
     "to exhaust," was often used in Chinese aesthetics to
     refer to bringing something to completion and fulfillment.
121 monkey <acc.> listen / abandoned-child to autumn 's /
   wind how
   • Autumn: autumn wind (*akikaze**). 1684. In *Journal of
     Bleached Bones in a Field*. Early in his first travel jour-
     nal, Bashō meets a baby abandoned by the roadside. He
     mourns for the baby, ponders the cause of its situation,
     declares "this is from heaven," and then continues on
     his own journey, which was designed to expose himself
     to life's impermanence. (For a discussion of this poem,
     see Barnhill, "Impermanence, Fate, and the Journey.") It
     was a tradition in Chinese poetry to listen to the sad
     cries of monkeys.

122 roadside 's / rose-of-sharon as-for horse by / eaten
- Autumn: rose of sharon (*mukuge**). 1684. The blossoms of the rose of sharon withers after only one day—and in this poem it does not even last that long. According to an unsubstantiated legend, Bashō told the Zen master Butchō, who had disapproved of poetry, that haikai was simply what happens here and now. Butchō pointed to the rose of sharon and asked for a hokku, and Bashō composed this verse. The Zen master was deeply impressed. In *Journal of Bleached Bones in a Field*.

123 horse on sleep / lingering-dream moon distant / tea 's fire
- Autumn: moon. 1684. Du Mu was a Chinese Tang poet. Bashō refers to his poem "My whip dangling, I trust the horse, / Riding miles without cockcrow. / In the woods I drowse in dream; / leaves fly about, and I am startled awake." In *Journal of Bleached Bones in a Field* and the haibun "Dozing on My Horse."

124 last-night-of-month moon is-not / thousand-year 's *sugi* <acc.> / hold windstorm
- Autumn: moon. 1684. Bashō draws on a poem by Saigyō: "Entering deeply, / searching out the depths / of the pathway of the gods: / high above, over all, / a mountain peak with pine wind" (*fukaku irite / kamiji no oku o / tazunureba / mata ue mo naki / mine no matsukaze*). In *Journal of Bleached Bones in a Field*.

125 potato wash women / Saigyō if-be / poem write
- Autumn: washing potatoes. 1684. Waka is the classical five-line verse form used by Saigyō. This hokku has been interpreted three main ways: "if I (Bashō) were Saigyō, I'd write a waka"; "if Saigyō were here, he would write a waka"; and "if Saigyō were here, the women would write a waka." In *Journal of Bleached Bones in a Field*.

126 orchid 's fragrance ! / butterfly 's wings to / incense do
- Autumn: orchid. 1684. In *Journal of Bleached Bones in a Field*. Butterfly (*chō*) by itself is a spring season word.

127 ivy plant / bamboo four-or-five stalks 's / windstorm
- Autumn: ivy (*tsuta**). 1684 (late Eighth Month; October). A greeting poem for the haikai master Roboku

(1628–1706) of Ise. In *Journal of Bleached Bones in a Field*.

128 hand in if-take / will-disappear tears ! hot / autumn 's frost
   • Autumn: autumn frost. 1684 (8th of Eighth Month; October 16). In *Journal of Bleached Bones in a Field*, when Bashō has returned to his home village and been given the white hair of his recently deceased mother. The passage in the journal refers to the legend of Urashima, who rescued a turtle, who in gratitude took Urashima to the Dragon Palace. He spent some time there and was given a treasure box, which he was warned not to open. When he returned home he found that everything had changed, and when he opened the box, instantly he became an old man with white hair.

129 cotton bow ! / lute by console / bamboo 's interior
   • Autumn: cotton-beating bow. 1684. The bow was used to make soft cotton yarn, and made a sound that resembled a lute. In *Journal of Bleached Bones in a Field* and the haibun "Deep in Bamboo."

130 monk morning-glory / how-many die-return / Buddhist-law 's pine
   • Autumn: monrning glory (*asagao**). 1684. The passage refers to a story in the *Zhuangzi* in which an ancient tree is so huge that oxen can hide behind it. In the *Zhuangzi*, the tree lives long because it is useless—thus proving the usefulness of uselessness. Bashō turns the story into a Buddhist one. In *Journal of Bleached Bones in a Field*.

131 winter not-know / hut ! hulling-rice / sound hail
   • Autumn: hulling rice. 1684. In the haibun "The Sound of Hulling Rice," where Bashō praises a man in a mountain village for going to unusual lengths to ensure the comfort of his mother at all times.

132 fulling-block hit / me to make-hear ! / temple 's wife
   • Autumn: fulling block (*kinuta**). 1684 (mid-Ninth Month; October). Bashō was in Yoshino, rich in poetic and religious traditions. Clothes were pounded on a fulling block to clean and soften them, and in the poetic tradition the sound was associated with loneliness. The fulling block was not commonly used in Bashō's time,

but he wishes to hear its sound in order to feel deeply what was considered the essential nature of Yoshino in autumn. There is an allusion to a waka by Fujiwara Masatsune (1170–1221): "At Yoshino / the mountain wind / deepens into the night, / and in the old village / a fulling block is struck" (*miyoshino no / yama no akikaze / sayo fukete / furusato samuku / koromo utsunari*). In *Journal of Bleached Bones in a Field* and the haibun "Preface to 'beat the fulling block.'"

133 dew drip drip / trial as floating-world / would-that-I-could wash
   • Autumn: dew (*tsuyu**). 1684. Bashō alludes to a waka attributed at that time to Saigyō: "Trickling down, / pure spring water falls / over the mossy rocks, / not enough to draw up / for this hermit life" (*tokutoku to / otsuru iwama no / koke shimizu / kumihosu hodo mo / naki sumai kana*). In *Journal of Bleached Bones in a Field*. Bashō repeats the phrase *tokutoku* three times in this passage.

134 imperial-tomb years pass / remember as-for what <acc.> / remembrance-grass
   • Autumn: fern of longing (*shinobugusa**). 1684. In *Journal of Bleached Bones in a Field*.

135 Yoshitomo 's / heart to resembles / autumn 's wind
   • Autumn: autumn wind (*akikaze**). 1684. During the Hōgen Disturbance of 1156, Yoshitomo (1123–60) fought and killed his father, Tameyoshi, the leader of the powerful Minamoto clan. Two years later, he was defeated in the Heiji Disturbance and fled to Owari Province, experiencing the cold loneliness that autumn wind suggests. Yoshitomo was assasinated in Owari, and soon after Tokiwa, his mistress, was murdered, perhaps by robbers. Arakida Moritake, a Shinto priest at the Ise Shrine, was one of the founders of haikai poetry. In *Journal of Bleached Bones in a Field*.

136 autumn-wind ! / bamboo-thicket also farm-fields also / Fuwa 's Barrier
   • Autumn: autumn wind (*akikaze**). 1684 (late Ninth Month; October-November). Fuwa Barrier was located

near Sekigahara-machi in Mino Province. It was an important government checkpoint in ancient times, but was abandoned in the Heian period so that it was in ruins when Fujiwara Yoshitsune wrote the following waka: "The guardhouse abandoned, / the shingled eaves at / Fuwa Barrier / have fallen to ruin, / leaving only autumn's wind" (*hito sumanu / fuwa no seki-ya no / itabisashi / arenishi nochi wa / tada aki no kaze*). In *Journal of Bleached Bones in a Field*.

137 die-even-not-do / journey 's end ! / autumn 's evening
 • Autumn: autumn evening *(aki no kure*)*. 1684 (late Ninth Month; October–November). In *Journal of Bleached Bones in a Field*, where Bashō recalls the opening hokku of the journal (see hokku 117). Tani Bokuin (1646–1725) was a haikai poet.

Winter 1684–85

138 harsh / sound ! hail 's / cypress-hat
 • Winter: hail. 1684–85.

139 winter peonies / plovers ! snow 's / cuckoo
 • Winter: winter peony (*botan**). 1684–85. A greeting verse for his host Koeki (d. 1709). Peonies normally bloom in summer, the season for the cuckoo, while the winter peony, with small white flowers, bloom in the season of plovers (*chidori**). In *Journal of Bleached Bones in a Field*. An earlier version has the interrogative *ka* instead of the exclamatory *yo* in the second line.

140 dawn ! / whitefish white / thing one-inch
 • Winter: whitefish (*shirauo**). 1684–85 (early Eleventh Month; December). In *Journal of Bleached Bones in a Field*. This verse alludes to a poem by Du Fu, which has the couplet "Each whitefish has its life / by nature one inch."

141 horse <acc.> even / gaze snow 's / morning !
 • Winter: snow morning. 1684–85. A greeting poem for his host Tōyō (1653–1712), a haikai leader in Atsuta. His residence has such beauty even a horse has allure. In *Journal of Bleached Bones in a Field*.

142 long-for even / withered rice-cake buy / inn !
- Winter: withered fern of longing (*shinobugusa**). 1684–85. In *Journal of Bleached Bones in a Field*, where Bashō describes the dilapidated state of the shrine. In an earlier version, the second line has "selling" (*uru*) instead of "buying" (*kau*).

143 hat even is-not / me ! winter-shower ? / this as-for what <quote>
- Winter: winter showers (*shigure**). 1684–85. In another version, the last line is literally "what what" (*nan to nan to*).

144 wild-poem / winter-wind 's / body as-for Chikusai to / resemble !
- Winter: winter wind (*kogarashi**). 1684–85 (Eleventh Month; December). In a popular story, Chikusai was a comical doctor who lost his patients because he kept indulging in "wild poetry." (*Kyō* means both crazy and comic.) Like Chikusai, Bashō "looked very shabby" as he traveled to Nagoya, where he gave this poem to his host. There is an unresolved debate whether the line "wild poem" is part of the first line of the hokku or functions as a title. In *Journal of Bleached Bones in a Field* and the haibun "Preface to 'mad poem—in winter's winds.'"

145 grass pillow / dog also rained-on ? / night 's voice
- Winter: winter showers (*shigure**). 1684–85. Grass pillow is an epithet for sleeping on a journey and therefore of travel. In *Journal of Bleached Bones in a Field*.

146 city-people ! / this hat I'll-sell / snow 's umbrella
- Winter: snow. 1684–85 (Eleventh Month; December). The *kasa* hat is a broad hat made of bamboo. Another word pronounced *kasa* means umbrella. In *Journal of Bleached Bones in a Field*.

147 snow and snow / tonight twelfth-month 's / bright-moon ?
- Winter: snow; Twelfth Month. 1684–85. The snow is so bright it seems as if the full moon is shining.

148 sea darken / duck 's voice / faintly white
- Winter: duck. 1684–85. In *Journal of Bleached Bones in a Field*.

149 year ended / hat wear sandals / wearing
   • Winter: year's end. 1684–85. In *Journal of Bleached Bones in a Field*.

Spring 1685

150 who 's son-in-law ! / ferns with rice-cake carry / ox 's year
   • Spring: Fern fronds. 1685. It was a New Year's custom for a son-in-law to bring these gifts to his wife's family. In *Journal of Bleached Bones in a Field*.

151 travel-crow / old-nest as-for plum into / has-become
   • Spring: plum (*ume**); old nest. 1685. Written while Bashō was sojourning in his native village.

152 spring is ! / name also is-not mountain 's / thin-mist
   • Spring: spring; mist (*kiri**). 1685. In *Journal of Bleached Bones in a Field*. An earlier version has for the last line, "morning mist" (*asagasumi*).

153 water-dipping ! / ice 's monk's / clog 's sound
   • Spring: water-drawing rite. 1685. The water-drawing celebration is held the first two weeks of the Second Month at Tōdaiji in Nara. The particular ritual mentioned here occurs in the middle of the night as monks run around the altar. The second line also could mean "the frozen monks." In *Journal of Bleached Bones in a Field*.

154 world in scent / plum-blossoms one-branch 's / wren
   • Spring: plum (*ume**) blossom. 1685. Single Branch Eaves was the name of the house of the doctor Genzui that Bashō praises in the haibun by that name. "Single branch" is an image in the *Zhuangzi* in which a bird is content with using but one branch of a tree. The influence of the modest doctor's virtue spreads throughout the land. In the haibun "Single Branch Eaves." *Misosazi* is the Winter Wren (*Troglodytes troglodytes*), a tiny bird with ebullient song found in North America.

155 plum white / yesterday ! crane <acc.> / probably-have-stolen
   • Spring: plum (*ume**). 1685. Shūfū was a wealthy merchant in Kyoto and patron of poetry. In this greeting

poem, Bashō compares him to the Chinese Song recluse poet Lin Hejing, who was famous for both his plum trees and cranes (*tsuru**). In *Journal of Bleached Bones in a Field*.

156 oak 's tree 's / flowers to indifferent / appearance !
- Spring: blossoms. 1685. Probably another greeting poem for his host Shūfū, praising his venerable simplicity in comparison to the showy blossoms. *Kashi* refers to several species of evergreen oak with leathery leaves that grow wild in mountainous regions. In *Journal of Bleached Bones in a Field*.

157 my clothes on / Fushimi 's peach 's / dew do <command>
- Spring: peach (*momo**). 1685. The poet could be asking the Priest to use the dewdrops (*tsuyu**), or could be asking the peach tree itself. The distinction is not significant, since this is a greeting poem praising the monk by associating him with the peach blossoms for which Fushimi was famous. In *Journal of Bleached Bones in a Field*.

158 mountain-path come / somehow appealing / wild-violet
- Spring: violets. 1685. *Sumire* (*Viola mandshurica*) is a three inch high perennial that produces deep purple blossoms April to May in lowlands and hills. In *Journal of Bleached Bones in a Field*.

159 Karasaki 's / pine as-for blossoms more-than / vague is
- Spring: blossoms; vagueness. 1685 (early Third Month; early April). Karasaki, on Lake Biwa, is famous for picturesque pines and beautiful scenery. Nearby is Mt. Nagara, known for hazy cherry blossoms. Haze is traditionally associated with spring evenings. This hokku alludes to a waka by Emperor Go-toba (1180–1239): "At Karasaki / the green of the pine / is also in haze / extending from blossoms: / spring dawn" (*karasaki no /matsu no midori mo / oboro nite / hana yori tsuzuku / haru no akebono*). The modern hokku poet Masaoka Shiki (1867–1902) criticized Bashō's poem as plagiarism. In *Journal of Bleached Bones in a Field*.

160 azalea arrange / this shadow in dried-codfish / cut-up
     woman
     • Spring: azalea. 1685. This hokku is said to portray a
       rustic scence with a feeling of *wabi***. In one version of
       Journal of Bleached Bones in a Field.

161 mustard field in / flower-viewing-faces is / sparrow !
     • Spring: mustard blossoms. 1685. In one version of *Jour-
       nal of Bleached Bones in a Field*. This plant with four-
       petaled yellow blossoms is also called "rape," "rape-
       seed," and "Chinese colza" (*Brassica campestris*).

162 life two 's / between in lived / cherry-blossom !
     • Spring: cherry blossom (*sakura**). 1685. The friend is
       Hattori Dohō (or Tohō) Bashō, 1657–1730). In *Journal
       of Bleached Bones in a Field*.

163 butterfly 's fly / only mid-field 's / sunlight !
     • Spring: butterfly (*chō**). 1685.

164 iris / me in hokku 's / thought is
     • Summer: iris (*kakitsubata**). 1685. The hokku refers to
       The Tales of Ise, chapter 9, where Ariwara Narihira and
       several friends stopped on a journey near some blos-
       soming irises, and the poet is asked to compose a waka
       on the subject of "traveler's sentiments" beginning each
       line with a syllable from the word "iris."

Summer 1685

165 well together / barley-ears let's-eat / grass pillow
     • Summer: barley (*mugi**). 1685. For "grass pillow," see
       notes to hokku 145. In *Journal of Bleached Bones in a
       Field*.

166 plum long-for / deutzia bow / tears !
     • Summer: deutzia (*unohana**). 1685 (5th of Fourth
       Month; May 7). Plums (*ume**) bloom in First Month,
       when Daiten died. Bashō heard the news in the Fourth
       Month, the time of deutzia blossoms. Both blossoms are
       white. In *Journal of Bleached Bones in a Field*.

167 white-poppy for / wing tear-off butterfly 's / memento
     • Summer: white poppy (*keshi**). 1685. Presented to his
       friend and disciple Tsuboi Tokoku (d. 1690). In *Journal
       of Bleached Bones in a Field*.

168 peony pistil deep / withdraw bee 's / regretful-farewell !
  • Summer: peony (*botan**). 1685 (early Fourth Month;
    May). The extended rhythm of 8–8–5 syllables may sug-
    gest the difficulty of departure. An earlier version reads:
    "separating from the peony's pistils, / crawling out, the
    bee's / reluctant parting" (*botan shibe wakete / haiizuru
    hachi no / nagori kana*). In *Knapsack Notebook*.

169 go horse 's / barley with solace / lodging !
  • Summer: barley (*mugi**). 1685. A greeting poem for his
    host. In *Journal of Bleached Bones in a Field*.

170 summer-robe / still lice <acc.> / unpicked
  • Summer: summer robe. 1685. Lice appeared in Chinese
    poems about wayfarers and recluses. The final poem in
    Journal of Bleached Bones in a Field: what began in
    dark intensity ends in humor.

Summer 1685

171 clouds time-time / people <acc.> give-rest / moonviewing !
  • Autumn: moonviewing. 1685 (The full moon was Sep-
    tember 13). I have included the headnote to an earlier
    version of the poem, which has a slightly different
    verbal ending (*yasumuru* instead of *yasumeru*). The
    hokku alludes to a verse by Saigyō: "Clouds appearing /
    now and then / covering its light / entertain the moon /
    and adorn its beauty" (*nakanaka ni / tokidoki kumo no
    / kakaru koso / tsuki o motenasu / kazari narikere*). In
    the haibun "Three Names."

172 wine-cup in / three 's names <acc.> drink / this-evening !
  • Autumn: this evening's moon. 1685. The cup suggests
    moon (*tsuki*), and three suggests full (*mitsu*). The verse
    of the Chinese poet Li Bo is: "A bottle of wine under the
    blossoms, / drinking all alone. / Raising the cup to the
    bright moon, / with the shadow we become three." The
    image of a single moon reflected in multiple objects was
    a traditional symbol of unity-with-multiplicity charac-
    teristic of East Asian metaphysics. In the haibun "Three
    Names."

Spring 1686

173 how-many frost in / spirit-banana 's / pine decorations
- Spring: New Year's pine decorations. 1686. The pine, which remains green through winter, was decorated for New Year's. The hokku employs an old-style pivot word in which *kokorobase* (spirit, mettle) blends with *baseo* (an old way of writing *bashō**).

174 old field ! / shepherd's-purse pick-go / males
- Spring: plucking sheperd's purse. 1686. One of the "seven herbs of spring," the shepherd's purse (*Capella bursapastoris*) produces many, small, white, four-petaled flowers in racemes on stems up to sixteen inches long.

175 well if-look / shepherd's-purse flower bloom / hedge !
- Spring: sheperd's purse blossom. 1686 (First Month). Concerning "looking closely," see notes to hokku 197.

176 sick-when / rice-cake <acc.> also not-eat / peach 's blossom
- Spring: peach (*momo**) blossoms. 1686.

177 Kannon 's / roof-tile look-out / blossom 's cloud
- Spring: clouds of blossoms. 1686.

178 old-nest just / pathos will-be / next-door !
- Spring: old nest. 1686. "Old nest" refers to a place someone has lived in a long time.

179 land on fall / root to approach blossom 's / departure !
- Spring: blossoms. 1686. There is a saying that "a flower returns to its roots" when it falls and dies.

180 old pond ! / frog jump-in / water 's sound
- Spring: frog. 1686. For comments on this poem, see the introduction, pp. 12–13.

Autumn 1686

181 east west / pathos one / autumn 's wind
- Autumn: autumn wind (*akikaze**). 1686. *Aware* is generally associated with the beauty-tinged sorrow of the impermanence of things.

182 bright-moon ! / pound <acc.> circle / all-night
- Autumn: harvest moon. 1686 (October 2).

183 blind-man ? <quote> / person to appears-as / moonviewing !
   • Autumn: moon viewing. 1686.

184 thing one / my house as-for light / gourd !
   • Autumn: gourd. 1686. There is an earlier version: "my
     one possession: / this gourd makes for / a light world"
     (*mono hitotsu / hisago wa karoki / waga yo kana*). In
     the haibun "Gourd of the Four Mountains."

185 dawn-going ! / 27th night also / three-day 's moon
   • Autumn: crescent moon. 1686.

Winter 1686–87

186 flower all wither / pathos <acc.> spill / grass 's seed
   • Winter: withered grass. 1686–87.

187 water is-cold / enter-sleep difficult / gulls !
   • Winter: cold. 1686–87.

188 water-jar crack / night 's ice 's / waking !
   • Winter: frozen. 1686–87? It is not clear whether Bashō
     is awake when the jar cracks, or the sound wakes him.

189 first snow ! / fortunately hut at / be-at
   • Winter: first snow. 1686–87. In the haibun "First
     Snow."

190 first snow ! / narcissus 's leaves 's / bend as-far-as
   • Winter: first snow; narcissus (*suisen**). 1686–87 (18th of
     Twelfth Month; January 31, 1687).

191 sake when-drink / more cannot-sleep / night 's snow
   • Winter: snow. 1686–1687. Commentators differ on
     whether Bashō is kept awake by the wine, the beauty of
     the scene, or an inner distress. In the haibun "Warning
     on Solitary Living."

192 you fire <acc.> burn / good thing will-show / snowball
   • Winter: snowball. 1686–87. In the haibun "Snowball"
     in which Bashō good Sora visits him after a snowfall.

193 moon snow <quote> / having-everything-my-way / year 's
   end
   • Winter: year's end. 1686–87. The end of the year is a
     time to look back. *Nosabaru* implies an arrogant indif-
     ference to others, making this one of Bashō's periodic
     self-deprecations.

Spring 1687

194 village 's children ! / plum break-remain / ox 's whip
- Spring: plum (*ume**). 1687.

195 absence in come / plum even distant 's / hedge !
- Spring: plum (*ume**). 1687. This is the haibun "Plums by the Fence."

196 forget do-not ! / grove 's within is / plum 's blossom
- Spring: plum (*ume**) blossoms. 1687. An earlier version has "please visit again" (*mata mo toe*) for the first line and was included in the haibun "Plum in a Grove." In that haibun, Bashō is visited by a monk on a pilgrimage to the north country. The plum blossom is said to signify Bashō.

197 flower in play / horsefly don't eat / friend-sparrow
- Spring: blossoms. 1687. *Tomosuzume* can mean "flock of sparrows" (*suzume**) but in this context the phrase implies being a friend to the horsefly and all beings. The title refers to a line found in various Daoist texts and Chinese poems, including the Chinese philosopher Cheng Mingdao (1032–85): "when one looks with tranquility, one sees that all things are self-content." They are content because they are self-realized, an idea that resonates with the Buddhist notion of original enlightenment. Bashō alludes to this phrase also in hokku 175 and in the haibun "Postscript to an Essay on a Bagworm." See also hokku 175, 218, and 443. An earlier version has the verb "to eat" (*suu*) instead of "to play" in the first line.

198 stork 's nest also / seen blossom 's / through-branches !
- Spring: blossoms. 1687. Storks nest high in tall trees and are white like cherry blossoms.

199 flower 's cloud / bell as-for Ueno ? / Asakusa ?
- Spring: clouds of blossoms. 1687. Ueno and Asakusa had Buddhist temples and were famous for their cherry blossoms. Both were sections of Edo near Bashō's hermitage.

200 long day even / chirp insufficient / skylark !
- Spring: skylark (*hibari**). 1687. An earlier version had a slightly different first line that would be translated the same (*nagaki hi o*).

201 field-within ! / thing to even not-attached / cry skylark
- Spring: skylark *(hibari*)*. 1687.

Summer 1687

202 cuckoo / cry-cry fly ! / busy
- Summer: cuckoo *(hototogisu*)*. 1687.

203 hair grow / appearance pale / fifth-month-rains
- Summer: summer rains *(samidare*)*. 1687.

204 fifth-month-rains in / grebe 's floating-nest <acc.> / see to will-go
- Summer: summer rains *(samidare*)*. 1687. Of this poem Bashō is reported to have said "'A willow in spring rain' is wholly renga. 'A crow digging for mud-snails' is entirely haikai. This grebe hokku has no haikai diction, but 'I'll go view the floating nest' has something of haikai in it." The nest of a grebe *(Podiceps ruficollis)* is made of the stems of reeds and water oats. It floats on the water while attached to a living plant. Lake Biwa was sometimes called "Grebe Lake."

205 now ! I / good robe wear / cicada-kimono
- Summer: cicada robe. 1687. A *semigoromo* is a thin kimono that is said to look like cicada's wings. The hokku was given in gratitude to his disciple and patron Sugiyama Sanpū (1647–1732).

206 drink sleep / wild-pink bloom / rock 's top
- Summer: wild pink *(nadeshiko*)*. 1687.

207 melon grow / you <nom.> be would-that <quote> / evening cool
- Summer: melon *(uri*)*; cool *(suzumi*)*. 1687. Based on a poem by Saigyō: "In the evening coolness / on the bank of Iwata / by the roots of a pine / I think / 'I wish you were here'" *(matsu ga ne no / iwata no kishi no / yūsuzumi / kimi ga are na to / omohoyuru kana)*.

208 small-crab / leg crawl-climb / clear-water !
- Summer: clear water. 1687.

Autumn 1687

209 lightning <acc.> / hand into take dark 's / small-candle-
     light !
     • Autumn: lightning (*inazuma**). 1687. Rika was a disci-
       ple who lived in Edo.

210 morning-glory as-for / unskillful <nom.> draw even /
     pathos is
     • Autumn: morning glory (*asagao**). 1687. The morning
       glory blooms briefly and thus evokes a sense of the
       impermanence of life. Ransetsu (1654–1707) was an
       Edo disciple.

211 bush-clover-field ! / one night as-for give-lodging / moun-
     tain 's dogs
     • Autumn: bush clover *(hagi*)*. 1687. In *Kashima Jour-
       nal.* An earlier version reads: "even wolves: / be their
       shelter for a night: / within the bush clover" (*ōkami mo
       / hitoyo wa yadose / hagi ga moto*).

212 cut-began / surface-of-rice-field 's crane ! / village 's
     autumn
     • Autumn: autumn. 1687. In *Kashima Journal.*

213 poor 's child ! / rice husking-leaving / moon <acc.> see
     • Autumn: moonviewing. 1687. In *Kashima Journal.*

214 taro 's leaves ! / moon wait village 's / burned-fields
     • Autumn: moon, taro leaves. 1687. In *Kashima Journal.*
       Taro were sold during the harvest moon viewing festival
       of the Eighth Month. Japanese farmers used slash-and-
       burn agriculture for certain crops.

215 moon fast / branches as-for rain <acc.> / holding
     • Autumn: moon. 1687. In *Kashima Journal.*

216 temple at sleeping / true face is / moonviewing !
     • Autumn: moonviewing. 1687. Bashō was visiting the
       Priest Butchō (1643–1715) at Inkyoji Temple. *Makoto-
       gao* means a "pious face," but here also has overtones of
       the Buddhist notion of "one's true face." Written on the
       same evening as the previous hokku. In *Kashima Jour-
       nal.*

217 this pine 's / seedling did age ! / gods 's autumn
     • Autumn: autumn. 1687. In *Kashima Journal.*

218 bagworm 's / voice <acc.> hear to come / grass 's hut
- Autumn: bagworm. 1687. Concerning the title, see notes to hokku 197. The bagworm actually does not make any sound, but in Sei Shōnagon's *Pillow Book* it was said to make a faint plaintive cry of *chichiyo chichiyo* ("father! father!"). The title could also be translated "listening to the stillness." In the haibun "Postscript to 'Essay on a Bagworm.'"

219 rise-up / chrysanthemum faint is / water 's after
- Autumn: chrysanthemum (*kiku**). 1687. "Faint" could refer to the flower's fragrance, its slow rising, its general feminine character, the general atmosphere of the scene (e.g. twilight), and so forth.

220 emaciated yet / somehow chrysanthemum 's / bud !
- Autumn: chrysanthemum (*kiku**). 1687.

Winter 1687–88

221 traveler <quotative> / my name will-be-called / first-winter-rain
- Winter: winter showers (*shigure**). 1687–88 (11th of Tenth Month; November 15). The first poem of *Knapsack Notebook*. The hokku was written at a farewell party for him and used as the first poem in the journal. Bashō is reported to have said, "I wrote the hokku's last two lines to suggest in words the exhilaration I felt at the forthcoming journey."

222 one ridge as-for / winter-shower cloud ? / Fuji 's snow
- Winter: winter showers (*shigure**). 1687–88 (25th of Tenth Month; November 29). Bashō cited this poem as an example of the sensitivity to the dignity and scale of the land that haikai requires.

223 capital up-to as-for / still half-sky ! / snow 's clouds
- Winter: snow. 1687–88 (December 9). Bashō was staying at the home of Terashima Bokugen (1646–1736) in Narumi. The host showed him a waka written twenty-five years earlier by Asukai Masaaki (1611–79) when he was visiting there on a journey away from the capital: "Today the capital / seems even more distant / here at

Narumi Bay / looking across the vast sea / that separates me from home" (*kyō wa nao / miyako mo tōku / narumigata / harukeki umi o / naka ni hedatete*). In *Knapsack Notebook*.

224 star-cape 's / darkness <acc.> look <quote> ? / cry plover
  * Winter: plover (*chidori**). 1687–88. Star Cape, on Narumi Bay near Nagoya, is famous for plovers. In *Knapsack Notebook*.

225 cold-although / two-people sleeping night ! / pleasurable
  * Winter: cold. 1687–88. In *Knapsack Notebook*. An earlier version has for the second line "sleeping together on the journey" (*futari tabine zo*).

226 dried-pine-needles <acc.> burn / hand-towel dry-over-a-fire / coldness !
  * Winter: cold. 1687–88. A variant has "ice" (*kōri*) instead of "cold" (*samusa*) in the last line.

227 winter 's sun ! / on-horseback on frozen / shadow
  * Winter: winter sun/day; freezing. 1687–88. *Hi* could mean either sun or day. Composed at Awatsu Nawate in Toyohashi, known for cold winter winds from the sea. There are two variants: "cold rice-fields— / hunched on horseback, / my shadow" (*samuki ta ya / bashō ni sukumu / kagebōshi*) and "going along hunched, frozen on horseback: my shadow" (*sukumiyuku / bashō ni kōru / kagebōshi*). In *Knapsack Notebook*.

228 snow and sand / horse from fall ! / rice-wine 's drunk
  * Winter: snow. 1687–88.

229 hawk one / finding joy / Irago-cape
  * Winter: hawk (*taka**). 1687–88 (12th of Eleventh Month; December 16). Cape Irago, at the tip of a peninsula, was famous in waka for its hawks. It also was associated with the exiled Prince Ōmi in the early *Man'yōshu* poetry colllection, and at the time of this hokku Bashō was visiting a disciple Tokoku, who had moved to Irago after suffering financial difficulties. In *Knapsack Notebook*.

230 Cape-Irago / resemble thing even is-not / hawk 's voice
  * Winter: hawk (*taka**). 1687–88. In the haibun "The Village of Hobi."

231 dream more even / reality 's hawk ! / reassured
- Winter: hawk (*taka**). 1687–88 (12th of Eleventh Month; December 16). In the symbolic reading of the verse, Bashō had been dreaming of Tokoku (the hawk) but now feels reassured to see him in person.

232 plum camellia / early-bloom praise / Hobi 's village
- Winter: early blooming plum (*ume**) and camellia (*tsubaki**). 1687–88. In the haibun "The Village of Hobi."

233 polish-repair / mirror also clear / snow 's blooosom
- Winter: snow blossoms. 1687–88 (24th of Eleventh Month; December 28). Bashō was visiting the Shinto shrine in Atsuta, which recently had undergone repairs. In Japan, white is the color of purity (and of cherry blossoms). In *Knapsack Notebook*.

234 straighten / snowviewing to leave / paper-robe !
- Winter: snowviewing; paper robe. 1687–88 (28th day of Eleventh Month). In *Knapsack Notebook*.

235 well then / snow-viewing in tumble / extent until
- Winter: snow-viewing. 1687–88 (3rd of Twelfth Month; January 5). Written when Bashō was a guest at a snow-viewing party in Nagoya. Commentators differ on whether it is just Bashō falling, or he and his friends. There are two variants with different first lines: "hey let's head out" (*iza iden*) and "hey let's go" (*iza yukamu*), the latter appearing in *Knapsack Notebook*.

236 Hakone cross / person ! probably-is / morning 's snow
- Winter: snow. 1687–88. Hakone Pass is a steep barrier between Edo and Kyoto. In *Knapsack Notebook*.

237 scent <acc.> search / plum for warehouse see / eaves !
- Winter: plum (*ume**) blossom viewing. 1687–88. The hokku is an greeting verse for his host Bōsen, whose wealth is suggested by the warehouse. In *Knapsack Notebook*. An earlier version has "house" (*ie*) instead of "warehouse."

238 dew freeze / brush with draw-dry / clear-water !
- Winter: frozen. 1687–88. For a similar hokku and an allusion to a waka attributed to Saigyō, see hokku 277.

239 journey's-sleep doing / saw ! floating-world 's / house
cleaning
  • Winter: year-end house-cleaning. 1687–88 (13th day of
    Twelfth Month). In *Knapsack Notebook.*
240 walk if-be / staff-stab-hill <location> / horse-fall !
  • Miscellaneous: no season word. 1687. The pun-filled
    waka might be translated: "From Kuwana I came / with
    nothing to eat; / morning passed at Hoshikawa / and
    after an endless day / I came to Hinaga" (*kuwana yori /
    kuwade kinureba / hoshikawa no / asake wa suginu /
    hinaga narikeri*). In *Knapsack Notebook.*
241 old-village ! / umbilical 's tail at cry / year 's end
  • Winter: year's end. 1687–88. Bashō is visiting his home
    village and is given his umbilical cord that his family
    had saved. In *Knapsack Notebook* and the haibun "End
    of the Year."

1688–94

242 snow space from / thin purple 's / sprout udo !
  • Spring: space in the snow; *udo*. 1688–94. The *udo* is a
    vegetable with an edible stem and purple sprouts (some-
    what like a rhubarb) that emerge in spring.
243 borrow sleep / scarecrow 's sleaves ! / midnight 's frost
  • Winter: frost. 1688–94.

Spring 1688

244 second-day on also / blunder as-for not-do ! / flower 's
spring
  • Spring: blossoming spring; second day. 1688. It was tra-
    ditional to worshipfully greet the New Year at dawn. In
    Knapsack Notebook.
245 spring beginning / still nine-days 's / fields-mountains !
  • Spring: rising of spring. 1688. In *Knapsack Notebook.*
246 Akokuso 's / heart even not-know / plum 's flower
  • Spring: plum (*ume**) blossoms. 1688. Akokusa is the
    childhood name of the famous Heian poet Ki no
    Tsurayuki (883–946). The hokku draws on a waka by

Tsurayuki: "The hearts of people / we do not know, / yet in my native village, / the plum blossoms still / give off their scent" (*hito wa isa / kokoro mo shirazu / furusato wa / hana zo mukashi no / ka ni nioikeru*). In an earlier version of the hokku, the second line has *wa* (as-for) instead of the stronger *mo* (even, also).

247 scent with smell / coal mine hill 's / plum 's blossoms
   • Spring: plum (*ume**) blossoms. 1688.

248 nose blow / sound even plum 's / blossoming !
   • Spring: plum (*ume**) blossom. 1688. One of several hokku that emphasize the inclusive aesthetic vision of Bashō. This hokku was written during his journey that produced *Knapsack Notebook*, in which Bashō said that for one who has the poetic spirit, "nothing one sees is not a flower."

249 dead-grass ! / slightly heat-wave 's / one two-inch
   • Spring: heat waves (*kagerō**). 1688. *Shiba* is Japanese lawngrass (*Zoisia japonica*). In *Knapsack Notebook*. In an earlier version, instead of "faint" (*yaya*) the second line has "still" (*mada*), which suggests more directly the transitional nature of the image: heat waves are a spring image, but withered grass is winter. Spring is just beginning.

250 sixteen-feet to / heat-wave is-high / rock 's on
   • Spring: heat waves (*kagerō**). 1688. In *Knapsack Notebook*.

251 what's tree 's / flower <quote> not-know / scent !
   • Spring: blossoms. 1688. Written at the Ise Shrine, the hokku alludes to a waka Saigyō wrote at Ise: "What divine being / graces this place / I know not and yet / feeling so deeply blessed / my tears spill forth" (*nanigoto no / owashimasu ka wa / shiranedomo / katajikenasa ni / namida koboruru*). In *Knapsack Notebook* and the haibun "Visiting the Ise Shrine."

252 shrine-maiden 's / one tree lovely / plum 's blossom
   • Spring: plum (*ume**) flower. 1688. At the Ise Shrine Bashō finds no plum trees except one behind the shrine maidens' hall. Plum blossoms are white, the color of

purity. In *Knapsack Notebook*. An earlier version reads: "plums so scarce / just one, so lovely: / shrine maidens" (*ume mare ni / hito moto yukashi / okorago*).

253 curtain 's / interior deep / north 's plum
- Spring: plum (*ume**). 1688 (Second Month). The blossoms symbolize Sonome (1664–1726), Bashō's disciple and wife of a doctor named Ichiu in Ise Yamada. For a discussion of the complex wordplay involved here, see Shirane, *Traces of Dreams*, 165.

254 plum 's tree on / still mistletoe ! / plum 's blossom
- Spring: plum (*ume**) blossoms. 1688. A greeting poem about passing down poetic refinement across generations. Ajiro Minbu (1640–83) was a haikai poet and Shinto priest at Ise, and his son Ajiro Hirōji (1657–1717) used the pen name of Setsudō in writing haikai. In *Knapsack Notebook*.

255 thing 's name <acc.> / first ask reed 's / young-leaves !
- Spring: new leaves of the reeds (*ashi**). 1688. Ryū Shosha (1616–93) was a Shinto scholar and priest at Ise who was fond of haikai. In *Knapsack Notebook*. An earlier version has *ogi*, a different type of reed than *ashi*.

256 taro plant / gate as-for creeper 's / young-leaf !
- Spring: young leaves of creepers. 1688. A portrait of the quiet life of a recluse. The taro is similar to a potato. In *Knapsack Notebook*. An earlier version has the first line: "camellia blooms in a grove" (*yabu tsubaki*).

257 this mountain 's / sorrow tell ! / old-yam-digger
- Spring: digging wild potatoes. 1688. Bashō was visiting the ruins of the Bōdai (Buddhahood) Temple, built in the eighth century. In this context, "mountain" implies mountain temple, and an earlier version begins with "mountain temple" (*yamadera*). In *Knapsack Notebook*.

258 wine-cup in / mud don't drop don't / flock-of-swallows
- Spring: barn swallows. 1688. Kusube is just north of the Ise Shrine. *Tsubame* is the Barn Swallow common in North America, *Hirundo rustica*. Alternate versions conclude with "flying swallows" (*tobu tsubame*) and "fluttering swallows" (*mau tsubame*).

259 paper-robe <nom.> / although-wet will-break / rain 's
flowers
- Spring: blossoms. 1688. A greeting poem for his host
Rosō, a Shinto priest.

260 god-fence ! / unexpected / nirvana-picture
- Spring: picture of Buddha entering nirvana. 1688. The
15th of Second Month is the commemoration of the
Buddha entering into nirvana upon death. In *Knapsack
Notebook*.

261 naked in as-for / not-yet second-month 's / windstorm !
- Spring: Second Month. 1688. Bashō alludes to the story
of priest Zōga, on pilgrimage to the Ise Shrine, who
obeyed an order from a god to give all his clothes to
beggars. The name for Second Month, *Kisaragi*, literally
means "wear another layer of clothes." Mt. Kamiji, lit-
erally "path of the gods," is near Ise. In *Knapsack Note-
book*.

262 first-cherry-blossoms / just-now today as-for / good day is
- Spring: first cherry blossom (*sakura**). 1688.

263 various 's / thing recall / cherry-blossom !
- Spring: cherry blossom (*sakura**). Bashō was visiting his
home village. Tangan was the son of Sengin (Tōdō
Yoshitada, d. 1666), Bashō's master and haikai friend in
his youth. In *Knapsack Notebook*.

264 blossoms <acc.> lodging in / beginning end ! / 20–days
extent
- Spring: blossoms. 1688. Blossoms were said to last
twenty days from opening to falling. The hut belonged
to Taiso, a samurai and haikai poet in Iga Ueno.

265 yoshino in / cherry-blossoms will-show ! / cypress hat
- Spring: cherry blossom (*sakura**). 1688. The hokku was
occasioned by Tokoku joining Bashō on his journey.
Bashō gives a haikai twist to the phrase "two travelers,"
which conventionally refers to the Buddha and the soli-
tary Buddhist wayfarer. In *Knapsack Notebook*.

266 spring 's night ! / secluded-person intriguing / temple 's
corner
- Spring: spring evening. 1688. In the *Tale of Genji* and
later literature, court ladies are portrayed staying at the
Hase Temple for spiritual retreat. In *Knapsack Notebook*.

267 skylark more-than / sky in rest / mountain-pass !
  * Spring: skylark *(hibari*)*. 1688. An earlier version has
    "above" *(ue ni)* instead of "in the sky." In *Knapsack
    Notebook.*

268 dragon-gate 's / flower ! drinker 's / souvenir into will-make
  * Spring: blossoms. 1688. Dragon's Gate *(Ryūmon)* is the
    name of waterfall in Yoshino and also in China. The
    Chinese poet Li Bo was known for his love of waterfalls
    and wine. In *Knapsack Notebook.*

269 sake drinkers to / will-tell hang / waterfall 's blossoms
  * Spring: blossoms. 1688. In *Knapsack Notebook.*

270 blossom 's shade / nō-script like resemble / journey's-sleep !
  * Spring: blossoms. 1688. Nō plays often present a trav-
    eler spending the night in a strange place, which
    becomes the scene for the main action of the play.

271 fan with / sake drink shadow ! / scatter cherry-blossoms
  * Spring: falling cherry blossom *(sakura*)*. 1688 (late
    Third Month; late April). The hokku alludes to the
    practice in the Nō theatre of pulling a fan toward the
    mouth to suggest drinking sake. The poem is said to be
    an image of *yūgen* (mystery and depth). In *Knapsack
    Notebook.* An earlier version reads: "with a fan / drink-
    ing sake in the shade of / blossoming trees" *(ōgi nite /
    sake kumu hana no / ki kage kana)*.

272 voice if-good / would-chant however / cherry-blossom fall
  * Spring: falling cherry blossom *(sakura*)*. The scattering
    blossoms evoke the atmosphere of the Nō drama. The
    verb *utau* usually means to sing, but here it refers to
    chanting from a Nō libretto *(utai)*.

273 flutteringly / mountain-rose falls ! / rapid 's sound
  * Spring: mountain rose *(yamabuki*)*. 1688 (late Third
    Month; late April). Nijikō is an area of the Yoshino
    River known for powerful rapids. In the haibun "Petal
    by Petal," where Bashō refers to a waka by Ki no
    Tsurayuki: "At Yoshino River, / the mountain roses at
    the riverbank / in the blowing wind: / even the reflec-
    tions in the depths / are scattered" *(yoshino-gawa / kishi
    no yamabuki / fuku kaze ni / soko no kage sae /
    utsuroinikeri)*. Also in *Knapsack Notebook.*

274 cherry-blossom-viewing / commendable ! each-day on /
     five-ri six-ri
     • Spring: cherry blossom (*sakura**) viewing. 1688. A *ri* is
       a little over two miles. In *Knapsack Notebook*.
275 sun as-for flower on / darken lonely ! / false-cypress
     • Spring: blossoms. 1688. The *asunarō* or false cypress,
       Thujopsis dolobrata, looks like a hinoki cypress, a tree
       whose wood is highly prized, while that of the false
       cypress is not. Literally, *asunarō* means "tomorrow I will
       become," and the context implies "tomorrow I will
       become a cypress." The *asunarō* seems to be what it is
       not; it appears to fall short of what one might expect it
       to achieve. (For a discussion of the complex theme of
       incompletion in Bashō's writings, see Barnhill, "Bashō as
       Bat.") In *Knapsack Notebook*. Another version appears
       in the haibun "False Cypress": "loneliness— / among the
       blossoms, / a false cypress" (*sabishisa ya / hana no atari
       no / asunarō*).
276 spring-rain 's / under-tree to convey / pure water !
     • Spring: spring rain *(harusame**)*. 1688. Bashō is at the
       site of Saigyō's hut, which he also visited in *Journal of
       Bleached Bones in a Field*. Even today, clear spring
       water flows over mossy rocks, and this hokku is carved
       in a stone. The hokku alludes to a waka attributed to
       Saigyō: "Trickling down, / pure spring water falls / over
       the mossy rocks, / not enough to draw up / for this
       hermit life" (*tokutoku to / otsuru iwama no / koke
       shimizu / kumihosu hodo mo / naki sumai kana*). In
       Knapsack Notebook.
277 freeze melt / brush with draw dry / clear-water !
     • Spring: melting. 1688. See notes to the previous hokku.
278 flowers-in-full-bloom / mountain as-for every-day 's /
     dawn
     • Spring: flowers in full bloom. 1688.
279 still-more want-to-see / flower to dawn-going / god 's face
     • Spring: blossoms. 1688. In *Knapsack Notebook* and the
       haibun "Preface to 'all the more I'd like to see it.'" In
       the haibun, Bashō reports that "It is said that the god

here, Hitokotonushi-no-kami, has a hideous face, and
people of the world have reviled him.' "

280 father mother 's / intently love / pheasant 's voice
  • Spring: pheasant (*kiji**). 1688. Bashō was visiting Mt.
    Kōya, which contains the mausoleum of Kūkai
    (774–835) as well as the remains of Bashō's ancestors
    and thousands of others. Based on a waka by Priest
    Gyōgi (668–749): "A mountain pheasant / calls plain-
    tively; / hearing its voice I wonder, / is that my father? /
    is that my mother?" (*yamadori no / horohoro to naku /
    koe kikeba / chichi ka to zo omou / haha ka to zo
    omou*). In *Knapsack Notebook* and the haibun "Preface
    to 'Climbing Mt. Kōya.' "

281 going spring in / Wakanoura at / catch-up-with
  • Spring: departing spring. 1688. Wakanoura, south of
    Osaka, is a scenic bay and famous in Japanese literature
    since early times because it literally means "Poetry Bay."
    In *Knapsack Notebook*.

Summer 1688

282 one taking-off / behind in place / change-of-clothes
  • Summer: change of clothes. 1688. The first day of the
    Fourth Month was traditionally a day to change one's
    apparel to reflect the beginning of the summer season.
    On this journey Bashō lacks true summer clothes, so he
    simply removes one layer to fit the occasion. In *Knap-
    sack Notebook*.

283 Buddha's-birth 's / day on born / fawn !
  • Summer: Buddha's birthday. 1688. In *Knapsack Note-
    book*.

284 young-leaves doing / your-eyes 's drop / would-wipe-away
  • Summer: young leaves. 1688. In *Knapsack Notebook*.

285 deer 's horn / first one-branch 's / departure !
  • Summer: (new) horns of the deer (*shika**). 1688. In
    Knapsack Notebook. An earlier version reads: "at the
    road's fork / we part ways: / deer's horns" (*futamata ni
    / wakaresomekeri / shika no tsuno*).

286 tired-from-travel / lodging borrow time ! / wisteria 's flower
- Spring: wisteria. 1688 (11th of Fourth Month; May 10). In *Knapsack Notebook*. This hokku was actually written in the summer. The original version had the summer image "cuckoo" (*hototogisu*) for the first line. When Bashō changed the line to "travel weary," the remaining season word in the poem was wisteria, and so it became a spring poem.

287 villagers as-for / rice in song sing / capital !
- Summer: rice-planting songs. 1688. In the haibun "Preface to 'Villagers.'"

288 iris / talk also journey 's / one !
- Summer: iris (*kakitsubata**). 1688. The hokku refers to *The Tales of Ise*, chapter 9, where Ariwara no Narihira and several friends stopped on a journey near some blossoming irises, and the poet is asked to compose a waka on the subject of "traveler's sentiments" beginning each line with a syllable from the word "iris." Bashō's verse also could be read as "conversations *beside* iris." In *Knapsack Notebook*.

289 moon as-for is-yet / absence 's seems to-be / Suma 's summer
- Summer: summer moon. 1688. Suma was known for exquisite loneliness during the autumn, which is also the ideal poetic season for the moon. In *Knapsack Notebook*. An earlier version reads: "it's summer / yet there seems an absence: / moon over Suma" (*natsu aredo / rusu no yō nari / suma no tsuki*).

290 moon see although / thing lacking ! / Suma 's summer
- Summer: summer moon. 1688. In *Knapsack Notebook*.

291 fisher 's face / first is-seen ! / poppy 's flower
- Summer: poppy (*keshi**) blossoms. 1688. The faces of fishers are dark with suntan amid the white poppies. In *Knapsack Notebook*.

292 suma 's ama 's / arrow at cry ? / cuckoo
- Summer: cuckoo *(hototogisu**)*. 1688. In *Knapsack Notebook*.

293 Suma-temple ! / not-blow flute hear / tree-shade
   • Summer: darkness under trees. 1688. The Temple of
     Suma possesed the flute of Atsumori, Taira warrior who
     died in the battle of Ichi no Tani in 1184. There is a
     famous Nō play titled *Atsumori*. In *Knapsack Notebook*.

294 cuckoo / disappear-go direction ! / island one
   • Summer: cuckoo *(hototogisu*)*. 1688 (20th of Fourth
     Month; May 19). This hokku plays off of a waka by
     Fujiwara Sanesada (1139–91): "Cuckoo: / gazing in the
     direction / of its call / there is only the moon / lingering
     in the dawn" *(hototogisu / nakitsuru kata o / naga-*
     mureba / tada ariake no / tsuki zo nokoreru). There is
     also a waka by Emperor Gomizuno-o (1596–1680):
     "cuckoo *(hototogisu*)*, / its single call disappearing /
     behind an island, / and I think of the poet / of the Akashi
     Coast" *(hototogisu / shima kakure yuku / hitokoe o /*
     akashi no ura no / akazu shi zo omou). In *Knapsack*
     Notebook.

295 octopus-trap ! / brief dream <acc.> / summer 's moon
   • Summer: summer moon. 1688 (20th of Fourth Month;
     May 19). Pots were lowered into the sea in the after-
     noon. In the night, octupuses crawled in them, and in
     the morning the pots were pulled up. Akashi was
     famous as the place where the Heike warriors were
     slain. The Japanese poetic tradition emphasized the
     brevity of summer nights. In *Knapsack Notebook*.

296 fifth-month-rains in / not-hidden thing ! / Seta 's bridge
   • Summer: summer rains *(samidare*)*. 1688. The Seta
     bridge, across Lake Biwa near the Seta River, is famous
     for both its Chinese-style beauty and its length.

297 this firefly / each-field 's moon to / I-shall-compare
   • Summer: firefly *(hotaru*)*. 1688. Bashō was waiting to
     travel to Sarashina to see the autumn moon.

298 eye in remain / Yoshino <acc.> Seta 's / fireflies !
   • Summer: firefly *(hotaru*)*. 1688. Bashō recalls spring
     blossoms at Yoshino as he sees summer's fireflies at Seta.

299 grass's leaf <acc.> / fall then fly / firefly !
   • Summer: firefly *(hotaru*)*. 1688.

300 world 's summer / lake on float / wave 's top
- Summer: summer. 1688.

301 evening-face ! / autumn as-for various 's / gourd !
- Summer: moonflower (yūgao*). 1688. The moonflower plant, with uniform blossoms, produces gourds of various sizes and shapes in the autumn. The hokku draws on an anonymous waka: "All green, / in spring they seemed / one kind of grass, / but in autumn they've become / blooms of various colors" (midori naru / hitotsu kusa to zo / haru wa mishi / aki wa iroiro no / hana ni zo arikeru).

302 noon-face 's / short-night sleep / daytime !
- Summer: noonflower (hirugao*). 1688. Summer is known for short nights, while the noonflower has a dreamy appearance—from lack of sleep? A greeting poem depicting a relaxed atmosphere.

303 deceased person 's / clothes also now ! / summer-airing
- Summer: summer-airing. 1688. Doyō is a period of late summer considered to be the peak of summer's heat. It was customary to air out stored clothes at that time.

304 would-lodge / goosefoot 's staff into become / day until
- Summer: goosefoot. 1688. As it grows into autumn, the goosefoot's stem becomes long and stiff, useful as a staff. In the haibun "Praise for a Painting of 'I Would Lodge Here.'"

305 mountain-cove ! / body <acc.> would-nourish / melon-field
- Summer: melon (uri*). 1688. A greeting poem for his host.

306 fragile-person to / will-compare flower also / summer-field !
- Summer: summer field. 1688. A summer field is a wide expanse of grass, normally devoid of flowers.

307 temple-bell also / reverberate like is / cicada 's voice
- Summer: cicada's cry (semi no koe*). 1688.

308 castle remains ! / old-well 's clear-water / first will-seek
- Summer: clear water. 1688.

309 interesting / finally sad / cormorant-boat
   • Summer: cormorant fishing. 1688. Cormorants were
     used on the Nagara River on moonless nights to catch
     fish. Torchlight attracts the fish near the surface, and
     cormorants on leashes capture the fish and then regurgi-
     tate them. In the haibun "Cormorant Fishing Boat."
310 this area / eye to seen thing as-for / all cool
   • Summer: cool (*suzumi**). 1688 (Fifth Month; June). In
     the haibun "An Account of the Eighteen View Tower,"
     written in gratitude to his host Kashima.
311 summer come yet / just one leaf 's / one-leaf !
   • Summer: one-leaf fern, summer. 1688. The one-leaf fern
     (*Pyrrosia lingua*) produces a single undivided leaf at a
     time when other plants have many leaves, thus seeming
     to be lonely and incomplete. See notes to hokku 275.

                       Autumn 1688

312 anything 's / comparison to also not-resemble / third-day 's
     moon
   • Autumn: crescent moon. 1688 (3rd of Seventh Month;
     July 29). In Japanese literature, the crescent moon has
     been compared to many things, such as a sword, a bow,
     and the eyebrow of a woman. Two early versions have
     different words with essentially the same meaning: *ari to
     aru / mitate ni mo nizu / mika no tsuki* and *ari to aru /
     tatoe ni mo nizu / mika no tsuki*.
313 harvest after ! / early-rice one-side 's / snipe 's voice
   • Autumn: snipe, early rice. 1688. The hokku draws on a
     famous waka by Saigyō: "Even one who is / free of pas-
     sions / feels such sorrow: / a marsh where a snipe rises /
     into autumn evening" (*kokoro naki / mi ni mo aware
     wa / shirarekeri / shigi tatsu sawa no / aki no yūgure*).
314 good house ! / sparrow rejoice / back-door 's millet
   • Autumn: millet. 1688. An earlier version reads: "such a
     fine house— / sparrows (*suzume**) delight in the back-
     yard / in autumn" (*yoki ie ya / suzume yorokobu / sedo
     no aki*).

315 early-autumn ! / sea also green-rice-field / one-green
- Autumn: autumn. 1688. The hokku blends seasons as
  well as places and color: green rice fields (*aota*) is a season
  word for late summer; into autumn they will turn golden
  brown. There are two earlier versions: "autumn— / both
  ocean and rice fields / are green" (*hatsuaki ya / umi yara
  aota yara / midori kana*) and "Narumi lagoon— / becom-
  ing like the rice fields, / all one green" (*narumi kata ya /
  aota ni kawaru / hitomidori*).
316 journey on tired / today which day ? / autumn 's wind
- Autumn: autumn wind (*akikaze**). 1688 (10th day of
  Seventh Month; August 5).
317 lotus pond ! / not-pick this as / festival-of-spirits
- Autumn: Festival of Spirits (*tamamatsuri**). 1688. Cut
  lotus blossoms were among the offerings placed on the
  "spirit shelf" (*tamadana*) for this festival.
318 millet grass with / meager even is-not / grass 's hut
- Autumn: millet, grass. 1688. An earlier version has a
  different second line with virtually the same meaning:
  mazushiku mo nashi.
319 autumn <acc.> passing / butterfly also lick ! / chrysanthe-
  mum 's dew
- Autumn: butterfly (*chō**), chrysanthemum (*kiku**), dew
  (*tsuyu**). 1688? 1685? A butterfly in autumn is consid-
  ered to be old and weak, and drinking dew on a
  chrysanthemum is traditionally thought to bring long
  life.
320 not-conceal ! / house as-for vegetable-soup with / red-
  pepper
- Autumn: red pepper (*tōgarashi*). 1688. Another exam-
  ple of Bashō's praise for a simple lifestyle, in this case a
  greeting poem for his host, a doctor Usō.
321 see-off 's / back ! lonely / autumn's wind
- Autumn: autumn wind (*akikaze**). 1688. Yasui
  (1658–1743) of Nagoya was one of Bashō's disciples.
322 be-seen-off / parting-from result as-for / Kiso 's autumn
- Autumn: autumn. 1688. Bashō is leaving his friends in
  Gifu for Sarashina, a journey which resulted in
  Sarashina Journal. An alternative version in *Sarashina*

Journal has "parting from" (*wakaretsu*) instead of "being seen off" (*okuritsu*). *Hate* can be interpreted variously, for example, "the result," "the end," and "finally."

323 plants various / each each flower 's / achievement !

* Autumn: blossoming plants. 1688. The same context as the previous poem. The hokku has been read symbolically as refering to his disciples.

324 morning-glory as-for / drinking-carousal not-know / full-bloom !

* Autumn: morning glory (*asagao**). 1688. See notes to the previous hokku.

325 tremble tremble <adv.> / all-the-more dewy ! / lady-flower

* Autumn: lady-flower, dew (*tsuyu**). 1688. The slender lady flower (*Patrinia scabiosifolia*) is considered to have a delicate, dew-like beauty, and being bent with dew accentuates its feminine appeal. In sunny fields of lowlands and hills, it produces numerous small yellow flowers at the ends of branches, August through October. In one version of *Sarashina Journal*. A variant, which was a departure verse for his friends in Gifu, has a different second line: "bent down and dewy" (*kokete tsuyukeshi ya*).

326 that inside in / laquer want-to-paint / inn 's moon

* Autumn: moon. 1688. In *Sarashina Journal*, immediately after a passage where he praises the wine cups of the village, despite their being unusually large and ostentatiously laquered with gold leaf. A variant has a different first line: "inside the moon" (*tsuki no naka ni*).

327 hanging-bridge ! / life <acc.> entwine / ivy vine

* Autumn: ivy (*tsuta**). 1688. The particular suspension bridge in Kiso that Bashō crossed was known in Japanese literature as quite dangerous. In *Sarashina Journal*.

328 hanging-bridge / first comes-to-mind / horse meeting

* Autumn: encountering a horse. 1689. In ancient times, horses from the various parts of Japan were presented to the court in mid-Eighth Month, about the time this hokku was written. A court envoy would meet the horses at this bridge. In *Sarashina Journal*.

329 face ! / old-woman alone cry / moon 's companion
  - Autumn: moon. 1688 (15th of Eighth Month; September 9). The poem refers to a famous legend of a village with a custom of abandoning its old women. The custom was broken when one man returned to rescue his aunt the morning after he abandoned her on a moonlit night. The last line has been interpreted as the moon being the woman's companion, or the image of the woman being Bashō's companion as he views the moon. *Omokage* means face, but also shadow, trace, image. In *Sarashina Journal* and the haibun "The Moon on Mt. Obasute in Sarashina."

330 16th-night-moon even / still Sarashina's / district !
  - Autumn: moon of the 16th. 1688 (16th of Eighth Month). In *Sarashina Journal* and the haibun "The Moon on Mt. Obasute in Sarashina."

331 body into penetrating / radish is-bitter / autumn 's wind
  - Autumn: piercing the body; autumn wind (*akikaze**). 1688 (Eighth Month; September). In *Sarashina Journal*.

332 Kiso 's horsechestnuts / floating-world 's people's / souvenir !
  - Autumn: fruit of the horsechestnut. 1688. Because this tree (*Aesculus turbinata* or *A. chinensis*) grows only in remote mountains and its nuts are not as tasty as normal chestnuts (*kuri**), it is associated with the recluse life. Saigyō wrote: "Deep in the mountains, / I'll collect water / dripping from the rocks / while picking up horsechestnuts / that plop down from time to time" (*yama fukami / iwa ni shitadaru / mizu tomen / katsugatsu otsuru / tochi hirou hodo*). The floating world refers to the common life of pleasure and pain, especially in the city. For an interpretation of both poems, see William LaFleur, *Karma of Words* (Berkeley: University of California Press, 1983). In *Sarashina Journal*. Another version of the hokku reads: "for those of the world / I will take them: / horsechestnuts of Kiso" (*yo ni orishi / hito ni torasen / kiso no tochi*).

333 moon light ! / four-gates four-sects also / just one
  - Autumn: moonlight. 1688. People from various Bud-
    dhist groups practiced at Zenkōji. The image of four
    gates refers temples of four sects, Zen, Tendai, Jōdo, and
    Ji. In *Sarashina Journal*.

334 blow-away / rock as-for Asama 's / windstorm !
  - Autumn: windstorm (*nowaki**). 1688. There are several
    earlier versions, including: "blowing them away: / at
    Asama the rocks / in the autumn windstorm" (*fukiotusu
    / asama wa ishi no / nowaki kana*) and "autumn
    winds— / blowing down the rocks / of Mt. Asama"
    (*akikaze ya / ishi fukiorosu / asama yama*). In *Sarashina
    Journal*.

335 16th-night-moon 's / which ? morning in / remaining
     chrysanthemum
  - Autumn: remaining chrysanthemum (*kiku**); 16th night
    moon. 1688. The 9th day of Ninth Month is the
    Chrysanthemum Festival, when the blossoms are sup-
    posedly at their peak. Like the 16th night for the moon,
    the 10th day of the month is one day past prime for the
    blossoms. In both cases, beauty remains, tinged now
    with the sadness of their fading. The old master is his
    disciple Yamaguchi Sodō (1642–1707), and Mount Lu
    is a famous mountain in China visited by numerous
    poets. An earlier version reads: "the sixteenth night
    moon / —which to prize more? / lingering chrysanthe-
    mum" (*izayoi no / tsuki to mihayase / nokoru tsuki*).

336 Kiso 's gaunt / still not-recovered with / after 's moon
  - Autumn: late harvest moon. 1688 (13th of Ninth
    Month; October 6). While the harvest moon occurs in
    the Eighth Month, the full moon in the next month
    ("the latter moon") is also prized. Written in Edo a
    month after he had been travelling through the moun-
    tains of Kiso. In one version of *Sarashina Journal*.

337 ivy 's leaf as-for / past tinged-with / autumn-leaves !
  - Autumn: autumn leaves; ivy (*tsuta**). 1688. The more
    subdued color of the ivy in the midst of bright autumn
    foliage suggests the past with its antique look.

338 departing autumn ! / body onto pull-put-on / 90-centime-
ters-futon
   • Autumn: departing autumn. 1688. Narrow bedding is
      about ninety centimeters wide and usually is just one
      part of a futon bedding. A portrait of humble living.

339 chrysanthemum cockscomb / cut exhausted / anniversary
   • Autumn: Nichiren memorial. 1688 (13th of Tenth
      Month; November 5). Written on the anniversary of the
      death of priest Nichiren, when many flowers, such as
      the chrysanthemum (*kiku**), are offered to his spirit.

Winter 1688–89

340 winter-seclusion / again will-sit-close / this post
   • Winter: winter seclusion. 1688–89. The verb suggests a
      feeling of emotional as well as physical closeness.

341 five six / tea-cake by line / sunken-hearth !
   • Winter: sunken hearth. 1688–89. In the winter cold,
      warmth is found sitting around a table above a sunken
      fire.

342 that form / want-to-see old-wood 's / staff's length
   • Winter: withered tree. 1688–89. In the Buddhist tradi-
      tion, "withered" is a symbol of thorough realization. In
      the haibun "A Staff of Aged Wood."

343 put-on lie-down / futon ! cold / night ! terrible
   • Winter: futon, cold. 1688–89. Rika (dates unknown), a
      disciple from Edo, had recently lost his wife. Bashō
      likely had in mind a waka by Saigyō: "A tree on a cliff /
      rising by an abandoned field: / from it a dove's call /
      mournful for its mate— / desolate nightfall" (*furuhata
      no / soba no tatsu ki ni / iru hato no / tomo yobu koe no
      / sugoki yūgure*).

344 banked-charcoal even / make-disappear ? tear 's / boil
sound
   • Winter: banked charcoal. 1688–89 (Twelfth Month).

345 two-people saw / snow as-for this-year also / fallen ?
   • Winter: snow. 1688–89. Bashō and his disciple Ochi
      Etsujin (1656–1739) saw snow on the journey that
      resulted in *Knapsack Notebook*. In the haibun "Sent to
      Etsujin."

346 rice buy to / snow 's bag ! / winter-hood
   • Winter: snow; winter hood. 1688–89. A playful, pun-
     filled poem. Bashō is without rice or a winter hood and
     converts his empty rice sack into a hood. *Nagezukin*,
     one of several types of head-pieces used to keep out
     winter's wind and cold, had a long section draping
     down the back. *Dai* was a type of hood, and also the
     word for "topic" for a poem. *Yuki* here means both "to
     go (buy rice)" and "snow." In the haibun "Eight Beg-
     gars of Fukagawa."

347 hidden-away / creepers 's companion ? / winter-green selling
   • Winter: winter greens. 1688–89. Bashō is living in
     winter seclusion, with no visitors and his hut covered
     with creepers. Farmers would walk around selling the
     meager winter vegetables, such as Chinese cabbage. A
     scene of a someone living secluded in humble circum-
     stances.

Spring 1689

348 New-Year's-Day as-for / each-field 's sun <emphasis> /
     longing
   • Spring: New Year's Day. 1689 (New Year's Day; Febru-
     ary 20). Sarashina was famous for a view of moonlight
     reflected on rice paddies. In one version of *Sarashina
     Journal*.

349 interesting ! / this-year 's spring also / journey 's sky
   • Spring: spring. 1689. Sent to his disciple Mukai Kyorai
     (1651–1704) to indicate his intention to leave for
     another journey (to the Deep North).

350 morning evening <acc.> / who wait island ! / unrequited-
     love
   • 1689. Miscellaneous (no season word). *Matsu* means
     both "wait" and "pine," and Matsushima is a cluster of
     pine clad islands famous for its beauty. Bashō yearned
     for it so much it seemed that a beautiful lover was there
     waiting for him.

351 heat-waves <nom.> / my shoulder on rise / paper-robe !
   • Spring: heat waves *(kagerō*)*. 1689 (7th day of Second
     Month; March 27). An opening hokku for a linked

verse at the inn where Tōzan, a poet from Ōgaki, was
staying in Edo.

352 red-plum ! / not-see love create / bead-blind
  - Spring: red-blossom plums (*ume**). 1689. The bead
    blinds were decorated blinds used by court ladies. Said
    to be a poem that captures the elegant charm of classi-
    cal Japanese literature, with the mere presence of blos-
    soms and beautiful bead blinds suggesting an alluring
    lady concealed inside.

353 doubt not / tide 's blossoms also / bay 's spring
  - Spring: spring on the bay. 1689. Just off the coast of
    Futamigaura, near the Grand Shrine at Ise, are the
    Wedded Rocks (*meoto-iwa*), two rocks of different sizes
    tied together by gigantic ropes. It is considered a beauti-
    ful and spiritual spot, especially to see New Year's
    dawn. "Doubt it not" is an expression used in religious
    discourse.

354 creepers even / young-leaves as-for lovely / broken-down
house
  - Spring: new leaves on creepers. 1689. Someone is away
    serving the Shōgun in Edo.

355 skylark cry / inside 's beat ! / pheasant 's voice
  - Spring: skylark (*hibari**); pheasant (*kiji**). 1689.

356 moon flower also / is-not sake drink / alone !
  - Miscellaneous (no season word). 1689.

357 grass 's door also / residence-change time ! / doll 's house
  - Spring: dolls. 1689 (3rd of Third Month; May 12). The
    first hokku in *Narrow Road to the Deep North*, coming
    after the famous opening passage about the transitory
    character of life. *Yo* here can mean "world," "period,"
    or "generation." 3rd day of Third Month was the Doll's
    Festival, when various dolls were displayed. With spring
    having arrived and Bashō giving up his hut to a family,
    it is time of changing residence, but it is also a world in
    which change is predominant and fundamental, seen in
    generation after generation.

358 sweetfish 's child 's / whitefish see-off / departure !
  - Spring: sweetfish, whitefish (*shirauo**). 1689 (27th of
    Third Month; May 16). Young sweetfish are said to

head upstream about a month after the whitefish go up
to spawn. Written at the time of his departure to the
Deep North, it is an earlier version of the following
hokku. The hokku is read symbolically, as representing
Bashō leaving his younger disciples.

359 go spring ! / / bird crying fish 's / eye as-for tear

- Spring: departing spring. 1689 (late Third Month; early
  May). The hokku alludes to famous lines from Du Fu's
  "A Spring View": "The nation broken, mountains and
  rivers remain; / spring at the old castle, the grasses are
  deep. / Lamenting the times, flowers bring forth tears; /
  resenting separation, birds startle the heart." The first
  two lines are quoted by Bashō in a later section of the
  journal. See hokku 386. In *Narrow Road to the Deep
  North*.

360 heat-waves with / tie-attach / smoke !

- Spring: heat waves (*itoyū**). 1689. Muro no Yashima is
  a Shinto shrine (now Ōmiwa Shrine in the city of
  Tochigi). The *kami* enshrined there is Konohana Sakuya
  Hime (Princess of the Blossoming Trees), consort of the
  deity Ninigi no Mikoto. After he suspected that her
  pregnancy was not by him, she gave birth locked in a
  burning room in order to prove the divine nature of her
  offspring. As a result, poems related to this shrine often
  mention smoke.

361 about-to-enter / sun also heat-waves / departure !

- Spring: heat waves (*itoyū**). 1689. The poem evokes the
  consonance between the narrow band of sun as it sinks
  below the mountains and the threadlike heat waves (lit-
  erally "thread + play"), which also are gradually disap-
  pearing. An earlier version reads: "just about to sink /
  the sun too takes its time: / spring evening" (*irikakaru /
  hi mo hodohodo ni / haru no kure*).

362 bell not-ring / village as-for what <acc.> ? / spring 's
     evening

- Spring: spring evening. 1689 (29th of Third Month; May
  18). Temple bells usually ring at dusk.

363 sunset 's / bell also not-hear / spring 's evening

- Spring: spring evening. 1689 (29th of Third Month; May
  18).

Summer 1689

364 oh glorious / green-leaf young-leaf 's / sun 's light
- Summer: green leaves; young leaves. 1689 (1st of Fourth Month; May 19). Bashō is at Mt. Nikkō, which literally means "sun's light." It is the site of an ancient Buddhist temple established by Kūkai as well as a Shinto shrine and mausoleum of the founder of the Tokugawa shogunate, Ieyasu (1542–1616). The original version reads: "so holy: / down even to the darkness beneath the trees, / the sun's light" (*ara tōto / ko no shitayami mo / hi no hikari*). In *Narrow Road to the Deep North*.

365 for-a-while as-for / waterfall at secluded ! / summer-retreat 's beginning
- Summer: start of summer retreat. 1689 (2nd of Fourth Month; May 20). Bashō is at Urami (Rear View) Falls at Nikkō, where one can stand behind the falling water. Summer retreat is an annual Buddhist practice of ninety days of seclusion and ascetic practice (including standing in waterfalls) beginning the 16th day of Fourth Month. In *Narrow Road to the Deep North*.

366 fodder carry / person <acc.> guide 's / summer-field !
- Summer: summer moor. 1689. Suitō was a disciple who lived in the town of Kurobane. This was a greeting poem and opening hokku of a linked verse. In the haibun "Preface to 'a man carrying fodder.'"

367 mountain also garden in / move-into ! / summer-room
- Summer: summer drawing-room. 1689. A greeting verse for his host who lived in Kurobane. The hokku displays one aspect of Japanese house and garden aesthetics: "capturing" a distant scene within the aesthetic framework of the view. In the haibun "Concerning the Beautiful Views at Master Shūa's Residence." An alternate version reads: "mountains and gardens / both move into it— / parlor in summer" (*yama mo niwa mo / ugokiiruru ya / natsuzashiki*).

368 woodpecker also / hut as-for not-break / summer grove
- Summer: summer grove. 1689. Bashō received training in Zen meditation from Butchō around 1682. He visited him during his journey to Kashima shrine, and then in

the journey to the Deep North, and now he comes to see his former hermitage behind Unganji Temple in the town of Kurobane. In *Narrow Road to the Deep North*.

369 field ! barley ! / middle at also summer 's / cuckoo

- Summer: cuckoo *(hototogisu*)*; barley *(mugi*)*. 1689. Rice sprouts are green, and the ripened barley field is yellowish. Bashō arrives in summer at the Shirakawa barrier, famous in poetry for moving scenes in spring, winter, and especially autumn. The summerness of the scene before him contrasts with the literary conventions. In the haibun "Summer's Cuckoo."

370 summer-mountain in / clogs <acc.> pray / departure !

- Summer: summer mountain. 1689 (9th of Fourth Month; May 27). Bashō is visiting the Hall of the Ascetic *(Gyōjadō)* at the Kōmyō Temple in Kurobane, which housed a statue of En no Gyōja, a priest (ca. 700) who wandered widely in the countryside and founded the ascetic *shugendō* sect. His clogs were said to be unusually high and intentionally difficult to walk on, and Bashō's prayer to them was for strength and fortitude on his journey as he departed for the Oku region. In *Narrow Road to the Deep North*. An earlier version reads: "summer mountains— / at departure praying / to the high clogs" *(natsuyama ya / kadode ni ogamu / taka-ashida)*.

371 crane cries ! / that voice by banana / will-tear

- Autumn: banana *(bashō*)*. 1689. The leaves of the banana tear easily in the wind, which is one reason Bashō took it as his pen name. The poem was actually written in summer, but the image in the painting he was writing about was an autumn image.

372 field <acc.> side to / horse pull ! / cuckoo

- Summer: cuckoo *(hototogisu*)*. 1689 (16th of Fourth Month; June 3). The cuckoo was known for a plaintive song given during its horizontal flight, and for being difficult to glimpse. Written while traversing the Nasu Plain. A poem card was stiff paper for writing poetry, used especially when a verse was given as a gift. In

Narrow Road to the Deep North and the haibun "Preface to 'across the fields.'"

373 fall-come ! / Takaku 's lodging 's / cuckoo

- Summer: cuckoo *(hototogisu*)*. 1689 (16th–18th of Fourth Month; June 3–5). The word high *(takai)* is embedded in the place name Takaku, which is located northwest of Kurobane. The scene of a monk on pilgrimage stopping at a place where he encounters something unusual is typical of Nō plays, and there is a Nō play *Killing Rock*. See notes to the next hokku. In the haibun "Cuckoo at a Lodging in Takaku."

374 rock 's scent ! / summer-grass red / dew hot

- Summer: summer grass, heat. 1689. Located near the hot springs in Nasu, the Killing Stone is a boulder (about seven feet square and four feet high), around which noxious gases rise. A legend assigns the origin of the stone to a fox spirit that transformed itself into a beautiful woman, Lady Tamamo. She succeeded in becoming the favorite mistress of Emperor Toba (1103–56), but was exposed by an exorcist. The fox then fled to the Nasu Plain, where it was killed, its vengeful spirit taking the form of the stone. Dew *(tsuyu*)* is usually associated with the cool of autumn.

375 rice-field one / planting depart / willow !

- Summer: rice planting. 1689 (20th of Fourth Month; June 7). The hokku is an allusive variation of Saigyō's waka: "By the roadside / a crystal stream flowing / in the shade of a willow *(yanagi*)*: / 'Just a moment,' I thought— / yet I've lingered long" *(michinobe ni / shimizu nagaruru / yanagi kage / shibashi tote koso / tachidomaritsure.)* A Nō play, *The Wandering Priest and the Willow*, was based on Saigyō's verse. In *Narrow Road to the Deep North*.

376 west ? east ? / first rice-sprouts in also / wind 's sound

- Summer: rice sprouts. 1689. Bashō is at the famous Shirakawa Barrier in his journey to the Deep North.

377 *fūryū* 's / beginning ! deep-north 's / rice-planting-song

- Summer: rice planting. 1689 (22nd of Fourth Month; June 9). *Fūryū*** is an extraordinarily complex term, including associations of high culture, art in general, poetry, and music, as well as ascetic wayfaring and Daoist eccentricity. Bashō had just crossed the famous Shirakawa Barrier, the entrance to the deep north and the inspiration for many poems. The hokku was a greeting poem for his host Sagara Tōkyū (1638–1715), and it served as the opening hokku of a linked verse conducted at his house. In *Narrow Road to the Deep North* and the haibun "Rice Planting Songs in the Deep North."

378 world 's people 's / not-discovered flower ! / eaves 's chestnut

- Summer: chestnut blossom (*kuri no hana**). 1689 (24th of Fourth Month; June 11). Gyōgi was a Buddhist monk known for wandering the countryside and assisting villagers. In *Narrow Road to the Deep North*. There is a different version in the haibun "Hidden House": "hidden house: / inconspicuous blossoms / of a chestnut by the eaves" (*kakurega ya / medatanu hana o / noki no kuri*). That version was the opening hokku of a linked verse and was written in praise of his host, the monk Kashin, who had a chestnut by his house.

379 summer-rains: / waterfall fall-bury / water-volume !

- Summer: summer rains (*samidare**). 1689.

380 rice-seedling plant / hand ! old / longing-pattern

- Summer: planting rice sprouts. 1689 (2nd of Fifth Month; June 18). The hokku refers to a famous local custom of dyeing clothes by using the patterns on a large stone. Bashō, however, finds the stone fallen, its face buried in the earth. In *Narrow Road to the Deep North* and the haibun "The Pattern-Rubbing Stone."

381 pannier also sword also / fifth-month in display / paper-carp-streamers

- Summer: Fifth Month; paper carp. 1689. The hokku refers to the festival for boys held on the 5th day of Fifth Month, when families with boys raise paper carp streamers. Bashō is at the temple which had the sword of Minamoto Yoshitsune (1159–89), famous tragic warrior, and the wooden backpack of the monk Benkei, his loyal bodyguard. In *Narrow Road to the Deep North*.

382 cherry-blossom from / pine as-for two-trunks <acc.> /
three-month-past
- Summer (three months after cherry blossoms, *sakura**).
  1689. Bashō saw the cherries bloom in Edo, and now he
  has arrived at the famous Takekuma Pine. Tachibana no
  Suemichi had written a waka: "The Takekuma Pine /
  has twin trunks; / if those in the capital / ask of it, I'll tell
  them / I gazed upon it" (*takekuma no / matsu wa futaki
  o / miyakobito / ikaga to toeba / miki to kotaen*). Kusak-
  abe Kyohaku (d. 1696), a merchant and Bashō's disci-
  ple, gave the poem cited in the hokku's headnote to
  Bashō when he left Edo, and Bashō sent this hokku to
  him in a letter. The word *miki* means "saw," "trunks,"
  and "three trees." *Matsu* means both "pine" and "wait
  for." The pine had been replanted or re-grafted for cen-
  turies, and Bashō marvelled at its continuity. An earlier
  version has for the first line: (the cherry blossoms have)
  "completely scattered" (*chiriusenu*). In *Narrow Road to
  the Deep North*.
383 Rain-hat-island as-for / where fifth-month 's / muddy-road
- Summer: fifth month. 1689. Bashō had wanted to see
  Kasashima because it was the site of the grave of Fuji-
  wara Sanekata (d. 998), a poet who died in exile there,
  but the summer rains washed out the road. In *Narrow
  Road to the Deep North* and the haibun "Preface to
  'Rainhat Island.'"
384 iris / feet to will-tie / sandals 's cord
- Summer: iris (*ayamegusa**). 1689 (7th of Fifth Month;
  June 23). Written around the time of the Iris Festival (5th
  day of Fifth Month, also called the Boy's Festival), when
  irises were displayed on the eaves of houses to drive
  away evil spirits. His host, the painter Kaemon, had
  given him sandals with blue cords. In the *Narrow Road
  to the Deep North*, where Bashō praises Kaemon for
  being an exceptional follower of *fūryū***.
385 islands-islands ! / 1000–pieces broken / summer 's sea
- Summer: summer sea. 1689. Matsushima is a cluster of
  pine clad islands famous for its beauty. In the haibun
  "Matsushima."

386 summer-grass ! / noble-warriors 's / dream 's remains
- Summer: summer grass. 1689 (13th of Fifth Month; June 29). Bashō is at the Takadachi Castle where the tragic warrior-hero Yoshitsune and his retainers met their death. See hokku 359 for the poem by Du Fu that Bashō cites just before this hokku in *Narrow Road to the Deep North.*

387 summer-rain 's / fall-remain ? / light-hall
- Summer: summer rains (*samidare**). 1689 (13th of Fifth Month; June 29). Bashō is at the Chūsonji Temple in Hiraizumi. The Hall of Light, built in 1124, enshrines three generations of the Fujiwara family in a gold-leafed room. A protective outer structure was built in 1288. An earlier version reads: "summer rains— / year upon year falling / five hundred times" (*samidare ya / toshi-doshi furu mo / gohyaku tabi*). In *Narrow Road to the Deep North.*

388 fleas lice / horse 's pee do / pillow side
- Summer: fleas. 1689 (16th of Fifth Month; July 2). Shit-omae literally means "before the urine." In *Narrow Road to the Deep North.*

389 coolness <acc.> / my lodging into make / relax indeed
- Summer: cool (*suzumi**). 1689. A greeting poem to his wealthy host and poet Suzuki Seifū (1651–1721) in Obanazawa. Despite his wealth, Bashō says that he has the spirit of a recluse. In *Narrow Road to the Deep North.*

390 crawl-out ! / silkworm-hut 's underside 's / toad 's voice
- Summer: toad. 1689. The poem gives a haikai twist to a verse in the *Man'yōshū*: Morning mist: / under the silk-worm nursery / a frog calls out. / If I could but hear your voice / I'd feel no yearning (*asagasumi / kaiya ga shita ni / naku kawazu / koe da ni kikaba / ware koime ya mo*). In *Narrow Road to the Deep North.* An earlier version is: "crawl out here! / under the silkworm nursery, / a toad" (*haiide yo / kaiya ga shita no / hikigaeru*).

391 eye-brow-brush <acc.> / image into make / rouge-plant 's flower
- Summer: safflower. 1689. "Rouge-plant" is the literal rendering of the Japanese name for safflower, *Carthamus*

tinctorius, from which rouge was made. The shape of the flowers resembles thistles and reminds Bashō of brushes used for eyebrows. For Suzuki Seifū, see notes to hokku 389. In *Narrow Road to the Deep North*.

392 stillness ! / rock into penetrate / cicada 's voice

- Late-summer: cicada's cry (*semi no koe**). 1689 (27th of Fifth Month; July 13). Bashō composed this at Yamadera ("Mountain Temple"), also called Ryūshaku Temple. In *Narrow Road to the Deep North*. There are two earlier versions: "mountain temple — / sticking into the rocks, / cicada's cry" (*yamadera ya / iwa ni shimitsuku / semi no koe*) and "loneliness — / seeping into the rocks, / cicadas' cry (*sabishisa ya / iwa ni shimikomu / semi no koe*).

393 summer-rains <acc.> / gathering swift / Mogami-River

- Summer: summer rains (*samidare**). 1689 (29th of Fifth Month; July 15). In *Narrow Road to the Deep North*. The original version, with "cool" (*suzushi*) instead of "swift" (*hayashi*), was a greeting poem for his host Takano Ichiei who owned a boathouse on the river. (See Shirane, *Traces of Dreams* 171–73, for a discussion of the revision process.)

394 water 's deep / ice-house seek / willow !

- Summer: ice house. 1689. A greeting poem praising the clear, cool water passing by the willow (*yanagi**) tree at his host's home.

395 wind 's scent also / south to close / Mogami-river

- Summer: wind's fragrance. 1689 (1st or 2nd day of Sixth Month; July 17 or 18). Bashō alludes to a line from the Chinese poet Bo Juyi: "A fragrant wind wafts in from the south." Bashō also may have in mind a Chinese poem attributed to the Chinese poet Su Shi: "Everyone suffers from the heat / But I love this long day of summer. / Coming from the south a delightful breeze / makes the palace cool." Seishin was the pen name of Shibuya Kurōbei, a merchant and poet in Shinjō.

396 thanks ! / snow <acc.> perfume / South-valley

- Summer: fragrance of the south. 1689. For the season word, see notes to previous hokku. Bashō is spending two days at a temple in Minamidani, "South Valley." A greeting poem for Priest Ekaku (d. 1707), who hosted a linked verse party. In *Narrow Road to the Deep North*. There are two earlier versions: "so grateful— / perfumed with snow / the wind's sound" (*arigata ya / yuki o kaorasu / kaze no oto*); "so grateful— / the sound of wind / pushing round the snow" (*arigata ya / yuki o megurasu / kaze no oto*).

397 coolness ! / faint third-day-moon 's / Haguro-mountain

- Summer: cool (*suzumi**). 1689 (9th of Sixth Month; July 25). Mt. Gassan, Mt. Haguro, and Mt. Yudono are the three sacred mountains of Dewa Province. Bashō was asked by Priest Ekaku of Nyakuōin Temple to write a hokku on his visit to the area. Haguro literally means "Feather Black Mountain." Embedded in the poem is a wordplay, with *honomi(eru)* implying "faintly visible." In *Narrow Road to the Deep North*. An earlier version has the first line as "cool breeze—" (*suzukaze ya*).

398 cloud 's peak / how-many crumbling / moon 's mountain

- Summer: cloud peaks. 1689 (9th of Sixth Month; July 25). "Moon Mountain" is both the mountain in moonlight (after a day of cloud transformations) and (in Chinese-style pronunciation) the literal name of the mountain Bashō is observing, Gassan. In addition, there is wordplay in the word *tsuki*, which suggests "to be exhausted" (*tsuku*): the clouds have crumbled completely and disappeared. In *Narrow Road to the Deep North*.

399 cannot-speak / Yudono at wetten / sleeves !

- Summer: worshiping at Yudono. 1689 (9th of Sixth Month; July 25). In Bashō's time, visitors to the shrine were forbidden to tell about the sacred object of worship, which is a large red rock with hot spring water flowing over it. In *Narrow Road to the Deep North*.

400 this jewel ! / Haguro to returns / law 's moon.

- Autumn: moon. 1689. Written in commemoration of the late High Priest Tenyū of Mt. Haguro. The moon, a traditional Buddhist symbol of enlightenment, is presented here as the embodiment of the Buddhist law or teachings, and a representation of Tenyū's *tama* or spirit. The word Bashō actually uses is the homonym *tama* meaning jewel. In the haibun "Memorial on the High Priest Tenyū." Written in the summer (9th of Sixth Month; July 25), but, because it was written about Priest Tenyū, it uses the Buddhist image of the moon, associated with autumn.

401   moon ? flower ? / although-ask four-sleep 's / snore !
  • Miscellaneous. 1689. Written on a painting of four Buddhist monks sleeping.

402   surprising ! / mountain <acc.> depart 's / first-eggplant
  • Summer: early eggplant (*nasu**). 1689. *Ideha* is an alternative way of reading Dewa; it also implies "on departing" from the mountains. This poem is an opening hokku for a linked verse and a greeting poem for his host, Nagayama Shigeyuki, who had given Bashō the first eggplant of the season.

403   hot sun (day) <acc.> / sea into insert / Mogami-river
  • Summer: heat. 1689 (14th of Sixth Month; July 30). From Bashō's perspective at Sakata, the sun is setting where the Mogami River pours into the sea. *Atsuki hi* can mean "hot day" as well as "hot sun." In *Narrow Road to the Deep North*. An earlier version had the first line as "coolness—" (*suzushisa ya*).

404   Kisagata ! / rain in Xi Shi 's / silk-tree 's blossoms
  • Summer: silk-tree blossoms. 1689 (17th of Sixth Month; August 2). *Nebu* means both the "silk tree" (*Albizzia julibrissin*) and "asleep." The leaves of the silk tree close during the evening, suggesting sleep. Xi Shi was a famous Chinese beauty associated with great sorrow. She was given to a King, whose infatuation with her led to the downfall of his kingdom. It also is said that once when rain moistened her face while she was asleep, she became even more beautiful. Bashō alludes to a poem by Su Shi: "Ripples on glittering water—in fine weather, so beautiful. / Haze in the mountains—when raining, so wonderful. / Comparing the Western Lake to Xi Shi: / Both are lovely, whether heavy make-up or light." Kisagata, on the Sea of Japan, was Bashō's northernmost

stop on the journey to the Deep North. In *Narrow Road to the Deep North*. Another version reads: "Kisagata in rain—, / with Xi Shi asleep / a silk tree in bloom" (*kisagata no / ame ya seishi ga / nebu no hana*).

405 evening-clearing ! / cherry-blossoms under to-cool / wave 's flowers

- Summer: cool (*suzumi**). 1689. The evening sun sparkling on waves were "wave blossoms." There is an allusion to a poem by Saigyō: "At Kisagata / the cherry flowers are embedded / in the waves. / Rowing on top of the blossoms, / the fishermen's boats" (*kisagata no / sakura wa nami ni / umuzumorete / hana no ue kogu / ama no tsuribane*).

406 Shiogoshi ! / crane legs is-wet / sea cool

- Summer: cool (*suzumi**). 1689 (17th of Sixth Month; August 2). Shiogoshi, literally "shallows," is located in the Kisagata area. In *Narrow Road to the Deep North*.

407 Atsumi mountain ! / blow-bay as-far-as / evening-cool

- Summer: cool (*suzumi**). 1689. Atsumi is literally "hot," and Fukuura, south of Kisagata, means "blowing bay." In *Narrow Road to the Deep North*.

Autumn 1689

408 Seventh-month ! / sixth-day also usual 's / night to as-for not-resemble

- Autumn: Seventh Month. 1689 (6th of Seventh Month; August 20). The 7th day of Seventh Month, Tanabata, is the Star Festival (*tanabata**). In *Narrow Road to the Deep North*.

409 rough-sea ! / Sado over stretch-out / heaven 's river

- Autumn: Heaven's River. 1689 (7th of Seventh Month; August 21). See the opening comments in the Introduction. In *Narrow Road to the Deep North* and the haibun "Introduction to Silver River."

410 herbal-medicine-garden in / which 's flower <acc.> / grass-pillow

- Autumn: plant blossoms. 1689 (8th day of Seventh Month; August 22). A greeting poem for his host, a poet as well as doctor in Takada whose pen name was Tōsetsu. For "grass pillow," see notes to hokku 145. In the haibun "Preface to 'in your medicinal garden.'"

411 small-sea-bream pierce / willow cool ! / fisher 's wife
- Summer: cool (*suzumi**). 1689. Actually written in early autumn, it presents the image of coolness associated with relief from summer heat.

412 one-house in / play-girls also slept / bush-clover and moon
- Autumn: bush clover *(hagi*)*. 1689 (12ᵗʰ of Seventh Month: August 26). In *Narrow Road to the Deep North*, Bashō encounters traveling prostitutes ("play-girls") at an inn in Ichiburi. The next morning the prostitutes ask Bashō if they can follow him on their journey to the Shinto Shrine at Ise, but Bashō declines, saying "Just entrust yourself to the way others are going. Surely the gods will protect you from harm." This hokku follows. However, in the diary of his traveling companion Kawai Sora (1649–1710), there is no record of this event actually occurring. (For an interpretation of this hokku, see Barnhill "Impermanence, Fate, and the Journey.")

413 early-rice 's fragrance ! / divide-enter right as-for / storm-shore-sea
- Autumn: early rice. 1689 (15ᵗʰ of Seventh Month; August 29). Ariso-umi is the name of the sea near the port of Fushiki on Toyama Bay. It literally means "rough shore." An earlier version has "the fragrance of rice" (*ine no ka ya*) for the first line. In *Narrow Road to the Deep North*.

414 red-red -ly / sun as-for heartless yet / autumn 's wind
- Autumn: autumn wind (*akikaze**). 1689 (17ᵗʰ of Seventh Month; August 31). The hokku brings together two seasonal topics: the lingering heat (*zansho*) of autumn and autumn's wind. In *Narrow Road to the Deep North* and the haibun "Preface to 'red, red.'" In the haibun, Bashō alludes to a waka by Fujiwara Toshiyuki (d. 901): "That autumn has come / is not evident / to the eyes and yet / I am startled by the sound / of autumn winds" (*aki kinu to / me ni wa sayaka ni / mienedomo / kaze no oto ni zo / odorokarenuru*).

415 autumn is-cool / each-hand by peel ! / melon eggplant
- Autumn: cool (*suzumi**) of autumn. 1689 (20th of the Seventh Month; September 3). A greeting poem for his host Issen at a linked verse party at Shōgen-an in Kanazawa. In *Narrow Road to the Deep North*. An earlier version reads: "summer heat lingers, / let's set our hands to cooking / melons (*uri**) and eggplants (*nasu**)" (*zansho shibashi / tegoto ni ryōre / uri nasubi*).

416 grave also move / my cry voice as-for / autumn 's wind
- Autumn: autumn wind (*akikaze**). 1689 (22nd of Seventh Month; September 5). Bashō was told that Kosugi Isshō (1653–88) had hoped to meet him, but when Bashō arrived in Kanazawa he learned Isshō had died the previous year. In *Narrow Road to the Deep North*.

417 lovely / name ! small-pine blows / bush-clover pampass
- Autumn: bush clover (*hagi**). 1689. Komatsu, a place name, literally means "little pine." This is a greeting verse for his host, the Shinto priest Kosen of Hiyoshi Shrine, and the opening hokku of a forty-four stanza linked verse. In *Narrow Road to the Deep North*.

418 wet go ! / person also interesting / rain 's bush-clover
- Autumn: bush clover (*hagi**). 1689 (26th of Seventh Month; September 9). The opening hokku for a fifty-stanza linked verse gathering held in Kanazawa.

419 pitiful ! ! / helmet's under 's / cricket
- Autumn: cricket (*kirigirisu**). 1689 (early Eighth Month; September). Bashō is visiting the Tada Shrine in Komatsu, which housed the helmet of the famous warrior Saitō Sanemori (d. 1183). Sanemori died in the Battle of Shinohara at the age of seventy-three. In order not to appear old to his enemies, he dyed his hair black. When the victorious general saw the severed head of the old man, he cried out "So pitiful." Bashō presented the poem as a religious offering to the Tada Shrine. In *Narrow Road to the Deep North*. An earlier version has a differently worded first line with the same meaning: *ana muzan ya*.

420 Yamanaka ! / chrysanthemum as-for not-pluck / hot-
   spring 's scent
   • Autumn: chrysanthemum (*kiku**). 1689. Yamanaka was
   known for its hotsprings, therapeutic like the chrysan-
   themum. A greeting poem for his host, the thirteen-year-
   old haikai poet Kumenosuke. In *Narrow Road to the
   Deep North* and the haibun "In Praise of Hot Springs."
421 peach 's tree 's / these leaves scatter don't / autumn 's wind
   • Autumn: autumn wind (*akikaze**). 1689. Kumenosuke's
   pen name Tōyō includes the word "peach (*momo**),"
   which was also part of one of Bashō's poetic names,
   Tōsei.
422 fishing-fires by / bullhead ! wave 's / under choke
   • Autumn: bullhead. 1689. Bullhead *(Cottus pollux)* are
   freshwater fish that are caught as they are attracted to
   the light of a fire.
423 hot-spring 's departure / tonight as-for skin 's / cold
   • Autumn: cool skin. 1689. Bashō is leaving the hot
   springs at Yamanaka. Another greeting poem for his
   young host Kumenosuke.
424 hot-spring 's departure / how-many times see ! / mist 's
   under
   • Autumn: mist (*kiri**). 1689 (late Seventh Month; mid-
   September).
425 today from ! / inscription will-disappear / hat 's dew
   • Autumn: dew (*tsuyu**). 1689. The hokku is a present to
   his traveling companion Sora as he departs from Bashō
   due to illness. Earlier they had written on their bamboo
   hats: "between heaven and earth, without a fixed
   abode, two wayfarers" (*kenkon mujū dōgyō ninin*). The
   poem also is in response to verse Sora presented to
   Bashō: "going on and on, / even should I fall: / bush
   clover dew" (*yuki yukite / tarorefusutomo / hagi no
   tsuyu*). In Bashō's hokku, dew suggests his own tears
   while echoing Sora's poem. In *Narrow Road to the
   Deep North*. A different version appears in the haibun
   "Preface to 'loneliness,'" where the first line is: loneli-
   ness (*sabishigeni*).

426 Stone-Mountain 's / stones more-than is-white / autumn 's
     wind
  - Autumn: autumn wind (*akikaze**). 1689 (5th of Eighth
    Month; September 18). *Ishiyama* literally means "stone
    mountain." Bashō may see the stones at Nata Temple
    (built on a hill of whitish quartz trachyte) as whiter than
    the famous white stones of Stone Mountain near Lake
    Biwa in Ōmi Province, or he may experience the wind as
    whiter than the stones. In *Narrow Road to the Deep
    North*.

427 garden sweep / would-like-to-depart temple in / fall
     willow
  - Autumn: falling leaves. 1689. Bashō stayed overnight at
    Zenshō-ji temple, and as he left some young monks
    asked for a verse. It was customary for a traveling monk
    who spent the night at a temple to sweep the garden
    before he left. In *Narrow Road to the Deep North*.

428 thing write / fan tear-up / departure !
  - Autumn: discarding the fan. 1689. At Kanazawa, the
    poet Hokushi (d. 1718) went to see him off but decided
    to accompany him all the way to Maruoka, where
    Bashō says goodbye. As weather cools in autumn, the
    fan used for summer heat is discarded. Bashō had writ-
    ten something on it, however, making it difficult to part
    with. *Nagori* connotes sad departure and memories. In
    Narrow Road to the Deep North. An earlier version
    reads: "scribbled on, / now tearing off a sheet of the fan:
    / departure" (*mono kaite / ōgi hegiwakuru / wakare
    kana*).

429 Asamutsu ! / moonviewing 's journey 's / dawning-separa-
     tion
  - Autumn: moonviewing. 1689. Asamutsu literally means
    "shallow water," the poem implying the sound the shal-
    low water streaming under the bridge, which was
    famous in Japanese literature.

430 moonview / Jewel-Bay 's reeds <acc.> / not-cut before
  - Autumn: moonviewing; reed (*ashi**) cutting. 1689 (mid-
    Eighth Month). Tamae, literally "jewel bay," is famous
    for its reeds, which beautify the sight of the moon, espe-
    cially just as they form seeds during the Eighth Month.

431 tomorrow 's moon / rain forecast / Hina-ga-dake
- Autumn: moon. 1689. "Tomorrow's moon" is the full moon of the Eighth Month. The hokku involves word-play: *hi* of Hina is the word for "to compare," in this case rain and shine.

432 Yoshinaka 's / awaking 's mountain ? / moon is-sad
- Autumn: moon. 1689. Kiso Yoshinaka (1154–84) was a general who was killed by Minamoto no Yoshitsune soon after he became Shōgun. See hokku 498 and 531.

433 many-countries 's / eight-scenes furthermore / Kei 's moon
- Autumn: moon. 1689. Kei (or Kehi) is the ancient name for the port city of Tsuruga. The notion of "eight scenes" comes from the Chinese tradition of eight beautiful views at Xiao River, and various eight scenes were selected around Japan.

434 moon is-pure / Yugyō 's carry / sand 's on
- Autumn: moon. 1689. Yugyō means "pilgrimage," but it also is the honoric title of the chief priest at the Yugyōji Temple of the Ji sect of Buddhism. More particularly, it refers to Taa Shōnin (1237–1319), Yugyō II, who carried sand to the muddy grounds of Kei Shrine. His successors made this an annual ritual. In *Narrow Road to the Deep North* and in the haibun "In Tsuruga." There are two earlier versions: "ceaseless tears— / dew on the sand / carried by the Pilgrim Priests" (*namida shiku ya / yugyō no moteru / suna no tsuyu*) and "the moon so pure / dew on the sand / carried by the Pilgrim Priests" (*tsuki kiyoshi / yugyō no moteru / suna no tsuyu*).

435 bright-moon ! / north-country weather / unpredictable
- Autumn: harvest moon. 1689 (15th of Eighth Month; September 28). In *Narrow Road*, Bashō relates that the night before the moon shone brightly, but the landlord warned him against expecting the same for the famous moon of the fifteenth night of the Eighth Month. In *Narrow Road to the Deep North* and haibun "In Tsuruga."

436　moon where / bell as-for sink / sea 's bottom
- Autumn: moon. 1689 (15th of Eighth Month; September 28). In the haibun "In Tsuruga."

437　moon only neither / rain because-of sumō also / not
- Autumn: moon; sumō. 1689. Written at Tsuruga Bay at Kei beach.

438　old name 's / Deer-Antler – lovely / autumn 's moon
- Autumn: autumn moon. 1689. Tsunuga, "antler-deer," is an ancient name for Tsuruga, a port city in Echizen Province.

439　loneliness ! / Suma than triumph / beach 's autumn
- Autumn: autumn. 1689 (middle of Eighth Month; late September). While Tsuruga was relatively unknown, Suma was famous in classical literature for its desolate atmosphere in autumn, related to its use as a place of exile. Bashō not only establishes a new aesthetic quality for Tsuruga within the literary tradition, he judges it superior to Suma in *sabi***, his central principle of loneliness. In *Narrow Road to the Deep North* and the haibun "In Tsuruga."

440　wave 's space ! / small-shells in mix / bush-clover 's dust
- Autumn: bush clover *(hagi*)*. 1689 (16th of Eighth Month; September 29). Written at Ironohama, "Color Beach." See notes to the following hokku. In *Narrow Road to the Deep North*.

441　small-bush-clover drop / Masuho 's small-shell / small-cup
- Autumn: small bush clover *(hagi*)*. 1689. Bashō is at Ironohama ("Color Beach") in the port city of Tsuruga in Echizen Province. Masuho is a tiny pink shell which resembles the small blossoms of the bush clover. Bashō draws on a waka by Saigyō: "The small crimson shells / which dye the sea tides / are gathered here, / perhaps the reason this shore / is called Color Beach" (*shio somuru / masuho no kogai / hirou tote / ironohama to wa / iu ni ya aramu*). In the haibun "In Tsuruga."

442　butterfly into even / not-become autumn deepen / rape-worm !
- Autumn: autumn. 1689 (21st day of Eighth Month; October 4).

443 as-it-is ! / moon even not-depend on / Mt. Ibuki
- Autumn: moon. 1689. The poem echoes the famous waka by Fujiwara Teika (1162–1241): "I gaze around / there are no blossoms / or autumn leaves; / a grass-thatched hut by a bay / in autumn evening" (*miwataseba / hana mo momiji mo / nakarikeri / ura no tomaya no / aki no yūgure*). It also recalls prose and poetry in which Bashō states that all things are self-realized and content (hokku 175, 197 and 218).

444 secluded / tree 's fruit grass 's grain / would-that-I-could-pick
- Autumn: the fruit of trees, the grain of grass. 1689 (4th day of Ninth Month; October 17).

445 early bloom / ninth-day also is-close / chrysanthemum 's flowers
- Autumn: chrysanthemum (*kiku**). 1689 (4th day of Ninth Month; October 17). The 9th day of Ninth Month is the annual Chrysanthemum Festival. An earlier version reads: "bloom quickly, / the ninth is near: / chrysanthemum by the house" (*hayō sake / kunichi mo chikashi / yado no kiku*).

446 wisteria 's fruit as-for / haikai into will-make / flower 's after
- Autumn: wisteria bean. 1689. "After the blossoms" refers not only to auturmn fruiting after spring flowering, but to the courtly aesthetic of the renga poet Sōgi as well. Once Sōgi crossed the Ōsaka Barrier and saw white wisteria blossoms, which called to mind the White Wisteria Slope on the Kii peninsula. He wrote: "crossing the barrier, / here too is a White / Wisteria Slope" (*seki koete / koko mo fujishiro / misaka kana*). The post-medieval haikai aesthetic celebrates the more lowly wisteria bean. Sogyū (Hirose Gennojō, 1646–1711), a disciple of Bashō, later became known as Izen. His home town of Seki, in Mino Province, also means "barrier," relating him to Sōgi's poem.

447 hidden-house ! / moon and chrysanthemum and to / rice-field three-tan
- Autumn: chrysanthemum (*kiku**). 1689. A greeting verse for his disciple and host Bokuin of Ōgaki, praising his aesthetic rusticity.

448 Saigyō 's / straw-sandals too hang / pine 's dew
   • Autumn: dew (*tsuyu**). 1689. Dew hanging from a pine
     evokes autumn, and the sandals of the itinerant poet-
     monk Saigyō would further enrich the scene.

449 clam-shells 's / Futami for separating / departing autumn !
   • Autumn: departing autumn. 1689 (6th of Ninth Month;
     October 19). This is the final poem of *Narrow Road to
     the Deep North*, where Bashō bids goodbye to several
     disciples who had gathered to meet him as he sets off
     from Ōgaki for Ise. Futami, literally "two views," is the
     area around the Great Shrine at Ise, known for clams
     and for the Wedded Rocks: two boulders in the sea tied
     together with a huge rope. *Futa* also means a lid (in this
     case, of a clam), while *mi* can mean both "see" and
     "flesh"; *futa mi ni wakareru* means to divide the clam
     meat from the shell. The second hokku of this journal,
     in which Bashō leaves for the Deep North, begins
     "departing spring."

450 moon lonely <imperative> / Akechi 's wife 's / story tell
   • Autumn: moon. 1689. When Akechi Matsuhide fell into
     poverty, his wife secretly cut and sold her hair so he
     could afford to hold a linked verse gathering. He vowed
     that within fifty days he would rise to power and she
     would ride in a jewelled palanquin. He fulfilled his vow.
     In the haibun "Akechi's Wife."

451 holiness for / everyone push-each-other / shrine-renewal-
     ritual
   • Autumn: Ritual of Renewal. 1689 (mid-Ninth Month;
     late October). Both the Inner and the Outer Shrines at
     the Grand Shrine of Ise are rebuilt every twenty years. In
     1689, after the journey chronicled in *Narrrow Road to
     the Deep North*, Bashō went to witness the ritual of
     changing from the old to the new shrines. He arrived on
     the 11th of Ninth Month, one day after the renewal
     ritual for the Inner Shrine. The ritual for the Outer
     Shrine was on the 13th.

452 autumn 's wind / Ise 's graveyard / still-more severe
   • Autumn: autumn wind (*akikaze**). 1689 (Ninth
     Month). Bashō likely had in mind a waka by Saigyō: "A

tree on a cliff / rising by an abandoned field: / from it a dove's call / mournful for its mate— / desolate nightfall" (*furuhata no / soba no tatsu ki ni / iru hato no / tomo yobu koe no / sugoki yūgure*).

453 inkstone ? thinking / pick-up ! hollow / stone 's dew
- Autumn: dew (*tsuyu**). 1689. Futami is the coastal area near Ise. It was said that when Saigyō lived in seclusion at Futami, he used a rock with a depression on its top as his inkstone.

454 gate into when-enter / cycad by orchid 's / scent !
- Autumn: orchid. 1689. *Sotetsu* is a cycad, or Japanese sago palm (*Cycas revoluta*). Shuei-in is a Pure Land Buddhist Temple in Ise.

455 shape-of-tree 's / day each <adv> change / cotton rose
- Autumn: cotton rose. 1689. The cotton rose (or Confederate rose, *Hibiscus mutabilis*) is a deciduous shrub whose pink or white flowers bloom in the morning and wilt in the evening, with new blooms coming the next day in different places. An earlier version reads: "transforming itself / day after day: / a cotton rose" (*edaburi no / hi ni hi ni kawaru / fuyō kana*).

Winter 1689–90

456 first-winter-shower / monkey too small-coat <acc.> / wants
- Winter: winter showers (*shigure**). 1689–90 (late Ninth Month; November). Written while Bashō was traveling from Ise to his hometown of Ueno in Iga Province.

457 people ! / winter-rain ! house as-for / cold-although
- Winter: winter showers (*shigure**); cold. 1689–90. Disciples are at a poetry gathering (in Bashō's hometown of Ueno in Iga Province) and will benefit from feeling the *wabi*** of winter showers.

458 mushroom-gathering ! / danger thing in / evening-winter-shower
- Winter: evening winter showers (*shigure**). 1689–90.

459 winter garden ! / moon also thread become / insect 's song
- Winter: winter garden. 1689–90. The sounds of insects are almost gone with the coming of winter, as a crescent

moon hangs in the sky. The opening hokku for a eight-
een-stanza linked verse in Ueno.

460 folding-screen on as-for / mountain <acc.> paint / winter
     seclusion
     • Winter: winter seclusion. 1689–90. For a similar verse
       written four years later, see hokku 646.

461 first-snow in / rabbit 's fur / beard make
     • Winter: first snow. 1689–90. A different version has the
       first line as "out in the snow" (*yuki no naka ni*).

462 now children / run walk / hail
     • Winter: hail. 1689–90 (1st day of Eleventh Month;
       December 12). In his hometown of Ueno, Bashō is at a
       linked verse gathering with disciples. They may be the
       "children" of the poem. Ryōbon was the pen name for
       Tomoda Kakuzaemon (1666–1730).

463 first-snow ! / when great-Buddha 's / column-erection
     • Winter: first snow. 1689–90. When Bashō visited the
       bronze Great Buddha at Tōdaiji Temple in Nara (the
       ancient capital), it remained in disrepair — without a
       head – and exposed to the elements. The earlier version
       of the hokku reads: "the snow is sad: / when will the
       Great Buddha / have its tiled roof?" (*yuki kanashi / itsu
       daibutsu no / kawarabuki*).

464 mountain-castle to / go-out 's palanquin borrow / winter-
     shower !
     • Winter: winter showers (*shigure**). 1689–90. *Ide* here
       means both "to go out" and the village of Ide, near
       Nara.

465 Chōshō 's / grave also walk-around ? / bowl-beating
     • Winter: bowl-beating. 1689–90. Bashō visited his disci-
       ple Kyorai in order to listen to the mournful sound of
       monks beating bowls for forty-eight nights starting the
       13th of Eleventh Month as part of an annual ritual to
       commemorate Saint Kūya (903–72). The monks didn't
       pass by Kyorai's house until nearly dawn. Chōshōshi
       (1569–1649) was a feudal lord who became a poet after
       a defeat in the famous battle of Sekigahara in 1600. He
       was known for a poem: "bowl-beating: / a single voice /
       at dawn / like a cuckoo singing / even on a winter night"

(*hachitataki / akatsukigata no / hitokoe wa / fuyu no yo
sae mo / naku hototogisu*).

466 hail if-do / wickerwork 's whitebait <acc.> / in will-put-out
• Winter: whitebait wickerwork, hail. 1689–90. The *ajiro*
is a device made of wicker for catching whitebait in river
shallows. Bashō's hut was at Gichūji Temple in Zeze.

467 what for this / 12th-month's market to / go crow
• Winter: Twelfth Month. 1689–90. The town market
was especially busy as New Year's approached. The
crow (*karasu**) has been read as representing Bashō.

Spring 1690

468 straw-mat <acc.> wearing / what-person is / blossom 's
spring
• Spring: blossom's spring. 1690 (1st of First Month; Feb-
ruary 9). In commenting on this hokku, Bashō lamented
that he lacked the ability to distinguish a mere beggar
from a sage, who may live in poverty. The "capital" is
the traditional capital of Kyoto.

469 otter 's / festival see let's-go / Seta 's depths
• Spring: Festival of the Otter. 1690. Seta is a town and a
river at the southern end of Lake Biwa, and the depths
of Seta are the interior recesses up in the hills. The festi-
val begins on the 16th day of First Month and lasts for
five days.

470 bush-warbler 's / hat drop / camellia !
• Spring: bush warbler (*uguisu**); falling-flowers of
camellia (*tsubaki**). 1690. Bush warblers were said to
stitch a hat with a plum blossom. Bashō gives a haikai
twist to this literary convention.

471 spring-rain ! / sprouts in sprout / eggplant-seed
• Spring: spring rain (*harusame**), eggplant (*nasu**)
seedling, three vegetables. 1690. This hokku was origi-
nally written on a sheet of paper along with the follow-
ing two hokku, each concerning one of the "three veg-
etables": eggplant, red pepper, and potato. An earlier
version reads: "the rain / has thinned—sprouts / of egg-
plant seeds" (*komaka naru / ame ya futaba no /
nasubidane*).

472 this seed <quote> / think-disparage / red-pepper
- Spring: red pepper (*tōgarashi*) seed. 1690. He respects this tiny seed in part because in autumn it will become a plant that burns the tongue, but also one theme in his writings is looking intently at and valuing all things, including those often overlooked. Another versions reads: "the red pepper / I do not belittle: / seedlings" (*tōgarashi* / *omoikonasaji* / *mono no tane*).

473 seed-potatoes ! / flower 's full-bloom with / sell-walk
- Spring: seed potatoes, cherries in full bloom. 1690. Traditionally, potatoes were planted during Second Month.

474 bank 's pine / blossom ! tree-deep / mansion-build
- Spring: blossoms. 1690. A greeting poem for Kōboku, a nineteen year old retainer at the Iga Castle. In East Asia there was a long tradition of making retreats in the city that mimicked a secluded dwelling in the mountains. In this case, the retreat was a manor surrounded by cherries and then pines on earthen embankments.

475 tree 's under in / soup also fish-salad also / cherry-blossom !
- Spring: cherry blossom (*sakura**). 1689 (Third Month; mid-April). *Namasu* consists of vegetables and raw fish in vinegar. The opening hokku for a linked verse composed in Ueno.

476 fitting ! / bean 's flour in / blossom-hunt
- Spring: blossom hunting. 1690. The simplicity of rice balls sprinkled with flour fits with flower viewing more than the common picnics with fancy food and large quantities of sake. "Blossom hunting" was another name for blossom viewing.

477 heat-waves ! / saiko 's thread 's / thin-cloud
- Spring: heat waves *(kagerō*)*; saiko. 1690. The saiko plant is a perennial medicinal herb with very thin leaves and a yellow blossom. Another term for heat waves is *itoyū*, "thin play."

478 butterfly 's wing <subj.> / how-many-times cross-over / wall 's roof
- Spring: butterfly (*chō**). 1690.

479 whole-village as-for / all blossom-guard 's / descendant ? !
  • Spring: blossom guards. 1690. In *Sand and Pebbles Collection* (*Shasekishū*, 1283) there is a story that the Empress Ichijō (988–1074) loved the cherry blossoms at Kōfukuji Temple in Nara so much that she wanted them transplanted to the capital of Kyoto. The monks strenuously opposed the plan. Impressed with their aesthetic sensitivity, she made the local village part of the temple so the trees would be remain protected. Guards were stationed by the trees during the height of their bloom.

480 snake eat <quote> / when-hear fearful / pheasant 's voice
  • Spring: pheasant (*kiji**). 1690.

481 four-directions from / blossom blowing-into / grebe 's wave
  • Spring: blossoms. 1690 (late Third Month; early May). "Grebe Lake" is another name for Lake Biwa. This is a greeting poem for his host Hamada Chinseki, a physician in Zeze, whose house commanded a broad view of the Lake Biwa area. In the haibun "An Account of Pure Washed Hall." A variant has the last line as "sea of grebes" (*nio no umi*).

482 go spring <acc.> / Ōmi 's people with / lament
  • Spring: departing spring. 1690 (late Third Month; early May). The "people of Ōmi" are said to include ancient poets there as well as Bashō's hosts and disciples.

483 alone nun / straw-hut aloof / white azalea
  • Spring: white azalea. 1690.

Summer 1690

484 dawn as-for / still lavender in / cuckoo
  • Summer: cuckoo (*hototogisu**). 1690. Murasaki Shikibu (d. 1014) is said to have written the *Tale of Genji* while secluded in this temple. "Murasaki" is the word for lavender, in this case the color of the dawn sky. Another version has "first of the month" (*tsuitachi*) rather than *murasaki*. Seta and Ishiyama are at the southern tip of Lake Biwa.

485 first rely / pasania 's tree also is / summer grove
  • Summer: summer grove; pasania (*shii**). 1690 (6th of Fourth Month; May 14). For three months Bashō stayed

in a hut known as "Unreal Dwelling," offered to him by his disciple Suganuma Kyokusui (1647?–1704) after his long journey to the Deep North. The evergreen pasania is situated amidst a dense grove of deciduous trees. Saigyō wrote the following waka: "Perched in a line / not separating from their friends / the titmice depend / for their nest on the lower branches / of the pasania" (*narabiite / tomo o hanarenu / kogarame no / negura ni tanomu / shii no shitaeda*). In the famous haibun "Account of an Unreal Dwelling."

486 you ! butterfly / I ! Zhuangzi 's / dream heart
   • Spring: butterfly (*chō**). 1690. Bashō sent this hokku to his disciple Dosui in a letter, where Bashō refers to the famous story in the *Zhuangzi* about someone who dreams he is a butterfly, and when he awakes he wonders whether he is in fact a butterfly who is now dreaming he is a person. Written in early summer, but reference to a butterfly makes it a spring verse.

487 summer-grass ! / I precede / snake will-hunt
   • Summer: summer grass. 1690.

488 evening to also / morning to also not-connect / melon 's flower
   • Summer: melon (*uri**) flower. 1690. The melon's yellow blossoms open in the heat of the day rather than the cool of morning or evening.

489 sun 's path ! / hollyhock turn / summer-rains
   • Summer: summer rains (*samidare**). 1690.

490 orange-tree ! / when 's field within 's / cuckoo
   • Summer: cuckoo (*hototogisu**), orange. 1690. Smelling the fragrant mandarin orange, associated with late Fourth Month, Bashō hears the cuckoo of the Fifth Month. The sensation gives rise to the feeling elicited by other occasions of hearing the call of the "bird of time" as distinctions between time and place blur. Bashō draws on a waka in the *Tales of Ise*: "When I breathe in the scent / of the mandarin orange blossoms / that await the Fifth Month, / I recall the fragrance of the sleeves / of one I loved long ago" (*satsuki matsu / hana tachibana*

no / ka o kageba / mukashi no hito no / sode no ka zo suru).

491 firefly-viewing ! / boatman drunk / unsteady
   • Summer: firefly *(hotaru*)* viewing. 1690. Seta, on the southern end of Lake Biwa, was known for fireflies around a Chinese-style bridge over the Seta River.

492 capital in though / capital long-for ! / cuckoo
   • Summer: cuckoo *(hototogisu*)*. 1690. The capital is Kyoto (which includes the word "capital," *kyō*) but the capital he longs for is that city in the past. The call of the seldom-seen cuckoo is associated with nostalgia for the past.

493 river-wind ! / pale-persimmon-robes wear / evening-cool
   • Summer: cool *(suzumi*)*. 1690. The "pale persimmon robes" are thin summer clothes made from hemp, light tan in color. In the haibun "The Evening Cool at Riverside, Fourth Avenue."

494 me to resemble don't / two into cut / musk-melon
   • Summer: musk melon *(uri*)*. 1690. Given to Emoto Tōko (1659–1712), a merchant who asked to be his disciple. "A melon cut in half" is a Japanese image for two people who are virtually identical. The *makuwauri*, musk melon, is *Cucumis melo var. makuwa*.

495 my hut as-for / mosquito 's smallness <acc.> / offering !
   • Summer: mosquito. 1690. Composed when Akinobō (d. 1718) visited Bashō at the Unreal Dwelling.

496 soon die / appearance as-for not-show / cicada 's voice
   • Summer: cicada's cry *(semi no koe*)*. 1690.

Autumn 1690

497 silk 's tree 's / through-leaves even dislike / star 's light
   • Autumn: Star Festival *(tanabata*)*. 1690. The silk tree *(Albizzia julibrissin)* has compound leaves with many leaflets (that might be used for peering through) as well as elegant red and white blossoms.

498 festival-of-spirits / today also crematorium 's / smoke !
   • Autumn: Festival of Spirits *(tamamatsuri*)*. 1690. Bashō was at the Gichūji Temple in Zeze, named for Kiso Yoshinaka, whose grave is located there.

499 dragonfly ! / cling-to not-able / grass 's on
   • Autumn: dragonfly. 1690.

500 wild-boars also / together with are-blown / windstorm !
   • Autumn: windstorm (*nowaki**). 1690.

501 here turn / I also lonely / autumn 's evening
   • Autumn: autumn evening *(aki no kure*)*. 1690.
      Unchiku lived 1632–1703. Dream was a major theme in
      Bashō's writings. In the haibun "Words on a Portrait by
      Unchiku."

502 white-hair pull / pillow 's under ! / cricket.
   • Autumn: cricket (*kirigirisu**). 1690. This was the open-
      ing hokku of a 18 stanza linked verse composed with
      Chinseki and Emoto Tōko (1659–1712) at Gichūji
      Temple at Zeze.

503 bright-moon ! / children in-a-line / temple 's veranda
   • Autumn: harvest moon. 1690 (15th of Eighth Month;
      September 17).

504 bright-moon ! / sea toward when-faces / seven Komachi.
   • Autumn: harvest moon. 1690 (15th of Eighth Month;
      September 17). The Seven Komachis is a poetic refer-
      ence to changes in the moon and the scenery below. It
      refers to the Heian poet Ono no Komachi (fl. ca. 850)
      whose semilegendary life is said to have gone through
      many stages, changing from youthful beauty to a poor
      hag living in seclusion.

505 moonviewing do / room at beautiful / face also is-not
   • Autumn: moonviewing. 1690. This hokku is said to be
      a revision of the two previous ones. Another version
      reads: "harvest moon— / in the room not a single /
      beautiful face" (*meigetsu ya / za ni utsukushiki / kao mo
      nashi*).

506 moon-about-to-appear ! / knees on hands <acc.> place /
   evening 's house
   • Autumn: moon about to appear. 1690. A greeting verse
      and opening hokku for a linked verse. Mizuta Masahide
      (1657–1723) was a physician in Zeze and a leader of a
      group of poets there.

507 paulownia 's tree by / quail call is / wall 's inside
  • Autumn: quail. 1690. The paulownia tree is *Paulownia tomentosa*, a deciduous tree whose large leaves turn yellow in autumn. The quail (*Coturnix coturnix*) is valued for its poignant call.

508 lightning with / not-enlightened person 's / admirable !
  • Autumn: lightning (*inazuma**). 1690. The brief flash of lightning was a conventional symbol for impermanence, one of the central Buddhist truths. The hokku was sent to his disciple Kyokusui in Edo in a letter dated 6th day of Ninth Month (October 7th). In it he criticized disciples in Ōmi who showed complacency in poetry and questionable behavior in their daily life.

509 sick goose <nom.> / night-cold from falling / journey-sleep !
  • Autumn: evening cold. 1690. One of the Eight Famous Scenes of Ōmi is wild geese (*kari**) flying down at Katada on the northwestern shore of Lake Biwa. Bashō visited some disciples at Katada in October of 1690 and became ill.

510 fisher 's house as-for / small-shrimp into mix / cricket !
  • Autumn: shrimp; cricket (*kirigirisu**). 1690. The last line could be read as one or many crickets.

511 morning-tea drink / monk is-quiet / chrysanthemum 's flowers
  • Autumn: chrysanthemum (*kiku**). 1690. Shōzui is a Zen temple.

512 butterfly also come / vinegar <acc.> drink chrysanthemum 's / vinegar-salad
  • Autumn: chrysanthemum (*kiku**). 1690. The salad is made of boiled chrysanthemum leaves, seasoned with vinegar. Bashō imagines that the butterflies are attracted to the fragrance of the chrysanthemum, a flower associated with seclusion and refined tastes. Awazu was a name used for the Gichūji Temple in Zeze.

Winter 1690–91

513 rain ! / field 's new-stubble 's / darken extent
  • Winter: winter showers (*shigure**). 1690–91.

514 cricket / forget-sound with cry / brazier !
- Winter: brazier. 1690–91. With the coming of winter, the cries of the cricket (*kirigirisu**), an autumn image, is heard only occasionally as if it has forgotten to cry.

515 frost 's after / pink bloom / wooden-brazier !
- Winter: frost; wooden brazier. 1690–91. After all blossoms have died with the coming of winter, the flower of a wild pink (*nadeshiko**) remains, painted on the round wooden brazier.

516 winter-wind ! / cheek-swollen hurt / person 's face
- Winter: winter wind (*kogarashi**). 1690–91.

517 first-snow ! / ascetic Koya-missionary 's / knapsack 's color
- Winter: first snow. 1690–91. Amidst the fluttering whiteness of the snow at the onset of winter, the muted color of a worn backpack on a monk suggests the aesthetic rusticity of *wabi***. *Kozō* is a monk from Mt. Koya who travels the country for missionary work and fundraising for his temple. *Oi* is wooden, lacquered backpack worn by priests while traveling.

518 snow fall ! / temporary-hut 's miscanthus 's / cut-remain
- Winter: snow. 1690–91. Miscanthus (*susuki**) was used for thatched roofs. The hut was a temporary storage building for a festival during Seventh Month at the Suwa Shrine in Shinano. Actually Bashō did not travel to Shinano.

519 plover rising / grow-late first-watch 's / Hiei wind-that-blows-down-a-mountain
- Winter: plover (*chidori**). 1690–91. Mt. Hiei to the northeast of Kyoto is the site of an extensive Tendai Buddhist monastery.

520 house-cleaning as-for / cedar 's tree 's space 's / windstorm !
- Winter: year-end house cleaning. 1690–91.

521 half-day as-for / gods <acc.> companion as ! / year-forgetting
- Winter: forgetting-the-year. 1690–91.

522 dried-salmon too / Kūya 's gauntness too / cold 's within
- Winter: deep winter; dried salmon. 1690–91. Kūya (903–72) was a famous ascetic pilgrim, and "Kūya

monks" wandered in the Kyoto area for forty-eight days at the end of the lunar year reciting sutras to commemorate Kūya's death. *Kan* was a thirty-day period considered the coldest time of winter, when monks practiced especially rigorous spiritual training. See the following poem and hokku 465.

523 fermented-soybean cut / sound for-a-while waiting / bowl hitting
  • Winter: bowl beating. 1690–91. In the early morning comes the sound of slicing soybeans for miso soup, a seasonal scene of winter. A pause allows one to hear the sound of the monks beating their bowls. See notes to hokku 465.

524 stone-mountain 's / stones on shower-down / hail !
  • Winter: hail. 1690–91. Stone Mountain, the site of a Buddhist temple on the southern shore of Lake Biwa, is known for its white rocks. Minamoto Sanetomo (1192–1219) wrote the following waka: "A warrior adjusts / his arrows, and onto / the armor on his arm, / hail storms down / in the bamboo field of Nasu" (*mononofu no / yanami tsukurou / kote no e ni / arare tabashiru / nasu no shinohara*).

525 every-day disliked / crow even snow 's / morning !
  • Winter: snow. 1690–91.

526 three-foot 's / mountain too windstorm 's / tree 's leaves !
  • Winter: tree leaf. 1690–91. "Three foot mountain" is an expression for a small hills.

527 Hira Mikami / snow between-carry across / snowy-egret 's bridge
  • Winter: snow. 1690–91. Hira and Mikami are mountains to the east and west of Lake Biwa. The pure whiteness of the scene creatively transforms the legend of *tanabata**, in which the bridge between the stars is made of black magpies.

528 admirable ! / snow not-fall day too / straw-coat and bamboo-hat
  • Winter: snow. 1690–91. Bashō is praising a portrait of the famous beauty and later crone Ono no Komachi, and in doing so praises the life of wayfaring associated

with the rainhat and sandals. In the haibun "On a Portrait of Sotoba Komachi."

529 hidden / twelfth-month 's sea 's / grebe
- Winter: twelfth lunar month; grebe. 1690–91 (late Twelfth Month; January). The scene is the cold waters of Lake Biwa as the year draws to a close, a time when most people are busy with financial and domestic affairs.

530 person to house <acc.> / buy-for I as-for / forgetting-the-year
- Winter: forgetting-the-year. 1690–91 (Twelfth Month; January). Kawai Otokuni was a wealthy patron in Ōtsu who bought a house for Bashō to stay at over New Year's.

Spring 1691

531 kiso 's character / snow ! sprout / spring 's grass
- Spring: spring grass. 1691. Bashō is at the grave of Kiso Yoshinaka at the Gichūji Temple. See notes to hokku 432.

532 plum young-greens / Mariko 's post-town 's / yam-porridge
- Spring: plum (ume*), young greens. 1691. Bashō sends off his disciple and patron Otokuni, who is about to journey along the Tōkaidō Road to Edo. Mariko is one of the stages along the way and was famous for its spicy yam porridge.

533 mountain-village as-for / Manzai-dancers late / plum 's blossoms.
- Spring: plum (ume*) blossoms. 1691 (mid-First Month; February). The itinerant Manzai dancers perform dances for households around New Year's, although they get to the countryside only after they have finished in the towns. The dances are said to bring good fortune.

534 moonwaiting ! / plum carry go / little-mountain-ascetics
- Spring: plum (ume*). 1691. Some people belonged to a religious association that would gather to await the rise of the moon, chanting prayers and devotions while enjoying food and drink. The yamabushi are mountain

ascetics who gain spiritual powers through their disciplines, but a novice still retains the soft grace of youth.

535 lazy ! / was-awakened / spring 's rain
- Spring: spring rain *(harusame*)*. 1691. There is also a slightly different earlier version: "so lazy— / helped out of bed: / spring rain" *(bushōsa ya / dakiokosaruru / haru no ame)*.

536 barley-meal by / emaciated love ? / cat 's wife
- Spring: cat in love. 1691.

537 years-years ya / cherry-trees <acc.> fertilize / blossom 's dust.
- Spring: cherry blossom *(sakura*)*. 1690. There is a Japanese proverb that "blossoms return to the roots."

538 drink-all-night-till-empty / flower-vase in will-make / two-shō barrel
- Spring: blossoms. 1691. A *shō* is about 1.8 liters. Bashō has in mind a line from a Du Fu poem: "a sake bottle is now made into a flower vase."

539 momentarily as-for / flower 's above is / moon-night !
- Spring: blossoms. 1691.

540 weak-from-old-age ! / teeth in bite-hit / seaweed 's sand
- Spring: seaweed. 1691. *Nori* is the thin sheet of dried seaweed used in sushi. An earlier version reads: "teeth biting into it, / my body's aging weakness — / sand in dried seaweed" *(kami atsuru / mi no otoroi ya / nori no suna)*.

541 mountain-rose ! / hat in should-insert / branch 's appearance.
- Spring: mountain rose *(yamabuki*)*. 1691.

542 mountain-rose ! / Uji's tea-oven 's / fragrance time
- Spring: mountain rose *(yamabuki*)*. 1691. Uji is a place in southern Kyoto area famous for its green tea.

543 dark 's night ! / nest <acc.> lose / cry plovers
- Spring: bird's nest. 1691. The poem has been interpreted in two ways: the plovers *(chidori*)* have lost track of their nests and cry in distress, and the plovers are distracting others from the nest by calling from elsewhere.

Summer 1691

544 sad node ! / bamboo 's child into become / person 's end

   • Summer: bamboo shoots. 1691 (19th of Fourth Month;
     May 16). *Fushi* are the joints in a bamboo stem. Bashō
     wrote this hokku after discovering the grave of Kogō no
     Tsubone. As told in the *Tales of the Heike*, she was once
     the favorite of Emperor Takakura (1161–81), but was
     forced by Taira Kiyomori (1118–81) to become a nun.
     Subsequently the Emperor fell ill and died, and Kogō
     drowned herself in the Ōi River. In *Saga Diary*.

545 Windstorm-mountain / grove 's rampant-growth ! /
     wind 's thread

   • Summer: rampant growth. 1691 (19th of Fourth Month;
     May 16). Arashiyama, "Windstorm Mountain," are the
     hills just west of Kyoto, where Bashō was staying during
     the time of the *Saga Diary*.

546 citron 's flower ! / old will-recall / food-preparation 's
     room

   • Summer: citron. 1691 (20th of Fourth Month; May 17).
     Bashō is staying at the now dilapidated "Villa of Fallen
     Persimmons," where the fragrant citron (or Chinese
     lemon) blossoms recall the prosperous days of old when
     servants prepared banquets in the room.

547 cuckoo / large-bamboo grove <acc.> / leak moonlight

   • Summer: cuckoo *(hototogisu*)*. 1691 (20th of Fourth
     Month; May 17). In *Saga Diary*.

548 wretched me <acc.> / make-feel-lonely <command> /
     mountain-cuckoo

   • Summer: mountain cuckoo. 1691 (22nd of Fourth
     Month; May 19). The mountain cuckoo (*Cuculus
     canorus*), rarely seen, is known for its deeply lonely
     song. In the *Saga Diary*, Bashō cites two waka by
     Saigyō: "Hoping no longer / for any visitors— / in this
     mountain village, / were there no loneliness, / dwelling
     here would be misery" (*tou hito mo / omoitaetaru /
     yamazato no / sabishisa nakuba / sumiukaramashi*); "In
     this mountain village / whom are you calling to / little
     birds? / I thought I would live / all alone" (*yamazato ni
     / tare o mata kowa / yobukodori / hitori nomi koso /*

sumamu to omou ni). In *Saga Diary*. An earlier version written in 1689 has "temple in autumn" (*aki no tera*) for the final line.

549 hand <acc.> when-hit / echo in to-dawn / summer 's moon
  • Summer: summer moon. 1691 (23rd of Fourth Month, May 20). In *Saga Diary*. A variant of this reads: "summer evening— / dawnlight in the echoes / of the clogs" (*natsu no yo ya / kodama ni akuru / geta no oto*).

550 bamboo 's child ! / childhood time 's / picture 's sketch
  • Summer: bamboo shoots. 1691 (23rd of Fourth Month; May 20). In *Saga Diary*.

551 barley 's ear ! / tears with dye / cry skylark
  • Summer: barley (*mugi**). 1691 (23rd of Fourth Month; May 20). The barley reddens as it matures, while the skylarks weep for the passing of spring. In *Saga Diary*.

552 one-day one-day / barley become-red / cry skylark
  • Summer: barley (*mugi**). 1691 (23rd of Fourth Month; May 20). See notes to the previous hokku. In *Saga Diary*.

553 talent without 's / want-to-sleep me <acc.> / noisy-birds
  • Summer: reed warbler. 1691 (23rd of Fourth Month; May 20). *Gyōgyōshi*, "clamorous birds," is another name for *yoshikiri*, Reed Warbler (*Acrocephalus spp*). In *Saga Diary*.

554 summer-rains ! / poetry-card peel-off / wall 's remains
  • Summer: summer rains (*samidare**). 1691 (4th of Fifth Month; May 31). In the haibun "Villa of Fallen Persimmons" and the final verse in *Saga Diary*.

555 rice-dumpling wrap / one-hand with put-between / forehead-hair
  • Summer: rice-dumping. 1691. *Chimaki* is a rice dumpling wrapped in sasa bamboo leaves, made particularly for the *Tango no sekku*, the Boy's Festival (also, Iris Festival) on the 5th day of Fifth Month. Bashō gives a haikai twist to the courtly tradition of a woman's hair draping down the sides of her face and put back behind her ears when she became involved in some aristoratic activity.

556 sixth lunar month as-for / flu victim 's / heat !
   • Summer: heat, Sixth Month. 1691. An earlier version
     has a different first line: "at noon, even greater" (*hiru
     wa nao*).

Autumn 1691

557 early-autumn ! / folded although 's / mosquito-net 's bed-
   covering
   • Autumn: autumn. 1691. With summer gone, the mos-
     quito net is folded up, but is then used for warmth as
     the autumn night turns cold.
558 begonia / watermelon 's color into / bloom
   • Autumn: begonia, watermelon. 1691. The pink color of
     the begonia flower (*Begonia evansiana*) resembles that of
     a watermelon. As the begonia blossoms just before the
     watermelon, it seems to grab the color of the melon
     flower before it can bloom.
559 autumn-wind 's / although-it-blows green / chestnut 's burs
   • Autumn: autumn wind (*akikaze**); chestnut (*kuri**).
     1691.
560 reed 's seed head ! / head <acc.> seize / Rashōmon
   • Autumn: seed head of a reed (*ogi**). 1691. Rashōmon
     was a run-down gate famous in medieval stories as a
     place where demons lived. In the Nō play *Rashōmon*,
     the armor of a warrior was seized by demons. Blown in
     the autumn wind, were the seedheads of the reeds suf-
     fering the same fate?
561 cowshed in / mosquito 's voices dark / lingering-heat !
   • Autumn: lingering summer heat. 1689 (mid-or-late Sev-
     enth Month; August). An earlier version reads: "in the
     cow barn, / the sound of mosquitoes is faint: / autumn
     wind" (*ushibeya ni / ka no koe kuraki / zansho kana*).
562 autumn 's color / rice-bran-mash pot even / is-not
   • Autumn: color of autumn. 1691. In chapter ninety-eight
     of the *Essays in Idleness* (1330–31), Yoshida Kenkō
     (1274–1338) gives five maxims, the second of which is,
     "He who looks to the next world must not own even a
     pot of rice-bran mash." Kukū was a disciple from
     Kanazawa. The first line refers to a poem by the priest

Jakuren (1139?–1202): "Loneliness— / something wholly devoid / of any color: / mountains cloaked in black pines / in autumn's evening" (*sabishisa wa / sono iro to shi mo / nakarikeri / maki tatsu yama no / aki no yūgure*).

563 loneliness ! / nail from hanging / cricket
- Autumn: cricket (*kirigirisu**). 1691 (15th of Eighth Month; September 7).

564 rice give / friend <acc.> this-evening 's / moon 's guest
- Autumn: this night's moon. 1691 (15th of Eighth Month; September 7). Bashō plays off on chapter 117 of *Essays in Idleness*, where Kenkō distinguishes various types of good and bad friends, as Confucius did before him in book sixteen of the *Analects*.

565 Mii-Temple 's / gate want-to-knock / today 's moon
- Autumn: tonight's moon. 1691 (15th of Eight Month; September 7). Written when Bashō held a moon-viewing party at Gichūji Temple, a few miles from Mii Temple on the southern shore of Lake Biwa. Bashō draws on lines from a Chinese verse by Jia Dao: "Birds sleep in trees by the pond. / Under the moon, a monk knocks on the gate."

566 lock open / moon shine-into / Ukimi-Temple
- Autumn: moon. 1691 (16th of Eighth Month; September 8). The 16th is the night after the harvest moon. The "Floating Temple" is located on Lake Biwa by Katada, and is reached by boat or bridge. In the haibun "At Katada, on the Night of the 16th."

567 easy-easy -ly / emerge 16th-night-moon / moon 's clouds
- Autumn: sixteenth-night moon. 1691 (16th of Eighth Month; September 8).

568 16th-night-moon ! / shrimp boil to-the-extent 's / tonight 's darkness
- Autumn: sixteenth-night moon. 1691 (16th of Eighth Month; September 8). Between the setting of the sun and the rising of the moon, there is a brief period when no light is in the sky, enough for his host to boil shrimp for his guests.

569 harvest-moon as-for / two-days pass even / Seta 's moon
   • Autumn: moon. 1691. During this year, there was an
     intercalary month, effectively repeating Eighth Month.
     Bashō came to Seta again after viewing the first harvest
     moon during the previous Eighth Month. Seta, at the
     southern end of Lake Biwa, is famous for its bridge and
     river by that name, where the harvest moon is beautiful
     even the second time around.

570 rice-plant sparrows / tea 's tree field ! / place-of-escape
   • Autumn: rice-field sparrows (*suzume**). 1691.

571 hawk 's eye also / now ! darken <quote> / cry quail
   • Autumn: quail. 1691. Quail were traditionally pre-
     sented as having a deeply poigniant cry.

572 buckwheat also see / make-envious / field 's bush-clover
   • Autumn: buckwheat blossoms (*soba no hana**); bush
     clover (*hagi**). 1691. A greeting poem for Sanshi, a
     farmer in Tatsugaoka in Ōmi who had invited Bashō
     and several disciples to his house.

573 grass 's door ! / day-darkening given / chrysanthemum 's
   wine
   • Autumn: chrysanthemum (*kiku**) wine. 1691 (9th of
     Ninth Month; October 29). It is the Chrysanthemum
     Festival, and people rise early in the morning to make
     the chrysanthemum wine, which is drunk to one
     another's longetivity. As the day ends, Bashō in his hut
     receives wine from them.

574 bridge-girder 's / endure as-for moon 's / departure !
   • Autumn: farewell moon. 1691. The "farewell moon,"
     also called "the latter moon" (*nochi no tsuki*), is the
     moon of the 13th night of Ninth Month and was prized
     for moon-viewing. At this time Bashō lived near the Seta
     Bridge. For *shinobu*, see the glossary.

575 nine time / awake although moon 's / four-o'clock !
   • Autumn: moon. 1691. Autumn nights were traditionally
     presented as long, after summer's brief nights.

576 mushroom ! / not-know tree 's leaf 's / stick
   • Autumn: mushroom. 1691.

577 noodles 's / beneath fire-raise / night-cold !
   • Autumn: evening cold. 1691. Bashō is staying up late into the cold of late autumn, and his disciple and host Kyokusui is cooking a night repast of noodles, miso, and vegetables.

578 autumn-wind ! / paulownia by moving / ivy 's frost
   • Autumn: autumn wind (*akikaze**); ivy (*tsuta**). 1691. A windblown paulownia tree (*Paulownia tomentosa*) is associated with the beginning of autumn, while frost is associated with the end of autumn, when ivy leaves turn red. The poem suggests the swift passage of autumn. An earlier version reads: "paulownia blown / at autumn's end— / frost on the ivy" (*kiri ugoku / aki no owari ya / tsuta no shimo*).

579 rice threshing 's / old-woman also auspicious / chrysanthemum's flower
   • Autumn: rice threshing; chrysanthemum (*kiku**) blossom. 1691. Chrysanthemums, associated with long life, bloom nearby an old woman vigorous enough to thresh rice. An earlier version has a different last line: "the garden's chrysanthemum" (*niwa no kiku*).

Winter 1691–92

580 hundred-year 's / appearance <acc.> garden 's / fallen-leaves !
   • Winter: falling leaves. 1691–92. This is a greeting hokku to his host Kōno Riyū (1662–1705) who was the chief priest at the temple and one of Bashō's disciples. In the haibun "Staying Over at Priest Riyū's at Meishōji Temple."

581 valuable / tears ? dye / fall autumn-leaves
   • Winter: falling maple leaves. 1691–92. Bashō is in the garden of a temple.

582 make-perform / garden <acc.> animate / winter-shower !
   • Winter: winter showers (*shigure**). 1691–92 (around the 10th of Tenth Month; November 29). A greeting poem for Kigai, chief priest at the Honryū Temple in Tarui, Mino Province.

583 leek white / washed-has-completed / cold !
- Winter: onion; cold. 1691–92 (around the 10th of Tenth Month; November 29). Bashō drew a painting of three leeks on a cutting board to accompany this hokku. The Tarui area, where this was written, was known for leeks with an underground stem that was white and up to a foot long (*nebuka* literally means "deep root").

584 time-time in / Ibuki <acc.> looking as-for / winter-seclusion
- Winter: winter seclusion. 1691–92 (middle of Tenth Month; late November/early December). A greeting poem praising not only the view from the host's house, but the host's leisurely life in winter seclusion.

585 withering-wind by / color ? attached / return-bloom
- Winter: withering winter wind (*kogarashi**); unseasonable flower. 1691–92. A greeting poem to his host, about whom we know nothing.

586 narcissus ! / white paper-screen 's / along-with-reflection
- Winter: narcissus (*suisen**). 1691–92 (20th of Tenth Month; December 9). Written at the house of Baijin in Atsuta, in appreciation of his parlor. A flower arrangement with a white blooming narcissus shines together with the whiteness of the paper screen. In Japanese culture, white suggests purity.

587 that color / peach more-than white / narcissus-flower
- Winter: narcissus (*suisen**) flower. 1691–92. Written on the occasion of Bashō giving poetic names to the two sons of his host, the poet Hakusetsu of Shinshiro in Mikawa Province. Each name contained the word "peach (*momo**)," like one of Bashō's sobriquets, Tōsei. The pure whiteness of the narcissus suggests the purity of the two youths.

588 capital in tire-of / this winter-wind ! / winter-living
- Winter: winter wind (*kogarashi**). 1691–92. Returning to Edo for the first time since his departure for the Deep North, Bashō stopped over at the home of Kōgetsu (Suganuma Gon-emon) of Shinshiro, Mikwawa Province.

589 snow <acc.> wait / wine-drinkers 's face ! / lightning
- Winter: snow. 1691–92.

590 winter-wind by / rock blow-sharpen / cedar-space !
   • Winter: winter wind (*kogarashi**). 1691–92. Written at Hōrai Temple near Shinshiro.

591 bedcover one / prayer present / journey-sleep !
   • Winter: bedcovering. 1691–92. His illness may have been gallstones.

592 inn rent / name <acc.> give-name / winter-shower !
   • Winter: winter showers (*shigure**). 1691–92. In the haibun "Winter Showers at Shimada."

593 somehow / not-becoming ! snow 's / withered-miscanthus
   • Winter: withered miscanthus (*susuki**); snow. 1691–92 (Eleventh Month; December). Composed soon after he returned to Edo (on the Musashi Plain) on the 29th of Tenth Month. In the haibun "Withered Miscanthus in Snow."

594 absent 's period in / wild god 's / fallen-leaves !
   • Winter: godless month; fallen leaves. 1691–92. During the Tenth Month, the gods were said to leave their local shrine to worship at the Grand Shrine at Izumo. This hokku has been read symbolically to reflect Bashō's long absence from Edo and his disciples there.

595 arrowroot 's leaf 's / face showing / morning 's frost
   • Winter: frost. 1691–92. Bashō provides a haikai twist to the convention of writing about the white underside of arrowroot leaves (*Pueraria thunbergiana*) exposed by the autumn wind.

596 geese clamor / Toba 's rice-field-surface ! / cold 's rain
   • Winter: cold rain. 1691–92. Toba, a place name, literally means "bird feathers," in this case geese (*kari**) that migrated to Japan in autumn.

597 fish bird 's / heart as-for not-know / year-forgetting
   • Winter: year-end party. 1691–92 (late Twelfth Month; February). At a "year-forgetting" party at Sodō's house with Matsukura Ranran (1647–93) and Kagami Shikō (1665–1731). In his *Account of My Ten Foot Square Hut (Hōjōki,* 1212), Kamo no Chōmei (1153–1216) wrote, "Fish never tire of water; no one other than a fish knows their heart. Birds love the woods; no one other

than a bird knows their heart. The same is true of those
who savor reclusion."

Spring 1692

598 person also not-see / spring ! mirror 's / behind 's plum
  • Spring: plum (*ume**); spring. 1692.

599 envious / floating-world 's north 's / mountain-cherry
  • Spring: mountain cherry blossoms. 1692. *Yamazakura*
    is a species of cherry common in low mountains (most
    famously at Yoshino) with pink blossoms. *Prunus
    jamasakura* or *P. donarium*.

600 bush-warbler ! / rice-cake on defecate / veranda 's edge
  • Spring: bush warbler (*uguisu**). Made for New Year's,
    rice cakes were put out on a veranda to dry. Bush war-
    blers were traditionally associated with elegant plum
    blossoms. Bashō considered this a successful example of
    his new style of lightness (*karumi***).

601 this heart / infer blossom with / begging-bowl one-set
  • Spring: blossoms. 1692. Bashō's poetic ideal of *fūga***
    involves both the religious discipline of austerity and the
    aesthetic refinement embodied in flowers. Bashō's disci-
    ple Shikō was departing for the Deep North.

602 cat 's love / end time bedroom 's / hazy-moon
  • Spring: cat in love; hazy moon. 1692.

603 count-come / house house 's / plum willow
  • Spring: plum (*ume**), willow (*yanagi**). 1692. Willows
    are just turning green as plums blossom.

604 both 's hands in / peach and cherry-tree ! / grass 's rice-cake
  • Spring: peach (*momo**); cherry blossom (*sakura**);
    mugwort rice-cake. 1692. Kikaku and Hattori Ransetsu
    (1654–1707) were two of his main disciples. Rice-cake
    with mugwort (*Artemsia princeps*) was a popular treat.

Summer 1692

605 cuckoo / cry sound ! old / inkstone-box
  • Summer: cuckoo (*hototogisu**). 1692 (9th day of Fourth
    Month; May 25). Fuboku, a Bashō disciple in Edo, died
    on the 9th day of Fourth month, 1691. At the gathering

was the inkstone box he used for writing poetry. The song of the cuckoo was associated with memories of the past.

606 cuckoo / cry ! five-foot 's / iris
- Summer: cuckoo *(hototogisu*)*, iris *(ayamegusa)**. 1692. The hokku is based on an anonymous waka: "The cuckoo sings— / in Fifth Month, / blue flags blooming, / I am lost in / an unknowing love" (*hototogisu / naku ya satsuki no / ayamegusa / ayame no shiranu / koi mo suru kana*). There is also a well-known statement by the poet and Emperor Go-Toba: "One should compose waka in the way one pours water on a five-foot blue flag."

607 sixth-month ! / sea-bream as-for there-is-yet / pickled-whale-meat
- Summer: Sixth Month; pickled whale meat. 1692. Sea bream is more of a delicacy, but for Bashō what fits the season and his aesthetics is the lighter fare of cold, white whale meat favored by the common people.

608 China gable 's / setting-sun ! pale / evening-cool
- Summer: cool *(suzumi*)*. 1692. Chinese-style of gable is often used for Shinto Shrines. Another version refers to the style of gable common among the people: "at the end of the gable / sunlight—weakening / in the evening cool" (*hafuguchi ni / hikage ya yowaru / yūsuzumi*).

Autumn 1692

609 wild-pink 's / heat forget / wildflower !
- Autumn: wildflowers of the fields. 1692. *Nokiku* (literally, field-chrysanthemums) is a general term for wildflowers of the Composite family that bloom in midautumn in mountains and fields. Their blossom colors may be pale lavender, white, or yellow, but in the poetry of Bashō's time they were considered as yellow. They bloom after the wild pinks (*nadeshiko**) that begin blooming in late summer.

610 third-day-moon under / earth as-for vague is / buckwheat 's flowers
- Autumn: crescent moon, buckwheat blossoms (*soba no hana**). 1692. An earlier version has a different last line: "buckwheat fields" (*sobabatake*).

611 banana-leaf <acc.> / pillar on hang / hut 's moon
   • Autumn: banana (*bashō**), moon. 1692 (Fourth
     Month). In the haibun "Words on Transplanting
     Banana Trees." The haibun gives an account of a third
     Bashō-an being built in Fukagawa nearby his earlier
     ones by several disciples. In the haibun, he extols the
     virtues of the banana plant, including its ability to
     accentuate the beauty of the moon.

612 harvest-moon ! / gate to rise-come / tide-head
   • Autumn: harvest moon. 1692 (15th of Eighth Month;
     September 25). Bashō's hut was near the mouth of the
     Sumida River.

613 green even-if / should-be thing yet / red-pepper
   • Autumn: red pepper (*tōgarashi*). 1692. This is the open-
     ing hokku of a linked verse held at Bashō's hut to wel-
     come his disciple Takamiya Shadō (d. 1737) from Ōmi.
     The pepper turns from green to red (and hotter) as it
     ripens. The verse is often interpreted allegorically, with
     red suggesting ambition, artificial adornment, undue
     enthusiasm, and so forth, with green being more natu-
     ral, unassuming, and so forth.

614 upriver and / this downriver ! / moon 's companion
   • Autumn: moon's companion. 1692.

615 autumn with accompany / would-go end as-for / Komat-
     sugawa
   • Autumn: autumn. 1692. Komatsugawa is a name for a
     river as well as a village along its banks. Bashō and his
     disciples Tōkei and Shadō were boating along the Ona-
     gizawa canal, which connected the Sumida and
     Komatsu rivers.

616 go autumn 's / still hopeful ! / green-tangerines
   • Autumn: green tangerines; departing autumn. 1692.
     Ripening tangerines are green in the decay of late
     autumn, and they eventually mature golden yellow.
     Written at the departure of his disciple Otokuni. An ear-
     lier version reads: "departing but also / something holds
     promise: / green tangerines" (*yuku mo mata / sue
     tanomoshi ya / aomikan*).

Winter 1692–93

617 today only / people also old / first-winter-shower
- Winter: winter showers (*shigure**). 1692–93 (3rd of Tenth Month; November 10). The poets at the gathering were Bashō, Kyoriku, Ranran, Shadō, and Taisui.

618 fireplace-opening ! / plasterer get-old / sideburns 's frost
- Winter: frost, opening the hearth. 1692–93. Opening the hearth refers to lighting the first fire of winter in the sunken hearth after it had been replastered. In the tea ceremony, this was done on the 1st day of Tenth Month, the first day of winter.

619 salt-sea-bream 's / gum also cold / fish 's shop
- Winter: cold. 1692–93 (early Twelfth Month; early January). The word "also" has been interpreted as linked to the rest of the scene (a cold day) and to the poet (having "entered into" the sea bream and become cold). Bashō stated that the everyday imagery of this hokku was characteristic of his late style of lightness (*karumi***), contrasting it with a more striking, Chinese-style verse by his disciple Kikaku: "its voice hoarse, / the monkey's teeth gleam white: / moon on the peak" (*koe karete / saru no ha shiroshi / mine no tsuki*).

620 garden sweep / snow <acc.> forget / broom !
- Winter: snow. 1692–93. Written on a painting by Bashō of Han Shan, who was a semilegendary Tang Dynasty Zen poet in China.

621 banked-charcoal ! / wall on as-for guest 's / shadow
- Winter: banked charcoal fire. 1692–93. At an inn, the host and guest talk by lamplight in the winter night.

622 moon flower 's / foolishness into needle will-stick / cold 's entrance
- Winter: beginning of deep winter. 1692–93. Acupuncture needles were used to strengthen one against infirmities and adversities and to loosen stiffness. *Kan*, literally "cold," was a thirty-day period considered the coldest time of the year. In that year, it began 29th of Eleventh Month (January 5).

623 very <adv.> / heart unusual / 12th-month !
   • Winter: Twelfth Month. 1692–93. Twelfth Month is
     normally a busy time when people set their affairs
     straight and prepare for New Year's. Bashō, however, is
     not bothered with all that and relaxes with a cask of
     wine his disciple Kyokusui had sent him. The hokku
     was included in a letter of thanks to Kyokusui.

Spring 1693

624 years-years ! / monkey on wear / monkey 's mask
   • Spring: (no specific season word). 1693 (1st of First
     Month; February 5). Of this hokku Bashō said, "I jotted
     down this poem because I grieved to see people stuck
     where they were, stumbling the same way year and
     year."
625 spring also gradually / appearance be-arranged / moon
     and plum
   • Spring: plum (ume*). 1693.
626 whitefish ! / black eye <acc.> open / law 's net
   • Spring: whitefish (shirauo*). 1693. Master Shrimp, a
     common subject of Zen painting, was a Five Dynasties
     Chinese monk who lived off of shrimp. Nori means law
     or Buddhist truth, as well as seaweed.
627 first horse on / fox <nom.> shave / head !
   • Spring: First Horse Day. 1693. Zekitsu was the atten-
     dant to Bashō's disciple Kikaku. First Horse Day is an
     annual festival at Inari Shrines. Inari, god of prosperity
     who protects rice, has fox spirits as attendants.
628 crane 's feather 's / black robe ! / blossom 's cloud
   • Spring: cloud blossoms. 1693. The monk's black robes
     rippling in the wind suggest crane (tsuru*) wings above
     white cherry blossoms, implying purity and nobility. In
     the haibun "Words of Farewell to monk Sengin."

Summer 1693

629 cuckoo / voice lie ! / water 's top
   • Summer: cuckoo (hototogisu*). 1693 (29th of Fourth
     Month; June 2). In a letter, Bashō noted that this hokku
     is based on lines by the Chinese poet Su Shi: "The moon

rises over the eastern mountain / and wanders among the stars. / White mist stretches out across the river, / and the water's brightness reaches to the heavens." Another version of Bashō's hokku reads: "a single call / stretches across the inlet— / cuckoo" (*hitokoe no / e ni yokotau ya / hototogisu*). He asked some fellow poets which of the two they prefered, and they agreed on the one given above. Both hokku were written on the topic of "cuckoo by the water."

630 wind-moon 's / riches also separate ! / peony
- Summer: peony (*botan**). 1693. "Wind and moon" is a metonym for the beauties of nature and implies also the poetic spirit that contemplates them. *Fukamigusa*, literally "deep-view-grass," is an alternative name for peony.

631 traveler 's / heart to also resemble / pasania 's flower
- Summer: pasania (*shii**) blossoms. 1693. An earlier version is found in the haibun "Words Sent to Kyoriku": "emulate the heart / of pasania blossoms: / a Kiso journey" (*shii no hana no / kokoro ni mo niyo / kiso no tabi*). Kyoriku (1656–1715) was a samurai from Ōmi who became Bashō's disciple in the summer of 1693. In the haibun Bashō describes Kyoriku's elaborate samurai dress as he departs for home, but Bashō claims that Kyoriku's true self is that of a wayfarer who embodies *wabi*** and *fūga***.

632 grieved person 's / journey from also learn / Kiso 's fly
- Summer: flies. 1693. Bashō's disciple Kyoriku was about to set off to the Kiso Road, a remote, mountainous road in central Honshu where lodging tended to be meager, lonely, and in the summer filled with flies. In the haibun "Words Sent to Kyoriku."

633 evening-face ! / drunk face put-out / window 's hole
- Summer: moonflower (*yūgao**). 1693. An earlier version had in the first line *ni* ("with") rather than the cutting-word *ya*.

634 children ! / noon-face bloomed / melon will-peel
- Summer: noonflower (*hirugao**), melon (*uri**). 1693. There are two slightly different earlier versions: "hey

children! / the noonflowers have bloomed, / and I'll peel a melon" (*iza kodomo / hirugao sakinu / uri mukan*) and "hey children! / if the noonflowers have bloomed / I'll peel a melon" (*iza kodomo / hirugao sakaba / uri mukan*).

Autumn 1693

635 high-water in / star also journey-sleep ! / rock 's on
  • Autumn: Star Festival (*tanabata**). 1693.

636 white-dew even / not-drop bush-clover's / swaying !
  • Autumn: bush clover *(hagi*)*; dew (*tsuyu**). 1693.

637 first-mushroom ! / still day-number not-pass / autumn 's dew
  • Autumn: first mushroom; dew (*tsuyu**). 1693. The opening hokku of a linked verse performed at Taisui's house in Fukagawa.

638 morning-glory ! / day as-for lock closed / gate 's fence
  • Autumn: morning glory (*asagao**). 1693. In the haibun "An Explanation of Seclusion."

639 morning-glory ! / this also again my / friend is-not
  • Autumn: morning glory (*asagao**). 1693.

640 fishy-smell / waterweed 's top 's / dace 's entrails
  • Autumn: waterweed blossom. 1693. Waterweed (*Monochoria vaginalis* var. *plantaginea*) is common in paddy fields and shallow ponds, with purple blossoms appearing in September and October. Dace are small fish without commercial value.

641 16th-night-moon as-for / little -ly darkness 's / beginning !
  • Autumn: 16th night moon. 1693.

642 autumn-wind in / broken sad / mulberry 's staff
  • Autumn: autumn wind (*akikaze**). 1693. Ranran, one of Bashō's earliest disciples ("like father and son," Bashō said), died suddenly at the age of forty-seven. Forty-eight is said to be the "age of mulberry." In the haibun "Lamenting the Death of Matsukura Ranran."

643 see ? that / seven-days as-for grave 's / third-day 's moon
  • Autumn: third-day moon. 1693. See notes to the previous poem. "Seventh night" is a memorial held seven

days after death. "Third-day moon" is the crescent moon, in particular the moon on the third day of the lunar month.

644 enter moon 's / after as-for desk 's / four corners !
- Autumn: setting moon. 1693. Enomoto Tōjun was Kikaku's father, who died on the 29th day of Eighth Month.

645 chrysanthemum 's flower / blossom ! stonemason 's / stone 's between
- Autumn: chrysanthemum (*kiku**). 1693.

Winter 1693–94

646 gold-screen 's / pine 's old ! / winter-seclusion
- Winter: winter seclusion. 1693–94. Four years earlier Bashō wrote a similar verse (hokku 460).

647 chrysanthemum 's scent ! / garden in worn-out / shoe 's bottom
- Autumn: chrysanthemum (*kiku**) fragrance. 1693 (9th day of Tenth Month; November 6). Bashō highlights the fact that this poem has an autumn season word but was written in winter (with a winter headnote).

648 winter-chrysanthemum ! / bran 's fall / hand-mill 's edge
- Winter: winter chrysanthemum (*kangiku**). 1693–94. The opening hokku for a two-person linked verse Bashō completed with Shida Yaba (1663–1740).

649 winter-chrysanthemum ! / sweet-wine make / window 's front
- Winter: winter chrysanthemum (*kangiku**). 1693–94. The sweet wine is made from rice and drunk hot on cold nights.

650 feather-robe in / wrap warm / duck 's feet
- Winter: duck. 1693–94.

651 saddle-seat on / little-boy ride ! / radish-pulling
- Winter: radish pulling. 1693–94 (8th of Eleventh Month; December 4). The parents harvest radishes as the boy sits in the saddle.

652 first-snow ! / make / bridge 's top
- Winter: first snow. 1693–94.

653 samurai 's / radish pungent / conversation !
- Winter: radish. 1693–94. A *daikon* is a large white radish. On the phrase in the headnote, see notes to hokku 42. An opening hokku for a linked verse conducted with two samurai.

654 peddler 's / geese pathos is / Ebisu-festival
- Winter: Festival of Ebisu. 1693–94 (20th day of Tenth Month; November 17). Ebisu is one of the Seven Deities of Good Fortune, and specifically the deity of commerce, fishing, and farming. An exuberant festival in his honor is held on the 20th day of Tenth Month. Geese (*kari**) would walk leashed to a pole as the peddler went around town hawking his goods.

655 Ebisu-festival / vinegar-sale to skirt / wear
- Winter: Festival of Ebisu. 1693–94. *Hakama* is a divided skirt, rather formal wear hardly usual for a peddler.

656 everyone go-out / bridge <acc.> receive / frost-road
- Winter: frost. 1693–94. An earlier version reads: "so thankful— / in gratitude they tread across / the frosty bridge" (*arigata ya / itadaite fumu / hashi no shimo*). This new bridge across the Sumida River was completed early in Twelfth Month.

657 living-while / one into frozen / sea-slug !
- Winter: sea slugs; frozen. 1693–1694.

658 housecleaning as-for / self 's shelf hang / carpenter !
- Winter: year-end house cleaning. 1693–94 (13th of Twelfth Month: January 8). 13th of Twelfth Month was an annual housecleaning day. The hokku is considered an example of Bashō's late style of lightness (*karumi***).

659 robber by / met night also is / year 's end
- Winter: year's end. 1693–94.

Spring 1694

660 paradise-decorations at / like-to-hear Ise 's / first-news
- Spring: Hōrai. 1694. *Hōrai* is the mythic land of Daoist immortals, but it also is a type of New Year's decora-

tions. They give rise to a feeling of solemnity and Shinto purity and make Bashō think of the Grand Shrine at Ise.

661 plum 's scent in / suddenly sun 's emerge / mountain-path !
- Spring: plum (*ume**) fragrance. 1694.

662 boil on / touch willow 's / bend !
- Spring: willow (*yanagi**). 1694. An earlier version switches the word order in the second line, with little change of meaning: *yanagi no sawaru*.

663 bush-warbler ! / willow 's behind / grove 's in-front
- Spring: bush warbler (*uguisu**); willow (*yanagi**). 1692–1694.

664 plum 's scent in / past 's one-character / pathos is
- Spring: plum (*ume**) fragrance. 1694.

665 nirvana-gathering ! / wrinkled-hands join / bead 's sound
- Spring: anniversary of the Buddha's death. 1694. The date of Buddha's death is memorialized as the day he entered nirvana, 15th of Second Month. An earlier version has a different first line: "Buddha's Birthday—" (*kambutsu ya*). That anniversary is held on 8th of Fourth Month.

666 eight-nine-ken / sky in rain falls / willow !
- Spring: willow (*yanagi**). 1694. A *ken* is length of about six feet. Commentators disagree whether the rain is still falling or has stopped, leaving the drops glistening in the tree. The hokku alludes to a lines from the Chinese poet Tao Qian: "A thatched hut eight or nine rooms / elm and willow hide the eaves behind the house."

667 spring-rain ! / wasp 's nest drip / roof 's leak
- Spring: spring rain (*harusame**), wasp nest. 1694.

668 green-willow 's / mud in hang-down / low-tide !
- Spring: low tide; green willow (*yanagi**). 1694 (3rd day of Third Month; March 28).

669 spring-rain ! / mugwort <acc.> extend / grass 's path
- Spring: spring rain (*harusame**). 1694. *Yomogi* (*Artemsia princeps*) is a vine conventionally associated in poetry with run-down houses and recluses.

Summer 1694

670 not-cold / dew ! peony 's / flower 's honey
- Summer: peony (*botan**). 1694. Dew is normally associated with the cool of autumn. Matsuo Tōrin was Bashō's cousin from Iga Ueno.

671 hidden-in-bushes / tea-pickers also hear ? / cuckoo
- Summer: cuckoo (*hototogisu**). 1694.

672 deutzia ! / dark willow 's / bending-back
- Summer: deutzia (*unohana**). 1694.

673 hydrangea ! / grove <acc.> little-garden 's / detached-room
- Summer: hydrangea (*ajisai**). 1694. A thicket with a hydrangea is used as a rustic garden for the hut. An opening hokku and greeting poem for his host and disciple Shisan (d. 1699), who held a farewell linked verse party for Bashō before he left for his hometown of Iga Ueno at the beginning of his final journey. Bashō offered this verse when asked about the style of lightness (*karumi***).

674 barley 's ears <acc.> / strength for grab / departure !
- Summer: barley (*mugi**). 1694 (11th of Fifth Month; June 3). Written on his departure for his home village of Iga Ueno at the start of his last journey. Another version has "depend on" (*tayori ni*) rather than "support" (*chikara ni*).

675 come-into-view / time ! especially / Fifth-Month Fuji
- Summer: Mt. Fuji in the Fifth Month. 1694. It is the rainy season, when Fuji is usually hidden in clouds.

676 bush-warbler ! / bamboo 's young grove in / age <acc.> cry
- Summer: old bush warbler (*uguisu**); bamboo shoots. 1694. While a bush warbler is an image of early spring, an aging bush warbler is an image of summer, here contrasted to the many young and fast-growing bamboo shoots.

677 summer-rains ! / silkworm ill / mulberry 's field
- Summer: summer rains (*samidare**). 1694. Commentators differ on whether there are one or many ailing silkworms.

678 Suru-road ! / orange-blossoms also / tea 's fragrance
  • Summer: orange blossoms. 1694 (17th of Fifth Month;
    June 9). Suruga was famous for both orange blossoms
    and tea. As Shirane notes (*Traces of Dreams*, 178), this
    is a greeting verse not for a person but for the land he is
    entering.

679 summer-rains 's / sky blow-throw-down / Ōi-River
  • Summer: summer rains (*samidare**). 1694 (around the
    17th of Fifth Month; June 9) . Bashō was confined for
    three days to the town of Shimada on the Ōi River,
    which was swollen by heavy rains.

680 world through journey on / field plough small-field 's / go-
    return
  • Summer: tilling the field. 1694. *Yo* can mean "life" as
    well as "world." *Kaku* here means plow a field of rice in
    preparation for transplanting, but there are also two
    homonyms, "to write" and "to paint," which connect
    agricultural work with artistic.

681 cool <acc.> / Hida 's carpenter 's / directions !
  • Summer: cool (*suzumi**). 1694 (23rd of Fifth Month;
    June 15). The legendary craftsman from Hida was the
    epitome of a skilled builder. Yasui (1658–1743) was a
    merchant in Nagoya and tea ceremony master. An ear-
    lier version reads: "it appears to be / a blueprint for
    coolness— / this dwelling" (*suzushisa no / sashizu ni
    miyuru / sumai kana*).

682 water-rail call (quote) / people (nom.) say ! / Saya-stop-
    over
  • Summer: water rail (*kuina**). 1694 (25th of Fifth Month;
    June 17). This is a greeting poem for his host, Yamada.
    Saya is just west of Nagoya.

683 coolness ! / naturally wild-pine 's / branch's shape
  • Summer: cool (*suzumi**). 1694 (11th of Intercalary Fifth
    Month; July 3). Bashō distinguishes between trained
    pines in gardens and this one that grows in its own nat-
    ural way. A greeting poem for his host, Hirooka Sesshi
    (1670–1711), a poet in Ueno.

684 brushwood attach / horse 's returning ! / rice-transplanting-cask

- Summer: rice planting. 1694. Apparently, brushwood was sold in town to pay for wine, which was drunk to celebrate the end of rice planting. Bashō was visiting Ensui (1640–1704), a wealthy merchant in Ueno who employed tenant farmers in his rice fields.

685 coolness <acc.> / picture into depict / Saga 's bamboo

- Summer: cool (*suzumi**). 1694. A greeting poem for Yamei (d. 1713), a samurai living in the Saga area of Kyoto.

686 clear-falls 's / water draw-up ? / jelly-noodles

- Summer: jelly noodles. 1694. The noodles are made from gelatine and served with vinegar. Kiyotaki, "clear waterfalls," is the name of a place in western Kyoto and a narrow stream running nearby that pours into the Ōi River. Given to his host Yamei in appreciation of a meal.

687 sixth-month ! / peak on clouds lay / windstorm-mountain

- Summer: Sixth Month. 1694 (15th of Sixth Month; August 5). Arashiyama, "windstorm mountain," is located just west of Kyoto and is famous for cherry blossoms and autumn foliage. Despite that name, in the summer heat, the clouds lie motionless on the summit as if placed there. Written at the Villa of Fallen Persimmons.

688 clear-waterfall ! / waves in fall-go-in / green-pine-needles

- Summer: falling pine needles. 1694. An earlier version written during Sixth Month reads: "clear cascade stream— / no dust in the waves, / summer moon" (*ōiyotaki ya / nami ni chiri naki / natsu no tsuki*). Later, Bashō wrote another hokku with the image of "no dust" (hokku 721), and then on the 9th of Tenth Month he revised this poem to remove that image, making this final version the last hokku he composed. For *kiyotaki*, see the notes to hokku 686.

689 morning-dew in / dirty cool / melon 's soil

- Summer: melon (*uri**); cool (*suzumi**). 1694. An earlier version reads: "morning dew (*tsuyu**)— / smooth and cool, / a mud-smeared melon" (*asatsuyu ya / nadete* *suzushiki / uri no tsuchi*). Another version has *doro* (mud) for the final word.

690 summer 's night ! / broken dawn / chilled-food
- Summer: summer evening. 1694. Cool food such as melon and eggplant was served at the conclusion of a banquet. This was a greeting poem for his host at a linked verse party.

691 rice fan / wife 's feast ! / evening-cool
- Summer: cool (*suzumi**). 1694. *Meshi* and especially *kaka* are somewhat vulgar terms that reflect the rustic topic.

692 plate-bowl also / dim -ly dark 's / evening cool
- Summer: cool (*suzumi**). 1694.

693 autumn near / heart <nom.> draw-near ! / four-and-a-half-mat-room
- Summer: autumn's approach. 1694 (21st day of Sixth Month; August 11). The four-and-a-half mat room refers to the small room (about nine feet square) of the tea ceremony. This was the opening hokku for a linked verse with Bokusetsu, Izen, and Shikō.

Autumn 1694

694 lightning ! / face 's place 's / miscanthus 's plume
- Autumn: lightning (*inazuma**); miscanthus (*susuki**). 1694. The preface refers to a story in the *Zhuangzi*: Zhuangzi used a skull for a pillow, and in a dream the skull reproached him for thinking that life is better than death. The hokku also refers to the legend about the beautiful poet Ono no Komachi: after death, miscanthus plumes grew up through the eyes of her skull. Lightning is a traditional image of impermanence. In the haibun "Preface to 'lightning—.'"

695 cool-cool ly / wall <acc.> placing-feet / noon-nap !
- Autumn: cool (*suzumi**). 1694 (early Seventh Month; August).

696 road narrow / wire-grass 's / flower 's dew
- Autumn: *sumotorigusa*; dew (*tsuyu**). 1694. *Sumotorigusa* is another name for *ohishiba* (*Eleusine indica*), a common weed in Japan.

697 star-festival ! / autumn <acc.> be-firmly-fixed / night 's
     beginning
     • Autumn: Star Festival (*tanabata**); autumn. 1694 (7th of
       Seventh Month; August 27). An earlier version has dif-
       ferent word order of the last line: *hajime no yo.* Yadō (d.
       1701) was a disciple living in Edo.

698 family as-for all / staff on white-hair 's / graveyard visit
     • Autumn: graveyard visit. 1694. Bashō's elder brother
       was Matsuo Hanzaemon (d. 1701).

699 number is-not / person <quote> not think / festival-of-
     souls
     • Autumn: Festival of Souls (*tamamatsuri**). 1694 (Sev-
       enth Month; early September). It is not known for cer-
       tain what was Bashō's relationship to Jutei; she may
       have been his mistress in years past or the wife of his
       nephew Tōin (1661–93). While Bashō traveled to his
       hometown of Ueno in Iga, she stayed in Bashō's hut.

700 lightning ! / darkness 's direction go / night-heron 's voice
     • Autumn: lightning (*inazuma**). 1694. The Black-
       crowned Night-Heron (*Nycticorax nycticorax*), found
       throughout most of the United States, often gives its
       hollow "qwock" sound as it flies during the night.

701 wind-color ! / confused -ly plant / garden 's autumn
     • Autumn: autumn. 1694.

702 village grow-old / persimmon 's tree not-have / house even
     not
     • Autumn: persimmon tree. 1694 (7th day of Eighth
       Month; September 25). This was a greeting poem for
       Katano Bōsui (1657?–1705) a merchant in Ueno, who
       hosted a linked verse gathering. The persimmon trees
       suggest that the village is prosperous.

703 winter-melon ! / mutual -ly change / face 's shape
     • Winter: winter melon (*uri**). 1694. Bashō has returned
       to his hometown of Iga Ueno. Winter melons are said to
       have a less attractive shape than autumn melons. Some
       classify this as an autumn verse, because it was written
       in autumn with an implicit comparison to autumn
       melons.

704 bright-moon under / foothills 's mist ! / field 's cloudiness
- Autumn: harvest moon, mist (*kiri**). 1694 (15th of Eighth Month; October 3).

705 bright-moon 's / flower ? as appear / cotton-field
- Autumn: harvest moon. 1694 (15th of Eighth Month; October 3).

706 cockscomb ! / geese 's come time / more red
- Autumn: cockscomb; geese (*kari**). 1694. Cockscombs (*Celosia cristata*) have reddish leaves all year, turning deeper red about the time that geese fly south to Japan as winter approaches. Bashō draws directly from the literal meaning of the Chinese name for cockscomb: "geese come red."

707 face to not-resemble / hokku also emerge / first-cherry-blossoms
- Spring: first cherry blossom (*sakura**). 1694. A spring poem written in autumn, when Bashō was in his home town of Iga.

708 new-rice-straw 's / begin-to-appear early / winter-shower !
- Autumn: new rice straw. 1694. A poem about seasonal transitions. *Shigure* are considered early winter showers but also can appear in late autumn as a sign of coming winter.

709 buckwheat as-for still / flower with entertain / mountain-path !
- Autumn: buckwheat flowers (*soba no hana**). 1694 (3rd of Ninth Month; October 21). It is still too early to serve buckwheat as food, so viewing their blossoms will have to do.

710 departing autumn ! / hands <acc.> open-out / chestnut 's burs
- Autumn: departing autumn, chestnut (*kuri**) burs. 1694 (5th of Ninth Month; October 23). Chestnut burs remain after the leaves fall, and some of them partially peel open like spreading palms.

711 "beee" cry / trailing-voice is-sad / night 's deer
- Autumn: deer (*shika**). 1694 (8th of Ninth Month; October 26). This was the first use in poetry of *bii* as onomatopoeic for a deer's call.

712 chrysanthemum 's scent ! / Nara in as-for old / Buddhas
- Autumn: chrysanthemum (*kiku**). (9th of Ninth Month; October 27). Bashō was in the ancient capital of Nara during the Chrysanthemum Festival.

713 chrysanthemum 's scent in / dark climb / festival !
- Autumn: chrysanthemum (*kiku**). 1694. Dark Pass is on Mt. Ikoma, which Bashō crossed on his way from Nara to Osaka soon after the Chrysanthemum Festival. Actually, Bashō crossed the pass during the day, but staged the poem in predawn darkness to fit the name of the pass.

714 wild-boar 's / bed into even enter ! / cricket
- Autumn: cricket (*kirigirisu**). 1694. Another version has the title "Shadō snoring by my pillow" and reads: "coming to my bed / mixing with the snoring: / a cricket" (*toko ni kite / ibiki ni iru ya / kirigirisu*).

715 measuring-box purchase / judgment change / moon-viewing !
- Autumn: moonviewing. 1694 (13th of Ninth Month; October 31). Boxes for measuring grain or liquid that were sold at the Sumiyoshi market were supposed to bring good fortune. Bashō was invited to a moon-viewing party at the home of Hasegawa Keishi (d. 1695?), but while visiting the market during the day, he fell ill and had to cancel.

716 autumn <emphasis> already / sprinkle rain in / moon 's form
- Autumn: autumn, moon. 1694 (19th of Ninth Month; November 6). An opening hokku for a linked verse at the home of Kiryū, a disciple in Osaka.

717 autumn 's night <acc.> / strike-demolish / talk !
- Autumn: autumn evening (*aki no kure**). 1694 (21st of Ninth Month; November 8). Bashō was in Osaka in part to resolve a dispute between two disciples. In the lonely night of autumn, the tension was suddenly broken.

718 this road ! / traveling person not with / autumn 's evening
- Autumn: autumn evening (*aki no kure**). 1694 (26th of Ninth Month; November 13). An earlier version reads:

"people's voices— / returning on this road / in autumn evening" (*hitogoe ya / kono michi kaeru / aki no kure*). There is also a version in which the first line is "along this road" (*kono michi o*).

719 pine-wind ! / eaves <acc.> go-around / autumn end
- Autumn: autumn ending (*aki no kure**). 1694 (26th of Ninth Month; November 13). The colloquial term "swirling" (*megutte*) gives a haikai twist to that traditional image of lonely tranquillity, wind in the pines.

720 this autumn as-for / why grow-old / cloud in bird
- Autumn: autumn. 1694 (26th of Ninth Month; November 13).

721 white-chrysanthemum <nom.> / eye in rises see / dust even is-not
- Autumn: chrysanthemum (*kiku**). 1694 (27th of Ninth Month; November 14). An earlier version had the exclamatory cutting word *ya* instead of *no* in the first line. This was the opening hokku of a linked verse and greeting hokku for his hostess Shiba Sono (1664–1726) of Osaka, one of Bashō's few female disciples. The poem alludes to one by Saigyō: "On a clear mirror / a speck of dust / appears at close view: / such, I think, / is this world" (*kumori naki / kagami no ue ni / iru chiri o / me ni tatete miru / yo to omowabaya*).

722 moon is-clear ! / fox fear / boy-lover 's companion
- Autumn: moon. 1694 (28th of Ninth Month; November 15). An opening hokku on the topic of love, in this case homosexual.

723 autumn is-deep / next-door as-for what <acc.> / do person ?
- Autumn: autumn. 1694 (28th of Ninth Month; November 15). This hokku was sent to the host of a poetry gathering, Negoro Shihaku (d. 1713), when illness prevented Bashō from attending.

Winter 1694

724 journey on be-sick / dreams as-for withered-field <loca-
    tion> / run-around

- Winter: withered field. 1694 (9th of Tenth Month;
  November 25). Written during the early hours of the
  day. Bashō died three days later.

MAJOR NATURE IMAGES
IN BASHŌ'S HOKKU

Note: The season poetically associated with the image is indicated in lower capitals. The numbers refer to poems the image appears in.

ajisai: hydrangea. The deciduous shrub up to five feet high with ball-shaped clusters of bluish flowers in June and July. It has become a common ornamental throughout the world. *Hydrangea macrophylla.* SUMMER. 92, 673.

aki no kaze; akikaze: autumn wind. Usually refers to the biting wind that connotes loneliness as well as cold. See also *kogarashi* and *nowaki.* AUTUMN. 1, 34, 77, 101, 135, 136, 181, 316, 321, 331, 414, 416, 421, 426, 452, 559, 578, 642.

aki no kure: autumn's evening. Refers both to an autumn evening and the evening of autumn, that is, late autumn. A principal image of tranquil loneliness. AUTUMN. 37, 38, 67, 137, 501, 718, 719.

asagao: morning glory, literally "morning face." The normally purple blossoms last only into mid-morning, and thus suggest impermanence. *Ipomoea nil, I. purpurea,* or *I. indica.* AUTUMN. 62, 63, 130, 210, 324, 638, 639.

ashi: reed. Up to 20" high, it is common by swamps, inlets, and ditches. *Phragmites communis.*
- *ashi no wakaba:* young leaves of reeds. SPRING. 255.
- *ashi kari:* cutting reeds. AUTUMN. 430.

ayamegusa: blue flag iris. Blooms purple May through July. 5th day of Fifth Month was the Iris Festival (also known as "Boy's Day"), and irises were displayed on the eaves of houses. Native to mountain meadows. *Iris sanguinea, I. nertschinskia,* or *I. sibirica.* Some authorities state that in Bashō's time, this word referred to sweet flags, *Acorus calamus.* See *kakitsubata.* SUMMER. 384, 606.

bashō: banana, plantain. Its long, broad leaves tear easily in wind and rain, thus suggesting transience and ascetic exposure to nature's elements. Used in Buddhist texts as a symbol for impermanence. In Japan, it rarely bears fruit. *Musa basjoo.* AUTUMN. 52, 58, 103, 371, 611.

botan: peony. A deciduous shrub usually around three feet high. Early summer blossoms of pink, red-purple, or yellow summer are luxuriant and suggest splendor. *Paeonia suffruticosa.* SUMMER. 139, 168, 287, 630, 670.

chidori: plover. Bird of the seashore, with a shrill, plaintive cry that evokes the loneliness of winter. Year-round resident that flocks in winter, with long legs and rather short bill. Refers to various species in the genus *Charadrius.* WINTER. 139, 224, 519, 543.

chō; kochō: butterfly. In Bashō's time, the butterfly was associated with the story in the *Zhuangzi,* in which Zhuangzi wakes after dreaming he was a butterfly, but then wonders whether he is actually a butterfly dreaming he is Zhuangzi. SPRING. 44, 45, 73, 86, 126, 163, 167, 319, 442, 478, 486, 512.

hagi: bush clover. A deciduous shrub up to seven feet high, with reddish-purple blossoms in early autumn. Associated with dew and the mournful cry of a stag in mating season. *Lespedeza bicolor.* AUTUMN. 211, 412, 417, 418, 440, 441, 572, 636.

hana: blossoms. Unless otherwise specified, *hana* refers to cherry blossoms (*sakura*). Moon (*tsuki*) and blossoms are the two principal Japanese images of nature, and as a pair they refer to nature's beauty and poetry about it. Cherry blossoms are known for scattering while at their peak, suggesting the combination of beauty and sadness central to

Japanese aesthetics. *Prunus spp.* SPRING. 4, 5, 9, 10, 11, 12, 14, 29, 72, 78, 82, 83, 86, 87, 88, 112, 113, 156, 159, 161, 177, 179, 186, 198, 199, 233, 244, 251, 259, 264, 268, 269, 270, 275, 278, 279, 306, 323, 356, 401, 105, 410, 446, 468, 473, 474, 481, 537, 539, 601, 622, 628.

harusame; haru no ame: spring rain. A soft, steady, quiet drizzle. See also *samidare* and *shigure*. SPRING. 84, 276, 471, 535, 667, 669.

hibari: skylark. A bird of meadows and fields known in poetry for singing cheerfully as it flies high into the sky. A year-round resident, it is about seven inches long, golden brown with white edges to tail and wings. *Alauda arvensis.* SPRING. 200, 201, 267, 355, 551, 552.

hirugao: noonflower, bindweed, literally "noon-face." A twining vine similar to the *asagao*, but opens in midday. Native to grassy fields and mountains, it is often associated with poor people. *Calystegia japonica.* SUMMER. 46, 47, 302, 634.

hotaru: firefly. Its many poetic associations include passionate love, the spirits of the dead, and a poor Chinese scholar who studied by the glow of fireflies. Ten luminous species in the family *Lampyridae* of the order *Coleoptera.* SUMMER. 55, 297, 298, 299, 491.

hototogisu: cuckoo. It is seldom seen, usually calling during flight in the evening in the mountains, so it is primarily an aural rather than visual image. Poets wait impatiently for its plaintive song, which announces the beginning of summer. The song often suggests a nostalgic sense of time past, and is associated with death. A summer visitor to Japan, it is greyish and about ten inches long. *Cuculus poliocephalus.* SUMMER. 48, 53, 69, 93, 139, 202, 292, 294, 369, 372, 373, 484, 490, 492, 547, 605, 606, 629, 671.

inazuma: lightning. Also *inabikari,* lightning flash. A symbol of impermanence. AUTUMN. 209, 508, 589, 694, 700.

kagerō and *itoyō*: heat waves. Distortion of the air caused by heat. SPRING. 249, 250, 351, 360, 361, 477.

kakitsubata: blue flag iris, rabbit-ear iris. Blossom is purple, up to twenty-eight inches high. Grows in wet soils (versus the *ayame*). *Iris levigata*. SUMMER. 6, 164, 288.

karasu: crow or raven. The crow or raven tends to be considered disagreeable and suggest desolation. *Corvus spp.* ALL SEASONS. 38, 158, 467, 525.

kari: wild geese. Migratory birds of various species that arrive in Japan in late autumn. AUTUMN. 509, 596, 654, 706.

- *kari no wakare* (departing geese): SPRING, indicating the birds' return to their summer home north of Japan. SPRING. 13.

keshi: opium poppy. The summer blossoms are of various colors, especially white (*shirageshi*). A petal that falls off a poppy is said to resemble a severed butterfly wing, and thus is associated with painful parting. *Papaver somniferum*. SUMMER. 167, 291.

kiji: pheasant. A bird of fields and farmlands known especially for its plaintive call that is suggested in the Japanese language as *horohoro*. The male is about thirty-one inches long, the female twenty-four inches, including their long tails. Year-round resident. *Phasianus colchicus*. SPRING. 280, 355, 480.

kiku: chrysanthemum. Blooms white or yellow in autumn, with beautiful fragrance. It is associated with aristocracy and purity, but also with the refined tastes of poetic reclusion as embodied in the Chinese poet Tao Qian (365–427). Drinking dew on a chrysanthemum was said to extend one's life, and even the fragrance was considered therapeutic. The chrysanthemum appears in Bashō's poetry more often than any other plant except cherry and plum trees. *Chrysanthemum morifolium*. AUTUMN. 49, 96, 99, 109, 219, 220, 319, 335, 339, 420, 445, 447, 511, 512, 573, 579, 645, 647, 712, 713, 721.

- *kangiku*: winter chrysanthemum. WINTER. 648, 649.

kinuta: fulling block. A wooden tool to pound cloth to make it soft and lustrous. Frequently appearing in classical literature, its sound was considered melancholy and it was associated with rural life. AUTUMN. 75, 105, 132.

kiri: mist. Traditionally mist (*kiri*) is associated with autumn, while haze (*kasumi, usugasumi,* hokku 152) is a spring phenomenon. It is uncertain whether *kasumi* and *kiri* are really different phenomena other than their seasonal associations. For an extensive discussion, see William J. Higginson, *Haiku World,* (Tokyo: Kodansha, 1996), 190–94. AUTUMN. 119, 120, 424, 704.

kirigirisu: cricket. Like the cicada (*semi*), crickets are primarily an aural image. Its strident cry is penetrating, and suggests age and loneliness. (In modern Japanese, *kirigirisu* means "grasshopper," while the cricket is *kōrogi*.) Various species and genera in the family *Gryllidae*. AUTUMN. 419, 502, 510, 514, 563.

kogarashi: winter wind. A harsh, withering wind. See also *akikaze* and *nowaki*. WINTER. 108, 144, 516, 585, 588, 590.

kuina: water rail. A small marsh bird with brownish body, about eleven inches long. Its call, transcribed as *katakata*, is said to be like the sound of tapping, suggesting someone visiting a recluse. *Rallus aquaticus.* SUMMER. 91, 682.

kuri: Japanese chestnut. The nuts, which have prickly husks, are used for food. The blossoms are inconspicuous. *Castanea crenata.* AUTUMN. 36, 559, 710.

• *kuri no hana* (chestnut blossoms): SUMMER. 378.

momo: peach. The pinkish-white blossoms appear in April and May and are associated with Girl's Day, 3rd of Third Month. *Prunus persica.* SPRING. 79, 157, 176, 421, 587, 604.

mugi: barley or wheat. Cultivated in dry fields and as a second crop in addition to rice. Eating ears of barley was an epithet for a poor man's journey. Harvested in summer, when the plant turns red. Various species. SUMMER. 53, 165, 169, 369, 536, 551, 552, 674.

mukuge: rose of sharon, rose mallow, hibiscus. Tall deciduous shrub sometimes planted as a hedge. Its two inch white or rose-purple flowers bloom and fade before the day is through, and thus was considered a symbol of impermanence. *Hibiscus syriacus.* AUTUMN. 35, 122.

nadeshiko: wild pinks. These 12–20 inch high plants native to the mountains have five-petaled pink (or white) blooms June through September. In classical poetry this late summer-early autumn plant was considered one of the "seven plants of autumn." *Dianthus superbus*. SUMMER. 206, 515, 609.

nasu: eggplant. A vegetable that ripens in late summer, when it is pickled, grilled, fried, or boiled. Smaller than Western varieties. *Solanum melongena*. SUMMER. 402, 415, 471.

nowaki: autumn windstorm. It is a severe windstorm generated by typhoons in autumn. See *akikaze* and *kogarashi*. AUTUMN. 58, 96, 334, 500.

ogi: reed. A plant that spreads quickly in marshy areas. *Miscanthus sacchariflorus*. AUTUMN. 52, 560.

sakura: cherry blossoms. See *hana*. SPRING. 3, 79, 80, 162, 262, 263, 265, 271, 272, 274, 382, 405, 475, 476, 537, 604, 707.

samidare: summer rains. Long, steady rains of the Fifth Month that can continue for several weeks. The monsoon season in Japan. Also written *satsukiame*. See *harusame* and *shigure*. SUMMER. 22, 54, 203, 204, 296, 379, 387, 393, 489, 554, 677, 679.

semi no koe: cicada's cry. Known as a symbol of impermanence because of the shell that remains after its short life, as well as for its penetratingly shrill songs in summer. Several species in the family *Cicadidae*. SUMMER. 205, 207, 392, 496.

shigure (verb: *shiguru*): early winter showers. Brief, intermittent, cold showers or drizzle of early winter and sometimes late autumn. WINTER. 42, 39, 143, 145, 2221, 222, 456, 457, 458, 464, 513, 582, 592, 617, 708.

shii: pasania. A tall, broadleaf evergreen tree with yellow flowers in May and June, and its inconspicuous but elegant blossoms are associated with SUMMER. It also produces nuts (*shii no mi*) in AUTUMN. The nuts and evergreen leaves suggest dependability. *Castanopsis cuspidata*. 485, 631.

shika: deer. Chestnut colored small deer less than five feet long. Mating season is October through December, when mournful calls are heard. *Cervus nippon*. AUTUMN. 16, 285, 711.

shinobugusa: fern of longing, hare's foot fern. *Shinobu* means both remember and to long for something. *Polypodium lineare, Davallia bullata,* or *D. mariesii*. AUTUMN. 134, 142, 574.

shirauo: whitefish, icefish. A small fish around two inches (one *sun*) long that is silvery with black eyes and nearly transparent in the water. *Salangichtys microdon*. Spring. 51, 140, 358, 626.

soba no hana: buckwheat blossoms. White blossoms appear in early autumn. They are considered rather commonplace, and buckwheat is used in making noodles. *Fagopyrum esculentum*. AUTUMN. 572, 610, 709.

suisen: Chinese narcissus. Blooms white in late winter, suggesting purity, with leaves up to sixteen inches long. *Narcissus tazetta* var. *chinensis*. WINTER. 190, 586, 587.

susuki (also *obana*): miscanthus, eulalia. One of the Seven Herbs of Autumn, it resembles our pampass grass and grows up to five feet high in hills and fields. Fluffy white blossoms in August through October gave rise to the alternate name, **obana** (tail flower). *Miscanthus sinensis*. AUTUMN. 53, 417, 518, 593, 694.

suzume: sparrow, Eurasian Tree Sparrow. A common bird of villages and towns, making nests near houses. *Passer montanus*. NO SEASON, but baby sparrows (*kosuzume*) is a spring image and sparrows in rice fields (*ina suzume*) is an autumn image. 81, 161, 197, 258, 314, 570.

suzumi: cool. Also *suzushi*. The experience of refreshing coolness during summer heat, often at night (*yūsuzumi* or *yoisuzumi*). Often used in greeting poems that praise a host's house or view. SUMMER. 18, 47, 116, 207, 310, 389, 397, 405, 406, 407, 411, 415, 493, 608, 681, 683, 685, 689, 691, 692, 295.

taka: hawk. Refers to various raptors of the order *Falconiformes*. WINTER. 229, 230, 231, 571.

tamamatsuri: Festival of the Dead, Feast of All Spirits, Bon Festival, *urabon.* A festival held in the middle of Seventh Month (in Bashō's day from the 13th to the 16th). It is a time when families offer services for ancestors who have returned as spirits to their old homes. AUTUMN. 317, 498, 699.

tanabata: Star Festival. On the 7th of Seventh Month, this festival celebrates the legend of the Oxhered Boy and Weaver Girl, represented as two stars, Altair and Vega. These two lovers are doomed to be separated by Heaven's River (the Milky Way) all year except on this day, when magpies form a bridge with their wings. AUTUMN. 408, 497, 697.

tōgarashi: red pepper. A hot-tasting red pepper with many varieties that suggest rustic simplicity. *Capsicum annum.* AUTUMN. 320, 472, 613.

tsubaki: camellia. Evergreen shrub blossoming February through April, familiar in the West as an ornamental. *Camellia japonica.* SPRING. 90, 232, 470.

tsuki: moon. Bashō's favorite image, and one of the two principal images in Japanese nature poetry, along with the cherry blossoms of spring. The phrase "moon and blossoms" is a metonomy for nature's beauty and for nature poetry. Unless otherwise specified, *tsuki* refers to the full moon in AUTUMN. 2, 19, 23, 30, 36, 95, 100, 112, 113, 123, 124, 193, 213, 214, 215, 289, 290, 291, 297, 326, 329, 333, 356, 398, 400, 401, 412, 431, 432, 433, 434, 436, 437, 438, 443, 447, 450, 459, 493, 506, 534, 539, 547, 564, 565, 566, 567, 569, 574, 575, 604, 611, 614, 622, 625, 630, 644, 716, 722.

- *izayoi no tsuki:* moon of the sixteenth night. Moon of the night after the full moon, usually the 16th of Eighth Month, which rises about an hour later than the moon of the 15th (and thus, literally, "hesitant moon"). AUTUMN. 330, 335, 566, 568, 641.
- *meigetsu:* harvest moon, literally, "bright moon." The full moon of the Eighth Month. AUTUMN. 147, 182, 435, 503, 504, 565, 569, 612, 704, 705.

- *mika no tsuki (mikazuki)*: crescent moon, literally, "third-day moon." AUTUMN. 63, 185, 312, 397, 610, 643.
- *nochi no tsuki* (later harvest moon) and *tsuki no nagori* (moon's farewell) refer to the moon of the 13th of the Ninth Month, which was also known as the "chestnut moon." AUTUMN. 336, 574.
- *oborozuki*: hazy moon. A SPRING image, because spring was the season of haze. 10, 602.
- *tsukimi*: moonviewing. A principal aesthetic pastime. AUTUMN. 171, 183, 216, 429, 430, 505, 715.

tsuru: crane. Includes seven species in the genus *Grus*, noted for beauty and a mournful, high-pitched screech. Particularly prized is *tanchō* (*Grus japonensis*: Japanese Crane). Said to live a thousand years, it is a symbol of longevity along with the tortoise (which lives ten thousand years). NO SEASON. 54, 155, 212, 371, 406, 628.

tsuta: Japanese ivy. Deciduous ivy that turns subdued colors, including red, in autumn. When associated with bamboo or a thatched hut, it suggests a simple, *wabi* life of a hermit living tranquilly in nature. *Parthenocissus tricuspidata*. AUTUMN. 127, 327, 337, 578.

tsuyu: dew. A symbol of impermanence. AUTUMN. 99, 133, 238, 319, 325, 374, 425, 448, 453, 636, 637, 670, 689, 696.

uguisu: Japanese bush warbler. Known for the beauty of its song, which is said to suggest the title of the Lotus Sutra (*Hokke-kyō*). Associated with plums blossoms in early spring. A common resident of Japan, about the size of a sparrow, colored olive-brown above and white below. *Cettia diphore*. SPRING. 68, 470, 600, 663, 676.

ume (or mume): plum (or Japanese apricot). Its fragrant white or red (*baika*) blossoms appear in early spring before leaves appear. It reaches a height of twenty feet. Associated with the bush warbler (*uguisu*) as the eagerly anticipated harbingers of spring. *Prunus mume*. SPRING. 69, 85, 89, 151, 154, 155, 166, 194, 195, 196, 232, 237, 246, 247, 248, 252, 253, 254, 352, 532, 533, 534, 598, 603, 625, 661, 664.

unohana: deutzia. Deciduous shrub of the mountains often used as a hedge. It produces small white blossoms in early summer. It is the poetic name for Fourth Month. *Deutzia scabra* or *D. crenata*. SUMMER. 166, 672.

uri: melon. A vegetable that blossoms (yellow) in early summer and ripen in late summer. It is often associated with coolness. SUMMER. 207, 305, 415, 488, 494, 634, 689.

yamabuki: mountain rose. Deciduous shrub of the rose family that reaches to seven feet high. Single, five-petaled yellow blossoms appear on the tips of branches in April and May. Native to mountainous areas and associated with streams. *Kerria japonica*. SPRING. 273, 541, 542.

yanagi: willow, especially the weeping willow. Prized for bright green leaves in spring. *Salix babylonica*. SPRING. 68, 84, 102, 375, 394, 411, 427, 603, 662, 663, 666, 672.

yūgao: moonflower, bottle gourd, literally, "evening-face." A gourd producing vine whose white blossoms of late summer resemble the morning glory (*asagao*, morning-face) and bindweed (*hirugao*, noon-face). The gourd is hollowed out for a container, and is traditionally associated with poor rural families. *Lagenaria sciceraria*. SUMMER. 56, 301, 633.

GLOSSARY

danrin. A popular school of haikai poetry established by Nishiyama Sōin (1605–1682). It gave poets greater freedom in subject matter, imagery, tone, and poetic composition than the earlier Teimon school. Bashō was a follower of this school before he set up his own, known as "Shōmon."

fūga. "The poetic spirit." A combination of "wind" and "elegance," this term refers to the aesthetic vitality and sensitivity found in haikai poetry as well as associated arts such as waka, landscape painting, and the tea ceremony.

fūryū. "Aesthetic elegance." It is an extraordinarily complex term, including associations of high culture, art in general, poetry, and music, as well as ascetic wayfaring and Daoist eccentricity. Bashō sees the roots of these in rural culture.

haibun. "Haikai prose-poems." Normally a brief prose text that exhibits haikai aesthetics and includes hokku. Bashō was the first great haibun writer.

haiga. "Haikai painting." A painting made in the haikai spirit, often accompanying a haikai poem.

haikai. "Comic, unorthodox." An abbreviation of *haikai no renga,* but also used as a general term for other genres and art forms that show *haikai no renga* aesthetics and what Bashō called the "poetic spirit" *(fūga).* In this general sense, it might be translated as haikai poetry or haikai art. For Bashō, it involved a combination of comic playfulness and spiritual depth, ascetic practice and involvement in the "floating world" of human society.

haikai no renga. "Comic renga," although "unorthodox" or "plebian" may be more accurate than "comic." A verse form, similar to traditional *renga*, that developed in the late medieval and Tokugawa periods. Compared to traditional *renga*, its aesthetics were more inclusive in subject matter and imagery, and more earthy and playful in tone. Parodies of the classical literature were common. Bashō was a master of *haikai no renga*.

haiku. An independent verse form with a 5–7–5 syllabic rhythm. A modern term, its was popularized by the great but short-lived poet Masaoka Shiki (1867–1902) who wanted to establish the haiku as a verse form that stands by itself, separate from the linked verses of a *renga*. Like its progenitor hokku, it is supposed to contain a season word (*kigo*). When the West first learned about Bashō and other pre-modern poets, the term haiku was anachronistically applied to their hokku. Properly speaking, haiku refers only to poems written since Shiki.

hokku. "Opening stanza." First stanza of a renga, thus with 5–7–5 rhythm. This stanza was considered the most important and was usually offered by the master poet at a linked verse gathering. A season word was required. Eventually poets wrote hokku as semi-independent verse: as potential starting verses for a renga sequence, to accompany prose in travel journals and haibun, or to be admired on their own.

karumi. "Lightness." An aesthetic characterized by greater attention to the mundane aspects of life, everyday diction, and generally avoiding the heavy, serious tone of some classical Japanese and Chinese poetry. Bashō promoted this aesthetic in his last years.

kasen. A thirty-six stanza *haikai no renga*, the most common form in Bashō's time.

kigo. "Season word." A word that in the literary tradition suggests a particular season (e.g. autumn) and possibly a part of a season (e.g., early spring), even if the object (e.g., moon or bush warbler) may be seen in other seasons. Season words may be an image derived from nature or human activity. Every hokku and haiku should contain a season word. Traditionally collections of Japanese hokku and haiku verse were organized by seasonal order. There are now numerous season words dictionaries (*saijiki* or *kigo jiten*).

renga. "Classical linked verse." Renga is a linked-verse or sequenced poem with multiple, alternating stanzas. The first stanza consists of a 5–7–5 syllabic rhythm. This is then coupled with another stanza with a 7–7 syllabic rhythm making a poetic unit of 5–7–5 and 7–7. Then comes the third stanza with a 5–7–5 rhythm. This is linked with the second stanza to make a poetic unit of 7–7 and 5–7–5, with the first stanza "forgotten." The linked-verse continues this way, usually up to one hundred or, in Bashō's time, thirty-six stanzas (called a "*kasen*"). Usually this was a group poem, with poets alternating stanzas. Modern renga is called "*renku*."

sabi. "Loneliness." The term suggests both sorrow and tranquility, a response to the realization and acceptance of the essential and shared loneliness of things. It can refer to an aspect of the fundamental nature of reality, a quality of a particular moment in nature, and the state of mind that apprehends and conforms to loneliness of the world. This term was a central spiritual-aesthetical ideal of Bashō's school.

teimon. An early school of haikai poetry established by Matsunaga Teitoku (1571–1653). It was characterized by verbal wit that was not allowed in traditional renga but depended on a knowledge of the classics and observed extensive rules of composition. The Danrin school was in part a reaction against the relative conservatism of this school. Bashō began as a Teimon poet.

wabi. "Aesthetic rusticity." A complex term that suggest simplicity and poverty, unadorned natural beauty, the elegant patina of age, loneliness, freedom from worldly cares, refined aesthetic sensitivity, and tranquillity. In some cases, it includes a tone of deprivation and desolation.

waka. "Classical Japanese verse." This poetic form consists of a
5–7–5–7–7 syllabic rhythm. It was the principal verse form
in the Heian and early medieval periods, and continues to
be written today (now called "*tanka*").

BIBLIOGRAPHY

SELECTED EDITIONS OF BASHŌ'S WORKS

Imoto Nōichi, Hori Nobuo, and Muramatsu Tomotsugu, eds. *Matsuo Bashō shū*. Nihon koten bungaku zenshū. Vol. 41. Tokyo: Shogakkan, 1972.

Imoto Nōichi, et al., eds. *Bashō bunshū; Kyoraishū*. Nihon no koten. Vol. 55. Tokyo: Kadokawa Shoten, 1985.

Imoto Nōichi, et al., eds. *Bashō kushū*. Nihon no koten. Vvol. 54. Tokyo: Kadokawa Shoten, 1984.

Komiya Toyotaka et al., eds. *Kōhon Bashō zenshū*. 10 Vols. Tokyo: Kadokawa Shoten, 1962–69.

Kon Eizō. *Bashō kushū*. Shinchō koten shūsei. Vol. 51. Tokyo: Shinchōsha, 1982.

Ōiso Yoshio and Ōuchi Hatsuo, eds. *Shōmon hairon haibunshū*. Koten haibungaku taikei. Vol. 10. Tokyo: Shūeisha, 1970.

Ōtani Tokuzō and Nakamura Shunjō, eds. *Bashō kushū*. Nihon koten bungaku taikei. Vol. 45. Tokyo: Iwanami Shoten, 1962.

Sugiwara Shoichiro, et al., eds. *Bashō bunshū*. Nihon koten bungaku taikei. Vol. 46. Tokyo: Iwanami Shoten, 1959.

Toyama Susumu. *Bashō bunshū*. Shinchō koten shūsei. Vol. 17. Tokyo: Shinchōsha, 1978.

SELECTED TRANSLATIONS OF BASHŌ'S HAIKU

Blyth, R. H., trans. *Haiku*. 4 vols. Tokyo: Hokuseidō, 1949–52.
———. *A History of Haiku*. 2 vols. Tokyo: Hokuseidō, 1963–64.

Carter, Steven, tr. *Traditional Japanese Poetry: An Anthology.* Stanford, CA: Stanford University Press, 1991.

Hamill, Sam, trans. *The Essential Bashō.* Boston: Shambhala, 1999.

Hass, Robert, ed. *The Essential Haiku: Versions of Bashō, Buson, and Issa.* Hopewell, NJ: Ecco Press, 1994.

Miner, Earl, and Hiroko Odagiri, trans. *The Monkey's Straw Raincoat.* Princeton, NJ: Princeton University Press, 1981.

Oseko, Toshiharu, trans. *Bashō's Haiku.* 2 volumes. Tokyo: Maruzen, 1900.

Shirane, Haruo, ed. *Early Modern Japanese Literature: An Anthology, 1600–1900.* New York: Columbia University Press, 2002.

Stryk, Lucien, trans. *On Love and Barley: Haiku of Bashō.* Hammondsworth: Penguin, 1985.

Ueda, Makoto, trans. *Bashō and His Interpreters: Selected Hokku with Commentary.* Stanford, CA: Stanford University Press, 1991.

SELECTED ENGLISH LANGUAGE SECONDARY SOURCES

Aitken, Robert. *A Zen Wave.* New York: Weatherhill, 1978.

Barnhill, David. "Bashō as Bat: Wayfaring and Anti-Structure in the Journals of Matsuo Bashō (1644–1694)." *Journal of Asian Studies* 49 (1990): 274–290.

———. "Impermanence, Fate, and the Journey: Bashō and the Problem of Meaning." *Religion* 16 (1986): 323–341.

———. "Of Bashōs and Buddhisms." *Eastern Buddhist* 32 (2000): 170–201.

Brazil, Mark A. *The Birds of Japan.* Washington, D.C.: Smithsonian Institution Press, 1991.

Foard, James. "The Loneliness of Matsuo Bashō." In *The Biographical Process: Studies in the History and Psychology of Religion,* 363–391. The Hague: Mouton, 1976.

Henderson, Harold G. *An Introduction to Haiku: An Anthology of Poems from Bashō to Shiki.* Garden City, New York: Doubleday, 1958.

Higginson, William J. *The Haiku Handbook*. New York: McGraw-Hill, 1985.

———. *Haiku World: An International Poetry Almanac*. Tokyo: Kodansha, 1996.

Keene, Donald. *Appreciations of Japanese Culture*. Tokyo: Kodansha, 1981.

———. *World Within Walls: Japanese Literature of the Pre-Modern Era, 1600–1867*. New York: Grove Press, 1976.

LaFleur, William. *The Karma of Words: Buddhism and the Literary Arts in Medieval Japan*. Berkeley, CA: University of California Press, 1983.

Miner, Earl. *An Introduction to Japanese Court Poetry*. Stanford, CA: Stanford University Press, 1968.

———. *Japanese Linked Poetry: An Account with Translations of Renga and Haikai Sequences*. Princeton, NJ: Princeton University Press, 1979.

Miner, Earl, and Hiroko Odagiri, trs. *The Monkey's Straw Raincoat*. Princeton, NJ: Princeton University Press, 1981.

Ōi [Ohwi], Jisaburo. *Flora of Japan*. Washington, D.C.: Smithsonian Institution, 1984.

Qiu, Peipei. *Adaptation and Transformation: Seventeenth Century Haikai and the Zhuangzi*. Honolulu: University of Hawaii Press, forthcoming.

Sato, Hiroaki. *One Hundred Frogs: From Renga to Haiku in English*. New York: Weatherhill, 1983.

Shirane, Haruo. *Traces of Dreams: Landscape, Cultural Memory, and the Poetry of Bashō*. Stanford, CA: Stanford University Press, 1998.

Ueda, Makoto. *Matsuo Bashō*. New York: Twayne, 1970. Reprinted Tokyo: Kodansha International, 1982.

Watson, Burton, trans. *The Complete Works of Chuang Tzu*. New York: Columbia University Press, 1968.

Wild Bird Society of Japan. *A Field Guide to the Birds of Japan*. Tokyo: Kodansha, 1985

INDEX TO BASHŌ'S HOKKU
IN TRANSLATION

Numbers refer to poem numbers.

a mountain rose— / I should stick it in my hat / just like a branch.
541

a narrow path, / wire grass blossoms / filled with dew. 696

a night of darkness— / having lost its nest, / a plover crying out. 543

a samurai gathering: / pungent as a radish is / their talk. 653

a sick goose / falling in the night's cold: / sleep on a journey. 509

a skylark's singing, / and keeping to its rhythm, / a pheasant's cry. 355

a spring night: / and with dawn on the cherries, / it has ended. 80

a spring unseen: / on the back of a mirror, / plum blossoms. 598

a squid-seller's call: / indistinguishable from the / cuckoo's. 93

a temple bell too / seems to be ringing: / cicada's cry. 307

a village grown old: / no house without / a persimmon tree. 702

a village where no / bells ring: what, then, / of spring evenings? 362

a wayfaring crow: / its old nest has become / a plum tree. 151

a whitefish— / opening its black eyes / in the net of the Law. 626

a whole rice paddy / planted — I depart / from the willow. 375

a wren of a single branch: / the fragrance of its plum blossoms /
throughout the world. 154

across the plain, / turn my horse over there! / cuckoo. 372

after the reaping— / from the side of a field of early rice / a snipe's
call. 313

against the brushwood gate / it sweeps the tea leaves: / windstorm. 40

ah spring, spring, / great is spring, / etcetera. 33

all the long day / singing, singing, yet not enough! / a skylark. 200

all the more I'd like to see it / with dawn coming to the blossoms: /
the face of the god. 279

all the summer rains: / have they left it untouched? / Hall of Light.
387

along the bridge beam / endures the fern of recollection: / farewell
moon. 574

among blossoms: / grieving that I can't even open / my poem bag. 11

an acupuncurist / pounding into my shoulder; / the cast off robe. 15

an orchid's scent— / its incense perfuming / a butterfly's wings. 126

and also a night / a thief came calling: / year's end. 659

and now also / the clothes of the deceased— / summer airing. 303

Arashiyama's / bamboo grove so dense— / the wind threading
through. 545

are needles falling / in the pine wind? / the water's cool sound. 116

are you a companion / to these creepers secluded away? / winter veg-
etable seller. 347

arriving when you were out, / even the plums are far away / beyond
the hedge. 195

arrowroot leaves / with their face exposed: / morning frost. 595

behold the moon! / while the reeds at Jewel Bay / are still uncut. 430
beneath a tree, / both soup and fish salad: / cherry blossoms! 475
beneath the noodles / building up the fire: / the night's cold. 577
between the waves— / mingling with tiny shells, / bits of bush clover
 blossoms. 440
biting deep within, / the pungent radish: / autumn wind. 331
Black Forest: / so now what are you called? / a morning of snow. 50
bleached bones / on my mind, the wind pierces / my body to the
 heart. 117
bloom quickly, / the ninth is near: / chrysanthemum blossoms. 445
blooming wildly / among the peach trees: / first cherry blossoms. 79
blossoming waves: / has snow returned to water, / flowering out of
 season? 12
blossoms as my lodging / from beginning to end— / twenty days. 264
blossoms at their peak, / with the mountains as always / at daybreak.
 278
blowing away / the rocks: Asama's / autumn windstorm. 334
blue flag irises / looking just like their images / in the water. 6
blue flag irises / stirring in my mind / a hokku. 164
Buddha's birthday: / on this day is born / a little fawn. 283
Buddha's Nirvana Day — / wrinkled hands together, / the sound of
 the rosaries. 665
burning pine needles / to dry my hand towel: / the cold. 226
bush warbler— / in a grove of bamboo shoots / singing its old age. 676
bush warbler— / pooping on the rice cake / at the edge of the
 veranda. 600
bush-warbler— / behind the willow, / in front of the grove. 663
butterflies and birds / ceaselessly fluttering — / clouds of blossoms. 86
butterflies only / fluttering in this field / of sunlight. 163
butterfly wings: / how many times fluttering / over the wall's roof.
 478
butterfly! butterfly! / I would ask you about / China's haikai. 45
buying a house, / and lending it to me: / seeing the year off. 530
buying a measuring box / I then changed my mind: / moonviewing.
 715
by a paulownia tree, / a quail is crying / inside the garden wall. 507
by the fishing fires, / a bullhead — under the waves / choking in tears.
 422
by the noonflower / a rice-pounder cools himself: / a sight so moving.
 47

Cape Irago: / nothing can match / the hawk's cry. 230
castle ruins— / pure water from the old well / is what I'll seek first. 308

cuckoo: / filtering through the vast bamboo grove / the moon's light. 547

cuckoo: / its call stretching out / across the water. 629

cuckoo: / now there are no / haikai masters. 48

cuckoo: / off where it disappears— / a single island. 294

cuckoo: / singing singing as it flies, / so very busy. 202

cuckoo, / were you invited by the barley / plumed with seed? 53

cuckoo cries— / five-foot spears / of blue flags. 606

dawn comes— / even on the night of the 27th, / a crescent moon. 185

day by day / the barley reddens toward ripeness: / singing skylarks. 552

daybreak— / a whitefish, whiteness / one inch. 140

daybreak: / in the lingering lavender / a cuckoo calls. 484

decorations of the immortals: / I'd love to hear from Ise / the first news of the year. 660

deep into autumn— / a butterfly sipping / chrysanthemum dew. 319

deepening autumn: / the man next door, / what does he do? 723

deep-rooted leeks / washed pure white: / so cold. 583

deer horns / developing their first branch: / our separation. 285

departing autumn— / with hands spread open, / chestnut burs. 710

departing autumn— / wrapping my body / in the narrow bedding. 338

departing spring— / birds cry, in the fishes' / eyes are tears. 359

departing spring— / I've finally caught up with it / here at Wakanoura. 281

deuztia— / over it, dark, a willow / bending back. 672

devoid of talent, / I wish only to sleep: / raucous warblers. 553

dew trickles down: / in it I would try to wash away / the dust of the floating world. 133

do not peek / even through silk tree leaves: / the stars' light. 497

do not think / you did not count: / festival of spirits. 699

do they extinguish even / the banked charcoal? / the sound of hissing tears. 344

don't take after me: / cut in two, / a musk melon. 494

don't drop your dirt / into my wine cup— / flock of swallows. 258

doubt it not: / the blossoms of the tide also show / spring upon this bay. 353

dozing on my horse, / with dream lingering and moon distant: / smoke from a tea fire. 123

dragonfly— / unable to hold on / to the grass blade. 499

drenched passersby— / they too are captivating: / bush clover in rain. 418

field of bush clovers— / be their shelter for a night: / mountain dogs. 211

finely-crafted, / now the garden is enlivened: / early winter shower. 582

firefly viewing— / the boatman is drunk, / the boat unsteady. 491

First Day— / deep in thought, lonely / autumn's evening. 67

first I'll ask / the names of things: these reeds / with new leaves. 255

first mushroom— / just a few days into the season, / autumn dew. 637

first snow— / coating the bridge / under construction. 652

first snow— / for the Great Buddha, when / will the columns be raised? 463

first snow— / great luck to be here / in my own hut. 189

first snow— / just enough to bend / narcissus leaves. 190

first snow— / the color of the knapsack / of a wandering priest. 517

first winter shower: / even the monkey seems to want / a little straw coat. 456

fish stench: / on top of waterweed / dace entrails. 640

fishes, birds, / their heart we do not know: / seeing the year off. 597

five or six of us / lined up before the tea cakes: / the sunken hearth. 341

fleas, lice, / a horse peeing / by my pillow. 388

flowers all withered, / spilling their sadness: / seeds for grass. 186

flying down / on the stones of Stone Mountain: / hail storm. 524

foolishly, in the dark, / he grabs a thorn: / hunting fireflies. 55

for a moment / it hangs above the blossoms: / the night's moon. 539

for a while / secluded at a waterfall— / start of the summer retreat. 365

for coolness / this craftsman from Hida / has the blueprint. 681

for half a day, / companions to the gods— / seeing the year off. 521

for holiness, / everyone's been shoving each other: / the Shrine Renewal. 451

for my father and mother / I yearn so deeply— / a pheasant's cry. 280

for now I'll rely / on the pasania tree: / summer grove. 485

for one who says / "I'm weary of my children" / there are no blossoms. 87

for the people in this house / send down winter showers / no matter the cold. 457

for the white poppy / it tears off its wing: / the butterfly's memento. 167

forty or fifty feet / in the sky, raindrops / in the willow. 666

fragrant orange— / when? in what field? / cuckoo. 490

freshly polished, / the sacred mirror too is clear: / blossoms of snow. 233

having carried brushwood, / the horse returns— / wine casks for rice-planting. 684

having planted the *bashō*, / now I despise them: / the reed sprouts. 52

heat waves / shimmering from the shoulders / of my paper robe. 351

heat waves! / the saiko's threadlike leaves / in a thin haze. 477

held in my eye: / with Yoshino's blooms / Seta's fireflies. 298

her face— / an old woman weeping alone: / moon as companion. 329

hermitage— / moon, chrysanthemums, / and an acre of rice. 447

hey kids! / let's run around / in the hail! 462

hey village kids, / leave some plum branches: / ox whips. 194

hidden / in the late winter waters: / a diving grebe. 529

hidden in the bushes, / do the tea-pickers too hear it? / cuckoo. 671

high hanging bridge: / what first comes to mind / is the Meeting with the Horses. 328

higher than the lark: / resting in the sky / at the pass. 267

his jewel-like spirit— / it returns to Mt. Haguro, / moon of the law. 400

hold for a moment / the sound of slicing soybeans: / bowl beating. 523

housecleaning: / hanging his own shelf, / a carpenter. 658

how easily it rose / and now it hesitates, / the moon in clouds. 567

how many frosts / has it endured — my banana plant / is my New Year's pine. 173

hydrangea— / and a thicket as a little garden / for the cottage. 673

hydrangeas— / at the time for summer clothes / pale blue. 92

I long to imagine / how you looked – your staff / of withered wood. 342

I would compare them / to a delicate child: flowers / of a summer field. 306

I would lodge here / until the days the goosefoot / has grown a staff. 304

I would sweep the garden / before departing: in the temple, / falling willow leaves. 427

I'd like to sleep / borrowing the scarecrow's clothes— / midnight frost. 243

I'll bind blue flags / around my feet: / sandal cords. 384

I'll fall asleep drunk, / the wild pinks blooming / over the rocks. 206

I'll serve buckwheat / while their blossoming: / mountain path. 709

I'll tell my drinking friends / of these blossoms hanging / over the waterfall. 269

I've hit the bottom / of my bag of discretion: / year's end. 107

ice is bitter / in the mouth of the rat / quenching its thirst. 60

Mount Atsumi— / all the way to Fuku Bay, / the evening cool. 407

mountain cove — / I would nourish my body / with this field of melons. 305

mountain roses— / when tea ovens at Uji / are so fragrant. 542

mountain village / and the New Year's dancers are late: / plum blossoms. 533

mountains too / move into the garden— / a summer parlor. 367

Musashi Plain— / just an inch, / the deer's voice. 16

Musashino fields— / no hindrances now, / your bamboo hat. 114

mushroom— / a leaf from an unknown tree / sticking to it. 576

mushroom— / it's become so ragged / it looks like a pine. 104

mushroom gathering— / in danger of getting drenched in / a cold evening shower. 458

my bedclothes are so heavy / perhaps I'll see the snow / from the sky of Wu. 66

my hair grown out, / my face pale: / summer rains. 203

my heart / so oddly at ease: / Twelfth Month. 623

my hut: / a square of light / from the window's moon. 100

my hut: / that the mosquitoes are small / is all I can offer. 495

my journey's horse / solaced with barley: / a night's lodging. 169

my native home— / weeping over my umbilical cord / at year's end. 241

my paper robe is wet, / but I'll go break a branch: / blossoms in the rain. 259

my sleeves, / dingy colored and cold: / darkest gray. 110

narcissus / and the white paper screen, / reflecting each other. 586

neither to evening / nor morning does it belong: / melon blossom. 488

nesting storks: / viewed through branches / of blossoms. 198

new rice-straw / is appearing . . . with / early winter showers. 708

New Year's Day: / it's the sun in each field / that brings such longing. 348

nine times awakened / yet it's still the moon / before dawn. 575

no moon, no blossoms, / just drinking sake / all alone. 356

no rain hat / in the winter showers? / well, well! 143

noonflower, / with a short night's sleep: / daytime. 302

not dead yet / at journey's end— / autumn evening. 137

not hidden / at this house: vegetable soup / with red pepper. 320

not just the moon: / because of rain, even sumō / has been called off. 437

not raining, yet / on bamboo-planting day / a raincoat and hat. 90

now look at me / in this fine summer robe! / a cicada kimono. 205

peach tree, / don't let your leaves fall: / autumn wind. 421

peasant boy— / husking rice, he pauses / to gaze at the moon. 213

penetrating even / the lair of a wild boar— / cricket's cry. 714

people of the world / don't discern this blossom— / chestnut by the eaves. 378

periodic rain / so no need to worry: / rice sprouts. 94

petal after petal / mountain roses flutter down: / the sound of the rapids. 273

pine of Karasaki: / more vague even / than the blossoms. 159

pine-filled berms / and blossoms – a manor built / deep in the forest. 474

planting seedlings / with the hands – ancient patterns / from the fern of longing. 380

plates and bowls too / faint in twilight: / evening cool. 692

please don't forget: / in the grove, / a plum blossom. 196

plovers rising: / as early evening deepens, / winds storm down Mt. Hiei. 519

plucking out white hairs— / under the pillow, / a cricket. 502

plum and camellia: / praise to their early bloom / here in Hobi Village. 232

plum blossoms and fresh greens / at the Mariko stopover / and that yam porridge. 532

potato-washing women: / were Saigyō here, / he'd compose a waka. 125

praying for a warm bed, / it has now appeared: / sleep along the journey. 591

putting up at an inn / I am asked my name: / early winter showers. 592

Rainhat Island— / where is it this rainy month / along muddy roads? 383

red-blossom plums— / unseen love engendered / by the courtly blind. 352

removing a one layer / I carry it over my shoulder: / clothes-changing day. 282

resting on my journey, / I watch the year-end housecleaning / of the floating world. 239

rice fields and barley— / and among them also / summer's cuckoo. 369

rice threshing, / an old woman's good fortune: / chrysanthemum blossom. 579

rice-field sparrows / in the tea fields— / their refuge. 570

rising again, / the chrysanthemums faint / after the rains. 219

slowly spring / is taking shape: / moon and plum. 625

smoothing it out, / I'm off to snowviewing: / my paper robe. 234

snow falling— / miscanthus for the shrine hut / still uncut. 518

snow morning: / alone, I manage to chew / dried salmon. 42

snow upon snow: / is tonight the twelfth month's / full moon? 147

so admirable— / even on a day without snow, / straw coat and bamboo hat. 528

so cold and yet / a night sleeping together: / so delightful. 225

so cool— / feet against a wall / in a midday nap. 695

so desirable— / inside his satchel, / moon and blossoms. 113

so enticing— / in the spring of this year too / the sky of wayfaring. 349

so enviable: / far north of the floating world, / mountain cherry blossoms. 599

so fascinating, / but then, so sad: / cormorant fishing boat. 309

so fitting— / bean-flour rice balls / while blossom hunting. 476

so grateful— / perfumed with snow, / the South Valley. 396

so harsh— / the sound of hail / on my cypress hat. 138

so holy: / green leaves, young leaves, / in sun's light. 364

so lazy— / finally roused from bed: / spring rain. 535

so many many / memories come to mind: / cherry blossoms. 263

so many plants, / each with its own / brilliant blossom. 323

so pitiful— / under the helmet, / a cricket. 419

so red, red, / the sun relentless and yet / autumn's wind. 414

so very precious: / are they tinting my tears? / falling crimson leaves. 581

somehow / still alive — snow on / withered miscanthus. 593

soon to die, / yet no sign of it: / a cicada's cry. 496

spend nights on a journey, / then you'll know my poems— / autumn wind. 77

spider, what is it, / in what voice — why — are you crying? / autumn wind. 34

spring begins— / in a new year, / ten quarts of old rice. 115

spring departs: / with those of Ōmi / I join the lament. 482

spring has risen / only nine days now and / these fields and mountains! 245

spring night— / someone in retreat, so mysterious / in a corner of the temple. 266

spring rain— / blowing back and forth like straw coats, / river willows. 84

spring rain— / dripping down the wasp's nest / from the leaking roof. 667

spring rain / flowing down the tree: / the pure water spring. 276

the blossoms are seen / even by the eyes of the poor: / demon thistle. 5

the blossoms at Dragon's Gate: / a splendid souvenir / for my drinking friends. 268

the color of autumn: / not even a pot / of rice-bran mash. 562

the color of the wind— / planted wild, / the garden in autumn. 701

the dew frozen, / I soak it dry with my brush: / the pure water spring. 228

the dignified stature / of the oak, indifferent / to the blossoms. 156

the Dutch consul too / lies prostrate before Him: / spring of the Shōgun's reign. 27

the Dutchmen too / have come for the flowers: / the horse saddle. 29

the eight scenes / of various provinces and now / the moon at Kei. 433

the faces of blossoms, / do they make you shy? / hazy moon. 10

the faces of the fishers / were seen first— / poppy flowers. 291

the first cherries blooming: / right now, today, / is such a fine day. 262

the fragrance of plums: / carrying me back / to the cold. 85

the gods gone / everything is desolate among / the dead leaves. 594

the hanging bridge— / grasping for dear life, / ivy vines. 327

the hawk's eyes / have darkened now: / calling quail. 571

the horse ambling, / I see myself in a painting: / summer moor. 70

the imperial tomb has stood / for ages: what do you recall, / fern of longing? 134

the ivy leaves / are tinged with the past: / autumn foliage. 337

the man wearing / a straw mat, who is he? / blossoms of spring. 468

the moon about to rise— / everyone with hands on knees / in the room. 506

the moon has set; / all that remains is / the four corners of his desk. 644

the moon is clear— / accompanying my boy lover / frightened by a fox. 722

the moon is here / yet there seems an absence: / summer in Suma. 289

the moon so pure / on the sand carried here / by the Pilgrim Priests. 434

the moon swift, / the branches still holding / the rain. 215

the moon's light— / four gates, four sects / yet only one. 333

the moon's your guide: / please come this way / to a traveler's inn. 2

the oars' sound striking the waves, / a bowel-freezing night — / and tears. 41

the old nest: / so lonely it will be / next door. 178

the old-lady cherry / in bloom: a remembrance / of her old age. 3

the pathos of / the birdseller's geese: / Festival of Ebisu. 654

the plums so white: / yesterday did someone steal / the cranes? 155

the rocks withered, / the waters wilted— / not even the feeling of winter. 43

with threads of / heat waves it is interwoven: / the smoke. 360
withered and bent over, / the whole world upside down: / bamboo in
     snow. 8
withered grass— / faint heat waves / one or two inches high. 249
withering frost: / melancholy blossoms / through the flower field. 9
without dropping / its bright white dew, / a bush clover sways. 636
wrapped warm / in its feather robe, / the duck's feet. 650
wrapping rice dumplings: / with one hand she puts back / her fallen
     hair. 555

Yamanaka— / no need to pluck chrysanthemums: / the fragrance of
     these springs. 420
year after year— / the monkey wearing / a monkey's mask. 624
year upon year— / fertilizing the cherry trees: / blossom dust. 537
year-end house cleaning: / through the cedar trees, / a windstorm. 520
yearning for the plum, / bowing before the deutzia: / eyes of tears.
     166
yes it's spring— / through nameless hills, / a faint haze. 152
Yoshitomo's heart / it does resemble: / autumn wind. 135
you start a fire, / I'll show you something fun: / a great ball of snow.
     192
you too come out, bat: / all these birds amid the blossoms / of this
     floating world. 83
you who raised melons: / "would that you were here" / in the evening
     coolness. 207
you're the butterfly / I'm Zhuangzi's / dreaming heart. 486
young sweetfish / seeing off the whitefish: / departure. 358

INDEX TO BASHŌ'S HOKKU
IN JAPANESE

ame oriori / omou koto naki / sanae kana. 94
ano naka ni / makie kakitashi / yado no tsuki. 326
aokute mo / arubeki mono o / tōgarashi. 613
aoyagi no / doro ni shidataru / shiohi kana. 668
ara nani tomo na ya / kinō wa sugite / fukutojiru. 26
arare kiku ya / kono mi wa moto no / furugashiwa. 71
arare seba / ajiro no hio o / nite dasan. 466
arashiyama / yabu no shigeri ya / kaze no suji. 545
ara tōto / aoba wakaba no / hi no hikari. 364
araumi ya / sado ni yokotau / amanogawa. 409
arigata ya / yuki o kaorasu / minamidani. 396
asacha nomu / sō shizukanari / kiku no hana. 511
asagao ni / ware wa meshi kū / otoko kana. 62
asagao wa / heta no kaku sae / aware nari. 210
asagao wa / sakamori shiranu / sakari kana. 324
asagao ya / hiru wa jō orosu / mon no kaki. 638
asagao ya / kore mo mata waga / tomo narazu. 639
asamutsu ya / tsukimi no tabi no / akebanare. 429
asatsuyu ni / yogorete suzushi / uri no tsuchi. 689
asa yosa o / taga matsu shima zo / katagokoro. 350
asu no tsuki / ame uranawan / hina-ga-dake. 431
atsuki hi o / umi ni iretari / mogamigawa. 403
atsumiyama ya / fukuura kakete / yūsuzumi. 407
awa hie ni / toboshiku mo arazu / kusa no io. 318
ayamegusa / ashi ni musuban / waraji no o. 384
ayu no ko no / shirauo okuru / wakare kana. 358

bashō-ba o / hashira ni kaken / io no tsuki. 611
bashō nowaki shite / tarai ni ame o / kiku yo kana. 58
bashō uete / mazu nikumu ogi no / futaba kana. 52
bii to naku / shirigoe kanashi / yoru no shika. 711
botan shibe fukaku / wakeizuru hachi no / nagori kana. 168
bushōsa ya / kakiokosareshi / haru no ame. 535
byōbu ni wa / yama o egaite / fuyugomori. 460
byōgan no / yosamu ni ochite / tabine kana. 509

chichi haha no / shikirini koishi / kiji no koe. 280
chidori tachi / fukeyuku shoya no / hiei oroshi. 519
chimaki yū / katate ni hasamu / hitaigami. 555
chi ni taore / ne ni yori hana no / wakare kana. 179
chiru hana ya / tori mo odoroku / koto no chiri. 78
chō mo kite / su o suu kiku no / namasu kana. 512
chō no ha no / ikutabi koyuru / hei no yane. 478

haiide yo / kaiya ga shita no / hiki no koe. 390
hakkuken / sora de ame furu / yanagi kana. 666
hakone kosu / hito mo arurashi / kesa no yuki. 236
hamaguri no / futami ni wakare / yuku aki zo. 449
hana mina karete / aware o kobosu / kusa no tane. 186
hana mukuge / hadaka warawa no / kazashi kana. 35
hana ni akanu / nageki ya kochi no / utabukuro. 11
hana ni asobu / abu na kurai so / tomosuzume. 197
hana no kage / utai ni nitaru / tabine kana. 270
hana no kao ni / hareute shite ya / oborozuki. 10
hana no kumo / kane wa ueno ka / asakusa ka. 199
hana o yado ni / hajime owari ya / hatsuka hodo. 264
hana wa shizu no / me ni mo miekeri / oni azami. 5
hanazakari / yama wa higoro no / asaborake. 278
hanjitsu wa / kami o tomo ni ya / toshiwasure. 521
haranaka ya / mono ni mo tsukazu / naku hibari. 201
hare mono ni / sawaru yanagi no / shinae kana. 662
haritate ya / kata ni tsuchi utsu / karakoromo. 15
haru mo yaya / keshiki totonou / tsuki to ume. 625
haru nare ya / na mo naki yama no / usugasumi. 152
haru no yo wa / sakura ni akete / shimaikeri. 80
haru no yo ya / komorido yukashi / dō no sumi. 266
harusame no / koshita ni tsutau / shimizu kana. 276
harusame ya / futaba ni moyuru / nasubidane. 471
harusame ya / hachi no su tsutau / yane no mori. 667
harusame ya / mino fukikaesu / kawa yanagi. 84
harusame ya / yomogi o nobasu / kusa no michi. 669
haru tachite / mada kokonoka no / noyama kana. 245
haru tatsu ya / shinnen furuki / kome goshō. 115
haru ya koshi / toshi ya yukiken / kotsugomori. 1
hashigeta no / shinobu wa tsuki no / nagori kana. 574
hasu ike ya / orade sono mama / tamamatsuri. 317
hatsuaki ya / tatami nagara no / kaya no yogi. 557
hatsuaki ya / umi mo aota no / hitomidori. 315
hatsushigure / saru mo komino o / hoshigenari. 456
hatsutake ya / mada hikazu henu / aki no tsuyu. 637
hatsu uma ni / kitsune no sorishi / atama kana. 627
hatsuyuki ni / usagi no kawa / hige tsukure. 461
hatsuyuki ya / hijiri kozō no / oi no iro. 517
hatsuyuki ya / itsu daibutsu no / hashiradate. 463
hatsuyuki ya / kakekakaritaru / hashi no ue. 652
hatsuyuki ya / saiwai an ni / makariaru. 189
hatsuyuki ya / suisen no ha no / tawamu made. 190

ikameshiki / oto ya arare no / hinokigasa. 138
ikauri no / koe magirawashi / hototogisu. 93
ikinagara / hitotsu ni kōru / namako kana. 657
iku shimo ni / kokorobase-o no / matsu kazari. 173
imo arau onna / saigyō naraba / uta yoman. 125
imo no ha ya / tsuki matsu sato no / yakibatake. 214
imo uete / kado wa mugura no / wakaba kana. 256
ina suzume / chanokibatake ya / nigedokoro. 570
inazuma ni / satoranu hito no / tattosa yo. 508
inazuma o / te ni toru yami no / shisoku kana. 209
inazuma ya / kao no tokoro ga / susuki no ho. 694
inazuma ya / yami no kata yuku / goi no koe. 700
ine koki no / uba mo medetashi / kiku no hana. 579
inochi futatsu no / naka ni ikitaru / sakura kana. 162
inochi nari / wazuka no kasa no / shita suzushimi. 18
inoshishi mo / tomo ni fukaruru / nowaki kana. 500
inoshishi no / toko ni mo iru ya / kirigirsu. 714
iragozaki / niru mono mo nashi / taka no koe. 230
iriai no / kane mo kikoezu / haru no kure. 363
irikakaru / hi mo itoyū no / nagori kana. 361
iru tsuki no / ato wa tsukue no / yosumi kana. 644
isaribi ni / kajika ya nami no / shita musebi. 422
ishi karete / mizu shibomeru ya / fuyu mo nashi. 43
ishi no ka ya / natsugusa akaku / tsuyu atsushi. 374
ishiyama no / ishi ni tabashiru / arare kana. 524
ishiyama no / ishi yori shiroshi / aki no kaze. 426
ite tokete / hitsu ni kumihosu / shimizu kana. 277
itoyū ni / musubitsukitaru / kemuri kana. 360
itsutsu mutsu / cha no ko ni narabu / irori kana. 341
iza kodomo / hashiri arikan / tamaarare. 462
iza saraba / yukimi ni korobu / tokoro made. 235
iza tomo ni / homugi kurawan / kusa makura. 165
izayoi mo / mada sarashina no / kōri kana. 330
izayoi no / izure ka kesa ni / nokoru kiku. 335
izayoi wa / wazuka ni yami no / hajime kana. 641
izayoi ya / ebi niru hodo no / yoi no yami. 568
izuku shigure / kasa o te ni sagete / kaeru sō. 39

jō akete / tsuki sashireyo / ukimidō. 566
jōroku ni / kagerō takashi / ishi no ue. 250

kabitan mo / tsukubawasekeri / kimi ga haru. 27
kachi naraba / tsue-tsuki-zaka o / rakuba kana. 240

kazu naranu / mi to na omoiso / tamamatsuri. 699
kegoromo ni / tsutsumite nukushi / kamo no ashi. 650
keitō ya / kari no kuru toki / nao akashi. 706
kesa no yuki / nebuka o sono no / shiori kana. 32
kiku keitō / kiri tsukushikeri / omeikō. 339
kiku no hana / saku ya ishiya no / ishi no ai. 645
kiku no ka ni / kuragari noboru / sekku kana. 713
kiku no ka ya / nara ni wa furuki / hotoketachi. 712
kiku no ka ya / niwa ni kiretaru / kutsu no soko. 647
kiku no nochi / daikon no hoka / sara ni nashi. 109
kiku no tsuyu / ochite hiroeba / nukago kana. 99
kimi hi o take / yoki mono misen / yuki maruge. 192
kimi ya chō / ware ya sōji ga / yumegokoro. 486
kinbyō no / matsu no furusa yo / fuyugomori. 646
ki no moto ni / shiru mo namasu mo / sakura kana. 475
kinuta uchite / ware ni kikase yo ya / bō ga tsuma. 132
ki o kirite / motokuchi miru ya / kyō no tsuki. 23
kirigirisu / wasurene ni naku / kotatsu kana. 514
kiri no ki ni / uzura naku naru / hei no uchi. 507
kirishigure / fuji o minu hi zo / omoshiroki. 119
kisagata ya / ame ni seishi ga / nebu no hana. 404
kiso no jō / yuki ya haenuku / haru no kusa. 531
kiso no tochi / ukiyo no hito no / miyage kana. 332
kiso no yase mo / mada naoranu ni / nochi no tsuki. 336
kitsutsuki mo / io wa yaburazu / natsu kodachi. 368
kiyotaki no / mizu kumasete ya / tokoroten. 686
kiyotaki ya / nami ni chirikomu / aomatsuba. 688
kōbai ya / minu koi tsukuru / tamasudare. 352
kochira muke / ware mo sabishiki / aki no kure. 501
kochō ni mo / narade aki furu / namushi kana. 442
kodai sasu / yanagi suzushi ya / ama ga tsuma. 411
kodomora yo / hirugao sakinu / uri mukan. 634
koe sumite / hokuto ni hibiku / kinuta kana. 75
koe yokuba / utaō mono o / sakura chiru. 272
kogakurete / chatsumi mo kiku ya / hototogisu. 671
kogarashi ni / iwa fukitogaru / sugima kana. 590
kogarashi ni / nioi ya tsukeshi / kaeribana. 585
kogarashi no / mi wa chikusai ni / nitaru kana. 144
kogarashi ya / hohobare itamu / hito no kao. 516
kogarashi ya / take ni kakurete / shizumarinu. 108
kohagi chire / masuho no kogai / kosakazuki. 441
kohōgen / dedokoro aware / toshi no kure. 111

magusa ou / hito o shiori no / natsuno kana. 366
masu kōte / funbetsu kawaru / tsukimi kana. 715
matsudake ya / shiranu ko no ha no / hebaritsuku. 576
matsudake ya / kabureta hodo wa / matsu no nari. 104
matsukaze no / ochiba ka mizu no / oto suzushi. 116
matsukaze ya / noki o megutte / aki kurenu. 719
mayuhaki o / omokage ni shite / beni no hana. 391
mazu tanomu / shii no ki mo ari / natsu kodachi. 485
meigetsu ni / fumoto no kiri ya / ta no kumori. 704
meigetsu no / hana ka to miete / watabatake. 705
meigetsu wa / futatsu sugite mo / seta no tsuki. 569
meigetsu ya / chigotachi narabu / dō no en. 503
meigetsu ya / hokkoku biyori / sadamenaki. 435
meigetsu ya / ike o megurite / yomosugara. 182
meigetsu ya / mon ni sashikuru / shiogashira. 612
meigetsu ya / umi ni mukaeba / nana komachi. 504
me ni kakru / toki ya kotosara / satsuki fuji. 675
me ni nokoru / yoshino o seta no / hotaru kana. 298
meshi augu / kaka ga chisō ya / yūsuzumi. 691
mezurashi ya / yama o ideha no / hatsunasubi. 402
michi hososhi / sumotorigusa no / hana no tsuyu. 696
michinobe no / mukuge wa uma ni / kuwarekeri. 122
midokoro no / are ya nowaki no / nochi no kiku. 96
miidera no / mon tatakabaya / kyō no tsuki. 565
mikazuki ni / chi wa oboro nari / soba no hana. 610
mikazuki ya / asagao no yūbe / tsubomuran. 63
mina idete / hashi o itadaku / shimoji kana. 656
minazuki wa / fukubyō yami no / atsusa kana. 556
minazuki ya / tai wa aredomo / shiokujira. 607
mi ni shimite / daikon karashi / aki no kaze. 331
minomushi no / ne o kiki ni koyo / kusa no io. 218
miokuri no / ushiro ya sabishi / aki no kaze. 321
mishi ya sono / nanuka wa haka no / mika no tsuki. 643
misoka tsuki nashi / chitose no sugi o / daku arashi. 124
miwataseba / nagamureba mireba / suma no aki. 31
mizu no oku / himuro tazunuru / yanagi kana. 394
mizu samuku / neiri kanetaru / kamome kana. 187
mizutori ya / kōri no sō no / kutsu no oto. 153
momo no ki no / sono ha chirasu na / aki no kaze. 421
momotose no / keshiki o niwa no / ochiba kana. 580
mo ni sudaku / shirauo ya toraba / kienubeki. 51
mon ni ireba / sotetsu ni ran no / nioi kana. 454
mono hitotsu / waga yo wa karoki / hisago kana. 184

nishi ka higashi ka / mazu sanae ni mo / kaze no oto. 376
niwa haite / idebaya tera ni / chiru yanagi. 427
niwa hakite / yuki o wasururu / hahaki kana. 620
nomiakete / hanaike ni sen / nishōdaru. 538
nomi shirami / uma no shitosuru / makura moto. 388
nō nashi no / nemutashi ware o / gyōgyōshi. 553
no o yoko ni / uma hikimuke yo / hototogisu. 372
nōren no / oku monofukashi / kita no ume. 253
nozarashi o / kokoro ni kaze no / shimu mi kana. 117
nurete yuku ya / hito mo okashiki / ame no hagi. 418
nusubito ni / ōta yo mo ari / toshi no kure. 659
nyūmen no / shita takitatsuru / yosamu kana. 577

ochikuru ya / takaku no shuku no / hototogisu. 373
ōgi nite / sake kumu kage ya / chiru sakura. 271
ogi no ho ya / kashira o tsukamu / rashōmon. 560
oi mo tachi mo / satsuki ni kazare / kaminobori. 381
okiagaru / kiku honoka nari / mizu no ato. 219
okiyo okiyo / waga tomo ni sen / nuru kochō. 44
okorago no / hito moto yukashi / ume no hana. 252
okuraretsu / okuritsu hate wa / kiso no aki. 322
omokage ya / oba hitori naku / tsuki no tomo. 329
omoshirōte / yagate kanashiki / ubune kana. 309
omoshiro ya / kotoshi no haru mo / tabi no sora. 349
oranda mo / hana ni kinikeri / umi ni kura. 29
oriori ni / ibuki o mite wa / fuyugomori. 584
otoroi ya / ha ni kuiateshi / nori no suna. 540

ran no ka ya / chō no tsubasa ni / takimono su. 126
ro no koe nami o utte / harawata kōru / yo ya namida. 41
robiraki ya / sakan oiyuku / bin no shimo. 618
rokugatsu ya / mine ni kumo oku / arashiyama. 687
rusu ni kite / ume sae yoso no / kakio kana. 195
rusu no ma ni / aretaru kami no / ochiba kana. 594
ryō no te ni / momo to sakura ya / kusa no mochi. 604
ryōmon no / hana ya jōgo no / tsuto ni sen. 268

sabishisa ya / kugi ni kaketaru / kirigirisu. 563
sabishisa ya / suma ni kachitaru / hama no aki. 439
saigyō no / iori mo aran / hana no niwa. 82
saigyō no / waraji mo kakare / matsu no tsuyu. 448
sakazuki ni / doro na otoshi so / muratsubame. 258
sakazuki ni / mitsu no na o nomu / koyoi kana. 172

shiodai no / haguki mo samushi / uo no tana. 619
shiogoshi ya / tsuru hagi nurete / umi suzushi. 406
shiorashiki / na ya komatsu fuku / hagi susuki. 417
shiore fusu ya / yo wa sakasama no / yuki no take. 8
shiraga nuku / makura no shita ya / kirigirisu. 502
shirageshi ni / hane mogu chō no / katami kana. 167
shiragiku no / me ni tatete miru / chiri mo nashi. 721
shiragiku yo shiragiku yo / haji nagakami yo / nagakami yo. 49
shiratsuyu mo / kobosanu hagi no / uneri kana. 636
shirauo ya / kuroki me o aku / nori no ami. 626
shiro ato ya / furui no shimizu / mazu towan. 308
shizukasa ya / iwa ni shimiiru / semi no koe. 392
shizu no ko ya / ine surikakete / tsuki o miru. 213
shukaidō / suika no iro ni / sakinikeri. 558
sō asagao / iku shinikaeru / nori no matsu. 130
soba mo mite / kenarigaraseyo / nora no hagi. 572
soba wa mada / hana de motenasu / yamaji kana. 709
sode no iro / yogorete samushi / koi nezumi. 110
sōkai no / nami sake kusashi / kyō no tsuki. 30
sono katachi / mibaya kareki no / tsue no take. 342
sonomama yo / tsuki mo tanomaji / ibukiyama. 443
sono nioi / momo yori shiroshi / suisenka. 587
sono tama ya / haguro ni kaesu / nori no tsuki. 400
suisen ya / shiroki shōji no / tomoutsuri. 586
sumadera ya / fukanu fue kiku / koshitayami. 293
suma no ama no / yasaki ni naku ka / hototogisu. 292
surugaji ya / hanatachibana mo / cha no nioi. 678
susuhaki wa / ono ga tana tsuru / daiku kana. 658
susuhaki wa / sugi no ki no ma no / arashi kana. 520
suzumeko to / koe nakikawasu / nezumi no su. 81
suzuri ka to / hirou ya kuboki / ishi no tsuyu. 453
suzushisa o / e ni utsushikeri / saga no take. 685
suzushisa o / hida no takumi ga / sashizu kana. 681
suzushisa o / waga yado ni shite / nemaru nari. 389
suzushisa ya / hono mikazuki no / haguroyama. 397
suzushisa ya / suguni nomatsu no / eda no nari. 683

tabi ni akite / kyō iku ka yara / aki no kaze. 316
tabi ni yande / yume wa kareno o / kakemeguru. 724
tabibito no / kokoro ni mo niyo / shii no hana. 631
tabibito to / waga na yobaren / hatsu-shigure. 221
tabigarasu / furusu wa ume ni / narinikeri. 151
tabine shite / mishi ya ukiyo no / susu harai. 239

tsuki mite mo / mono tarawazu ya / suma no natsu. 290
tsuki nomi ka / ame ni sumō mo / nakarikeri. 437
tsuki sabi yo / akechi ga tsuma no / hanashi sen. 450
tsuki shiro ya / hiza ni te o oku / yoi no yado. 506
tsuki sumu ya / kitsune kowagaru / chigo no tomo. 722
tsuki wa aredo / rusu no yō nari / suma no natsu. 289
tsuki yuki to / nosabarikerashi / toshi no kure. 193
tsuki zo shirube / konata e irase / tabi no yado. 2
tsukurinasu / niwa o isamuru / shigure kana. 582
tsuru naku ya / sono koe ni bashō / yarenubeshi. 371
tsuru no ke no / kuroki koromo ya / hana no kumo. 628
tsuta no ha wa / mukashi mekitaru / momiji kana. 337
tsuta uete / take shigo hon no / arashi kana. 127
tsutsuji ikete / sono kage ni hidara / saku onna. 160
tsuyu itete / hitsu ni kumihosu / shimizu kana. 228
tsuyu tokutoku / kokoromi ni ukiyo / susugabaya. 133

ubazakura / saku ya rōgo no / omoiide. 3
uguisu no / kasa otoshitaru / tsubaki kana. 470
uguisu o / tama ni nemuru ka / taoyanagi. 68
uguisu ya / mochi ni fun suru / en no saki. 600
uguisu ya / take no koyabu ni / oi o naku. 676
uguisu ya / yanagi no ushiro / yabu no mae. 663
uki fushi ya / take no ko to naru / hito no hate. 544
uki hito no / tabi ni mo narae / kiso no hae. 632
uki ware o / sabishigarase yo / kankodori. 548
uma bokuboku / ware o e ni miru / natsuno kana. 70
uma ni nete / zanmu tsuki tōshi / cha no keburi. 123
uma o sae / nagamuru yuki no / ashita kana. 141
ume ga ka ni / mukashi no ichiji / aware nari. 664
ume ga ka ni / notto hi no deru / yamaji kana. 661
ume ga ka ni / oimodosaruru / samusa kana. 85
ume koite / unohana ogamu / namida kana. 166
ume no ki ni / nao yadorigi ya / ume no hana. 254
ume shiroshi / kinō ya tsuru o / nusumareshi. 155
ume tsubaki / hayazaki homen / hobi no sato. 232
ume wakana / mariko no shuku no / tororojiru. 532
umi kurete / kamo no koe / honoka ni shiroshi. 148
unohana ya / kuraki yanagi no / oyobigoshi. 672
uo tori no / kokoro wa shirazu / toshiwasure. 597
urayamashi / ukiyo no kita no / yamazakura. 599
uri tsukuru / kimi ga are na to / yūsuzumi. 207
ushibeya ni / ka no koe kuraki / zansho kana. 561

yoru hisokani / mushi wa gekka no / kuri o ugatsu. 36
yoshinaka no / nezame no yama ka / tsuki kanashi. 432
yoshino nite / sakura mishō zo / hinokigasa. 265
yoshitomo no / kokoro ni nitari / aki no kaze. 135
yōte nemu / nadeshiko sakeru / ishi no ue. 206
yūbare ya / sakura ni suzumu / nami no hana. 405
yūbe ni mo / asa ni mo tsukazu / uri no hana. 488
yūgao no / shiroku yoru no kōka ni / shisoku torite. 56
yūgao ya / aki wa iroiro no / fukube kana. 301
yūgao ya / yōte kao dasu / mado no ana. 633
yuki chiru ya / hoya no susuki no / karinokoshi. 518
yuki ma yori / usu murasaki no / me udo kana. 242
yuki no ashita / hitori karazake o / kami etari. 42
yuki no naka wa / hirugao karenu / hikage kana. 46
yuki o matsu / jōgo no kao ya / inabikari. 589
yuki to yuki / koyoi shiwasu no / meigetsu ka. 147
yuki ya suna / uma yori otochi yo / sake no yoi. 228
yuku aki no / nao tanomoshi ya / aomikan. 616
yuku aki ya / mi ni hikimatou / minobuton. 338
yuku aki ya / te o hirogetaru / kuri no iga. 710
yuku haru ni / wakanoura nite / oitsukitari. 281
yuku haru o / ōmi no hito to / oshimikeru. 482
yuku haru ya / tori naki uo no / me wa namida. 359
yuku koma no / mugi ni nagusamu / yadori kana. 169
yuku kumo ya / inu no kake-bari / murashigure. 24
yume yori mo / utsutsu no taka zo / tanomoshiki. 231
yu no hana ya / mukashi shinoban / ryori no ma. 546
yu no nagori / iku tabi miru ya / kiri no moto. 424
yu no nagori / koyoi wa hada no / samukaran. 423

zatō ka to / hito ni mirarete / tsukimi kana. 183

INDEX OF NAMES

Numbers refer to poem numbers.